THE CANARY ISLANDS

THE CANARY ISLANDS

A CULTURAL HISTORY

JUAN CRUZ RUIZ

Translated from the Spanish by James Womack

Overlook Duckworth
New York • London

This edition first published in hardcover in the United States and the
United Kingdom in 2017 by Overlook Duckworth, Peter Mayer Publishers, Inc.

NEW YORK
141 Wooster Street
New York, NY 10012
www.overlookpress.com
For bulk and special sales, please contact sales@overlookny.com,
or write us at the above address

LONDON
30 Calvin Street
London E1 6NW
info@duckworth-publishers.co.uk
www.ducknet.co.uk

Cataloging-in-Publication Data is available from the Library of Congress

Book design and typeformatting by Bernard Schleifer
Manufactured in the United States of America
ISBN US: 978-1-59020-219-7
ISBN UK: 978-0-7156-5222-0

FIRST EDITION
2 4 6 8 10 9 7 5 3 1

To Oliver Arenas Cruz. Welcome to the world.

CONTENTS

*Sometimes my childhood sends me
a postcard: Do you remember?*
—MICHAEL KRÜGER, *Wettervorhersage*

(*Translated by Richard Dove*)

LA PALMA

Roque de
los Muchachos
P. N. Caldera de Taburiente

Garafía

Barlovento

San Andrés
y Sauces

Santa Cruz
de La Palma

Los Llanos
de Aridane

Fuencaliente

ISLAS

LA GOMERA

Hermigua

Vallehermoso

Valle Gran Rey

P. N.
Garajonay

San Sebastián
de La Gomera

Playa de
Santiago

TENERIFE

San Cristóbal
de La Laguna

Puerto
de la Cruz

Icod de los Vinos

La Orotava

Santa Cr
de Teneri

Garachico

Parque Nacional
del Teide

Candelaria

Guía de Isora

Los
Cristianos

El Médano

Valverde

Frontera

El Tamaduste

Punta de
Orchilla

La Restinga

EL HIERRO

OCÉA

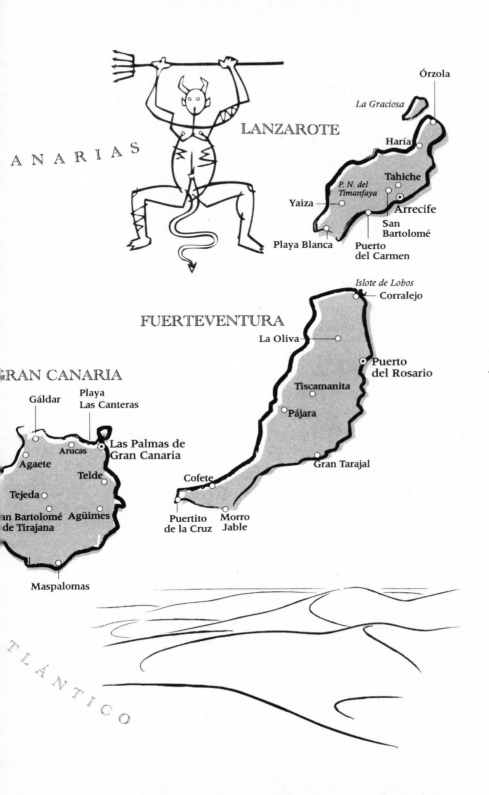

C A N A R I A S

LANZAROTE

Órzola

La Graciosa

Haría

P. N. del Timanfaya

Tahiche

Yaiza

Arrecife

San Bartolomé

Playa Blanca

Puerto del Carmen

FUERTEVENTURA

Islote de Lobos

Corralejo

La Oliva

Puerto del Rosario

Tiscamanita

Pájara

Gran Tarajal

GRAN CANARIA

Gáldar

Playa Las Canteras

Arucas

Las Palmas de Gran Canaria

Agaete

Telde

Tejeda

an Bartolomé de Tirajana

Agüimes

Cofete

Puertito de la Cruz

Morro Jable

Maspalomas

T L Á N T I C O

BEFORE LEAVING

SIXTY YEARS AGO, THE BASQUE WRITER IGNACIO ALDECOA TRAVELLED to the Canary Islands in search of what he had been told was paradise. He wrote a book, *A Tourist's Notebook*, which the publishing house Arión published in its series 'A Pilgrim in His Own Land'. I first came across this book many years later, in a second-hand bookshop in Madrid. I bought several copies, as many as I could find; I also tried to get some publishers interested in reprinting it, and I even got together a group of young filmmakers, led by Miguel García Morales, to film a documentary based on Aldecoa's sentimental journey to the place he did indeed end up believing was paradise.

Meanwhile, Peter Mayer, an editor whom I had met when he worked for Penguin, spoke to me once in Madrid about making a similar trip. He did not know Aldecoa's book, and on that occasion I didn't mention it to him, didn't mention this text that I had read with both gratitude and excitement some time before Mayer made his suggestion. One thing was definitely the case, that ever since Mayer spoke to me I had a clear idea in my head: to follow Aldecoa on his journey; to revisit the places he had been to; to rediscover, insofar as it was possible, the terrain he had covered, keen to lose himself in the landscape of the Islands.

The notes of the conversation I had with Peter Mayer about what he wanted from my journey got lost in a taxi somewhere, but could not be wiped from my mind. He said that he didn't want a general history, or a geography textbook, or a tourist guide: what he was keen on was a book of my memory of the Islands, the knowledge I kept in my mind's eye of their landscape, and that which I kept in my heart about the people there, my forefathers and my contemporaries. He didn't want a scholarly book either. He wanted a sentimental portrait of the Canary Islands. A sentimental journey, as I understood it.

These jottings were in a notebook I had taken out to record my conversation with Peter. The task was exciting and confusing all at once; it is very difficult to compress into a single journey, a single point of view, the whole extent of such a fragmented land. The Canary Islands are a group of seven large islands (plus two smaller ones and two islets) situated in a strategically significant part of the Atlantic, next to Africa, fragments sheared off that continent by geological processes; they are on the way to America, or to Europe, depending on the direction you're coming from, and they have a lot in common with all of these places: Africa, America, Europe. They have belonged to the Spanish Crown since the fifteenth century, and are a part of Spain, of the history, culture and language of Spain. Their relation with America (South America above all) has been essential for their development and for that of their language, their culture, their attitudes and their thought. And of course their relation with Europe, via tourism and other forms of human contact, has supported their development.

The whole region of the Canary Islands, which used to be divided into two provinces and which now is a part of the autonomous framework of democratic Spain, has been visited by writers, scientists, politicians, all kinds of people: the writers, over the course of their visits, have seen surreal spaces, extraordinary displays of the power of the earth, metaphors for both the sea and the land; artists have been struck by the variety of the landscape. And they have written, or painted, or sculpted—either while on the Islands themselves or basing their work on their experiences there—the impressions which have remained in their mind's eye or in their heart of these crags bathed by the Atlantic.

But there are not many people who have done as Aldecoa did, not even among the travellers from the Islands themselves; very few, at least very few that I know of, have travelled the full circle, have voyaged into the interior of the Islands and seen them from the outside as well, have learnt enough to be able to describe the Islands as a whole. Aldecoa's book, only fifty pages long in its first edition, is in this sense exceptional, and is a true guide for anyone who might want to make the incredible journey over the whole of the archipelago: high and low, far and wide.

If it had not been for Mayer's suggestion (visit all the islands, describe them all, with modern eyes but without discounting the views of the past), then I would never have undertaken this journey. Years ago, when Julio Cortázar published *The Autonauts of the Cosmoroute*, a book describing the sentimental journey he and his wife, Carol Dunlop, took along the highway from Paris to Marseilles, I decided to imitate the great author of *Hopscotch* and go on a circular trip over and around Tenerife, the largest island of the archipelago, where I was born. On the first day, along with my wife, Pilar Garcia Padilla, I came to a pretty spot in the northeast of the island, the hamlet of Masca, a beautiful place that I have since revisited in order to describe it to you in the book you now have in your hands. But the first time I was there, a group of thieves, who were staking out that part of the island with the aim of taking advantage of unwary tourists, stole everything that we had in the car, and so we called a halt to our adventure. The journey which I have now finally undertaken, travelling not just across Tenerife but through the whole region, had as its aim the same goals: to see, close-up, in as much detail as possible, the physical myth of the archipelago; to get as deep as possible into the land in order to be able to describe, or try to describe, its soul; to travel from the green forests to the geological rifts; to speak with the stones and the sea and the mountains; to see things in order to talk of them.

It was a very complex journey: it was not simply a question of looking at maps or searching for written and oral sources to guide me; Mayer's suggestion, which I took up, was that I should give a personal account, an extremely personal one, of what it was I found.

And what did I find? That time has passed since Aldecoa jotted down the results of his poetic investigation of the archipelago. Back in his day there were islands that it was impossible to visit, where storms blew in and boats did not dare drop anchor. Back in those days, the middle of the last century, not every island had its own airport, and the Atlantic is both fierce and treacherous. It was extremely difficult for Aldecoa to dock at El Hierro, and La Gomera resisted him as well. Nowadays, all the islands are far easier to reach, although the Atlantic remains fierce; the boats have been improved and are now much faster and safer, and every island has its own working airport. The region which the Basque author visited was one that was semi-feudal, where survival almost everywhere was dependent on agriculture; tourism had not yet started its exponential growth, and the customs which he noted are very different from those which can be seen nowadays on these islands where nearly two million people live, far more than the population of the archipelago when he travelled there.

So, to some degree, Aldecoa travelled to one set of islands and I visited another. Are they really so different, changed by the passing of time and the new impressions and sensations which it has laid down? I don't think so. The fundamental sentiment of the island dwellers (isolated as they are; landscape has a significant role to play in this) is still their melancholy (their *magua*, as it is called there) which Aldecoa so clearly identified, and which was visible in my parents, and in my older brothers and sisters, and in the countrymen and the fishermen whom you run into in the villages and who are still the archetypal representatives of the native islanders.

This is a sentimental journey: I began it (or began it again, as it is a journey which contains within it all the other journeys I have made to the Islands over the course of my life) in La Gomera, and have finished it in Gran Canaria: two islands which look similarly blunt, both striking like fists from the sea. But this is not a journey from island to island; that was not my aim. Just as memories do, the islands sometimes become confused with one another: they have a great deal in common. And so from time to time something that I see in one island will remind me of other physical aspects or feelings that are to be found in other parts of the archipelago.

The painter Pedro González said something to me when I told him that I was dedicating a great deal of space to the sea in this book: a phrase that I wanted to include here because to some degree it is the framework or leitmotif of my journey. 'The sea is the horizon for the Canary Islanders,' the great artist said, and then clarified his statement as we drank red wine in La Carrera, the main street in La Laguna on Tenerife, his home town. Like the sea, the horizon constantly changes for Canary Islanders: it can be in-your-face or oblique; it can embrace you or push you away; it breaks your heart or it consoles you. The sea is our common point; it encloses us and defines us; it frightens us and warns us. It makes us the people we are.

This journey has made me love my islands more because it has explained them to me; I am a little closer to their horizons because the islands themselves have shown their horizons to me.

While I wrote this book I needed a crutch to continue walking: an emotional crutch, words that would inspire me to carry on travelling down paths which one can only travel using the words that other wise men have previously uttered. And so, as well as Ignacio Aldecoa's book, I made a great deal of use of two other unique texts. One was *Journey to the Canary Islands* by the German naturalist Alexander Humboldt, who spent time in the Islands (Tenerife above all; he saw some of the other islands in passing) at the end of the eighteenth century, as he travelled towards America. It is an extraordinary book, in which the scientific traveller does not simply observe the geology of Mount Teide, the vast volcanic mountain of the Islands, which is his passion and the object of his investigation, but also deals in great detail with the character of the islanders who put him up or whom he meets in the streets. The other book is by one of my teachers, Domingo Pérez Minik (1903-1989), a self-taught and extremely articulate man who lived through the Spanish Civil War on the losing side and was one of the members of the committee that welcomed the pope of surrealism, André Breton, to Tenerife. Minik offered a vibrant discourse on the human condition of the island, a few fragments of which I share with the readers of this book, as they seem to show in great detail what it is to be an inhabitant of these Atlantic islands.

At the end of the book, my sensation as I finished was that I had embraced, or tried to embrace, the essence of an archipelago which offers as many surprises to the visitor as the people of the islands have impressions of the sea. Before leaving you with what I saw in La Gomera and on the rest of the islands, travelling back and forth over a period of time, halting when I needed to in my sentimental memories and in those of others, I would like to thank Peter Mayer for his commission, the sentimental importance of which I don't need to explain here, and also my dear companion, Pilar Garcia Padilla, through whose eyes I saw my own emotions anew as I travelled once again through these landscapes in which Aldecoa sought paradise and I found my horizons once again. Pilar also corrected what I wrote, gave coherence to the expression of a great number of my feelings and instilled logic in what were initially only side-tracks and suggestions. She was, if Peter will permit me to use the expression, the first editor of this book, which is dedicated to Oliver, my grandson, who, at the time of writing in January 2011, was as yet unborn, hanging safely in the belly of our daughter Eva. To some extent, this book is a form of letter to Oliver and to Eva, a letter which many people helped me to write: Yolanda Delgado, with her intelligent corrections, Ulises Ramos, Marian Montesdeoca, Carmelo Rivero and Leoncio González, who provided me with fertile literary materials to help me understand how foreigners approach and think about these islands.

IN CLOSING THIS INTRODUCTION I RECALL THE NAME OF THE COLLECTION in which Ignacio Aldecoa published *A Tourist's Notebook*: 'A Pilgrim in His Own Land'. And I realise that this is what I have been all this time as I travelled through the Islands, a pilgrim in my own land, in search of an ever-changing horizon which appears and disappears like the non-existent and mysterious island of San Borondón.

LOCAL FOOD

JUANA, THE WOMAN WHO RUNS THIS RESTAURANT WHERE I AM NOW, this restaurant on Mount Cedro in the Garajonay national park on La Gomera, served the same kind of food, during Holy Week, to the German chancellor Angela Merkel. The German governmental security services spoke to Juana, a native of La Gomera with pale eyes and hair that is already greying, they used helicopters to sweep the area, and then suddenly she appeared, in tall boots and with her husband: the most powerful woman in unified Germany.

It was a clear April day; Frau Merkel ate *papas con carne* (they call them *papas* on the Canary Islands and in South America, as well as in the west of Andalucia; they are just *patatas*, potatoes, in the rest of Spain); Juana also served *almogrote* (an extremely addictive blend of cheese, tomato, garlic and pepper), and the German leader also had space for some *papas arrugadas*, a speciality of the Canary Islands, which are made (ideally) by boiling the *papas* in a large pot of heavily salted water.

However, the good lady did commit one heresy at this meal, so exclusive and so typical of the Canary Islands (or rather, typical of La Gomera itself): she washed down the dishes—all of them extremely heavy in both salt and, probably, calories—with a glass of orange juice (which was, at least, freshly squeezed). And, however natural it might have seemed to her, to drink orange juice with such a meal in the Islands was a sacrilege that, at the very least, astonished the onlookers. This type of meal needs to be accompanied with wine; wine of any type, but if it is local, no matter whether smooth or sharp, then all the better; this land, at least in the mountains, demands wine; down by the shore one can drink the water that flows from the mountains, but the mountains of the Canary Islands are made for drinking wine.

She could have drunk the wine, which here, as throughout most of the islands, is fairly good, and which has even garnered a certain amount of literary fame in the past, for it is a wine that William Shakespeare gave Falstaff to drink. But no, Merkel only drank orange juice. She could have drunk any of the good vintages that have in recent years flourished on the islands, she could have drunk Juana's own wine: a popular wine that hangs around in the throat, as though begging for more food. Up there, in the mountain haze: wine, of any kind. German wine, even . . . but, unarguably, wine.

Angela Merkel ate this meal a few feet away from where I am now, on this August midday, in the height of summer, where in the capital of the island, San Sebastián de La Gomera, it is thirty-two degrees Centigrade under a torrid sun, and the cats and dogs seek refuge in the scarce shade offered by the old tiled roofs of the villa where Christopher Columbus stayed before he went off to discover America in 1492. Many years later, in *One Hundred Years of Solitude*, Gabriel García Márquez envisages the island: he sees it rising among the clouds, the same clouds which cover Mount Teide, the mythical mountain of Tenerife. Between Columbus's voyage of discovery and all the other related daydreams, the island has remained here, solid as a dun-coloured rock. Look at it now, from where Columbus saw it, and you will see it steep and dry, for it is summer; but you know that as soon as it rains, even a little, this drought-ridden appearance will give way to another landscape, a garden filled with cliffs as green as Garajonay itself, where Germans stop for lunch and drink orange juice.

When Angela Merkel had her meal the weather was fine, the sun came through the gaps in the thick Garajonay forest, almost four thousand hectares of untouched nature, ten per cent of the island's whole surface, and you could walk through the cliffs and the eternal springs that drape a sibilant, drowsy noise over the scrubland.

And it was April, mid-spring. But on this August day when Juana lays the table with the same food that back then nourished the woman who was in charge of Europe, the temperature outside must be around five degrees, there are occasional showers, the streams flow rapidly, stormily, and the ramblers who share this refuge with us—La Vista, it is called—dry themselves as rigorously as if they were entering a private home. They are shivering when they come in, and although the calendar shows that we are in midsummer, nature has spun on its heel and we are in midwinter again. This is the phenomenon we call the 'sea of clouds', produced by the trade winds which batter the island all year from the northeast and which, when they reach the Islands' tall peaks, condense and cause this typical phenomenon of the north faces of the more mountainous islands. The tourists, in their summer flip-flops, seek shelter here, and wine is a swift comforter. Juana is a strapping, healthy woman, who makes no distinction between her more illustrious guests and those who arrive with nothing more than the clothes on their backs. This is a trait of people who live in the Islands outside the cities: they seem to have a democratic attitude deeply fixed in their souls, which leads everyone to be treated in the same way, which is to say that they are treated well, but no one feels better or worse dealt with than anyone else; in the countryside everyone is equal, and the rain falls evenly on us all in any case.

IT IS HER OWN HOUSE, JUANA'S HOUSE. BEFORE REACHING IT, FOR ANYONE who has never before entered the tree-filled depths of Garajonay, the possibility of arriving in such a spot seems like a dream after nightmares of darkness or desert. But here is Juana, and she opens the door as though it were the door to a refuge, and the fog slides away, and it is as though one were entering a warm paradise in which anything she were to put before you on the table would be just what you wanted. More than anything else, you want that rough wine which La Merkel did not want to try: her loss.

And what Juana does place before you on the table, which has spent decades supporting the elbows of any number of tourists, is the gastronomic tradition of the island (and of most of the other islands as well). What she gives us—*papas arrugadas*, *almogrote*, meat—is very like what I used to eat at home in my little house in Puerto de la Cruz, in the touristic north of Tenerife, the island just across the way, which is where we have come from now in order to walk on this island with its many paths, this island which bade farewell to Columbus, who would, I imagine, have eaten here the same food as Angela Merkel.

My parents made their home next to the San Felipe ravine, where at times—days of my childhood—the emboldened water of the winter floods would carry everything away with it, flushing it down from the heights into the sea; from the roof of my house I saw sticks and furniture and sometimes dead bodies washed along by the flood. 'The ravine's running!' people would shout, and the spectacle, at once cruel and marvellous, would bring the children running to look; I grew up knowing these terrible marvels with which nature punished the people who lived on the edge of the ravines. I lived in this house, and I learnt to eat the food of the Islands there: *papas*, sardines both fresh and salted, *carne con papas*, fried eggs, fried *papas*, bananas, *gofio* . . . the food that instructed our taste buds and our stomachs. Now that I have come into Juana's house (my mother was called Juana as well), I have come back to the tastes of my own home; I don't tell Juana; I don't tell anyone: you travel with the knowledge of the food you have eaten, and there must always be a sentimental trigger that sends you back to its taste, which is not simply physiological: they are the tastes that life keeps in store for you and reveals at the right moment.

EVERY DAY MY MOTHER MADE US WHATEVER SHE HAD AVAILABLE IN HER larder, the larder of a poor woman with little money, to whom famine had given the ability to do much with very few resources. But everything tasted wonderful. She would boil the *papas* with coarse salt, which my father bought by the kilo in the village markets; she would serve meat only on Sundays, and she cooked it with chickpeas and paprika so that the whole dish took on the same colour and texture— halfway between red and brown and so reminiscent of warm earth— as the dish which Juana has just served me, accompanied, now as then, with carrots and other local vegetables which I can't quite iden- tify. I suppose that there must be *bubangos* (a variety of zucchini na- tive to the Canary Islands) chayote squash, red onion, a little cilantro; cilantro is wonderful: it gives a special flavour to everything it comes into contact with, as if instead of a herb it were a combination of every possible herb, as if the Atlantic and the Mediterranean were mixing together their stews, their meat, their fish, their salads. In Garajonay, Juana—this Juana from La Gomera—has put everything into the food: it is the custom here: when there was nothing, women would put whatever they had into the stew. And so their stews grew from nothing to become unforgettable. So unforgettable that, half a century later, the flavour comes back to me as though it were a word spoken by my mother back in my earliest childhood. The childhood of flavours.

BUT, AS I HAVE SAID, THIS MEAT, WHICH WE ARE EATING ON A WEDNES- day in August, in this winter which has been laid down on us by the strange and prehistoric climate of Garajonay, was something which we would only ever eat in my house on Sundays. The domestic econ- omy of those years (the post-war 1950s, which seemed to last forever in the Canary Islands for families of few resources) forced these diets upon us, and during the week we ate more improvised meals, which even so we thought tasted exquisite.

For example, my mother would buy salted fish, which was cheaper and which kept better. We would go to the discount shops, which still exist, places of scarcity and abundance at the same time: they had what they needed to have, but very little of it; this was where my mother would do her shopping, or send us to do her shopping for her. But I should probably tell you what we were eating, or what we ate at home, in order for you to understand why Juana was giving us so much food, so much good food, on this wintry August Wednesday.

My father would eat very early, as early as the uncertain dawn light would allow. He would get up alone. Making breakfast was back then the only obligatory task for people of his sex, so my father would make himself a huge cup of milky coffee; the milk came from a goat we kept outside the house, on a little hillock which was the site of what was to me a fascinating story, which I will soon tell you.

To his milk, my father would add salt and *gofio*. Salt? Yes, he never ate sugar, he hated sugar, and I never saw him eating sweet food; I don't even remember him bringing sweets home; he bought fruit; when oranges were cheap he would buy huge baskets of oranges, which my mother would then share out among our relatives and neighbours; my father had no sense of quantity, or money: he had no money, and when he had money he would spend it like a rich man. He was a robust man, a peasant, and as well as being a robust peasant he was sentimental and eccentric, a man who did not believe in death.

Which was why he lived so long.

But let's get back to his diet, his strange diet, strange as he was.

He would take this huge cup of coffee with goat's milk and would add several spoonsful of *gofio*, and then he would shave in front of a tiny mirror that showed only part of the face at a time, as in an old Western movie. He would walk over to the mirror in silence; sometimes he would talk to the mirror; he would address himself, like the colonel in that story by Gabriel García Márquez; in fact, the Islands are very like those unfarmed fields that appear in García Márquez's fiction, or the vibrantly fertile farms of Macondo, and my father was there, shaving, speaking to the man he saw in the mirror, as if he were bringing news from the dreams which had been inter-

rupted at four o'clock in the morning. He was not aware that the letter that would save him could never come, just as it never came for
García Márquez's colonel, but unlike the colonel, my father was by
now not waiting for any letter. Perhaps a letter from Venezuela, but
really he knew that he would not receive that letter that had come
through so many other doors: emigration papers, which (to a degree)
had solved the problems of so many Canary Island families in the hungry years after the Spanish Civil War.

I liked to watch him shave. I would be awake, studying by the light
of a single bulb which also helped him see his face better in the mirror.
And I watched him shave himself bit by bit, as he drank the milky
coffee which was now a solid mass that helped him break the fast of
the short night. Milk, *gofio*, salt. This was his way of greeting the
morning, when he started to work in the deep silence of the night. I suppose that the same rituals took place in every house: the fight for life
begins slowly, noiselessly, in the clinging dawns, around darkened
courtyards. There were other places, of course, but it was in a place
like this that I started to know what life was and the sounds that made
up the morning by the ravine, as the cocks all crowed and one could
hear, very softly, the sound of wind in the banana trees.

THE MILK, AS I HAVE SAID, CAME FROM THE GOAT, AN AGITATED BEAST
that kicked against the ground as though trying to summon its master,
or else sending messages to an underground world of chasms and lava,
the soil of the La Orotava valley, ground so fertile that if you threw
a seed down then a tree would surely sprout up; I planted an avocado
tree: I dropped an avocado stone in the banana plantation and a little
while later a tree grew up which became the avocado tree that gave
us all avocados until my father decided to cut it down and build the
driveway to a garage. The garden was dug out, and this was in some
way a symbol of the way in which things came to an end, and also
a metaphor of the development of the Islands, from agriculture to
asphalt.

But let's not talk about this for the moment. Let's get back to the goat's milk, the milk we all drank. Sometimes we got milk from cows, because there were all kinds of animals at my house, as there were back then at many houses in the Islands. There were goats, pigs, cows, chickens, and rabbits, cockerels, little baby chickens that ran ahead of my mother cheeping as though fleeing a fire; the noise of the farm was the sound of my childhood, before the radio came to my house bringing the whole world with it. When my father brought the radio home for the first time, my mother listened to it for a moment and said:

'The devil's in that thing.'

And she wanted to cast it out of the house, as one might cast out the devil; later she grew to like the devil, if I can put it like that, and listened to the radio serials with me in the quiet of the afternoons, all those fantasies that made us believe that the world was large, not confined to this house on the edge of the ravine.

The animals also used to rest in the afternoons, all of them: a Noah's Ark that my mother cared for as though they were also her children. There were four real children in the family, and then the animals, all the animals one can imagine; there were lizards as well, but they weren't tame; the pipes were full of lizards which came out to take the clean midday village sun: the sun that forced its way through persistent clouds which it eventually managed to beat into submission; the wild sun which was still a refuge for tourists who thought, when they reached my village, that they had reached the land where the clouds gather to rest. As if it were a single speck of light, the sun pushes its way through the clouds and Puerto de la Cruz is now a garden filled with light. Anyway, we were talking about the animals. The custom of having so many animals around the house dates back to the times of famine, which since before the dawn of Western civilisation has, along with all other kinds of epidemic, devastated these African islands, these lands so dun and irregular, so attractive and so defensive. If a war had taken place back then, if the island would have been doubly isolated, then we would have had enough raw material to survive for a year, or nearly; we had the banana plantation, tomatoes and lettuce; the garden was a jewel, my mother said, and looked after the various crops as though she were guarding some precious gem. There were vegetables, too: *bubangos*, chayotes, onions. My father was there, waiting for the letter which he did not know needed to come, going up into the mountains to gather pine needles which he would use to make manure that he sold to the landowners; my mother was there, on the edge of the ravine, feeding the animals which would later feed us, feeding them so that we could eat our stews, drink our milk. It was a subsistence economy. Years later, high up in Garajonay on La Gomera, the fragrant taste of the food we used to eat at home is still the only condiment we need.

MY MOTHER WAS THE ONE WHO MILKED THE GOAT; MY FATHER PREferred goat's milk because, according to him, it was salty as the salt that he put in the milk, salty as the *gofio*. The *gofio* was the same as *gofio* always had been, ever since it was invented by the Guanches, or the Romans, or the Phoenicians, or the Carthaginians, or the French, or the Genovese, or the Andalucians, or the Basques, etc.: all of the people who make up the disputed origins of the Canary Islands. All ancestors are our ancestors, and they came from everywhere: the Islands were crossing points; in the Islands, the sea becomes a concentric wheel: it is the Atlantic, but it is also a crossing point of lost highways: there were pirates around us (the British Admiral, Horatio Nelson, wanted to sack Tenerife and was wounded; he lost an arm, but then the islanders looked after him as they normally look after people; they gave him cheese and he gave us beer), but there were also friends, people who came in peace to discover the Islands and use them as a stepping stone from which to make further discoveries. This is what happened with Christopher Columbus, the admiral who set foot on La Gomera in order to make the world a larger place, to discover America.

Gofio, my father putting *gofio* in his goat's milk. *Gofio* has an origin closer to home, more immediate. Its origin is as follows: millet (corn, which came back with Columbus and his men from their trip to America) was taken to the mills, and was ground down there until it became a fine toasted flour, which I would try as it came out of the chutes, as if I were tasting an ice cream or some other product which derived its delicacy from its texture. My mother would send us to the mill; all the children of the village went there; we would stare at the mill covered from top to toe in flour; the dull sound of the mill itself, the dry smell of the toasted millet, and then the product itself coming down the chutes, ready to be eaten with milk, or cheese, or bananas, or wine. The raw material of life; the evocative symbol of the islanders' humble tables. The 'rough stuff' spoken of by the philosopher Miguel de Unamuno, who was exiled to Fuerteventura in the 1920s and who found there, in this delicacy that appeared almost skeletal, the best possible metaphor for that lonely island and, by extension, for the spirit—austere, essential—of the Canary Islanders themselves. *Gofio*. Wad of *gofio*, the island's skeleton.

But it should not be eaten alone, and far less alone and in large amounts; *gofio* was made to be mixed with water, with sugar, with milk, with bananas. Bananas, which came to the Canary Islands in a deliberate act of economic glaciation, after the failure of other products such as cochineal (an insect that is parasitic on plants such as the prickly pear, and which was used a lot in dye manufacture up to the nineteenth century), are fruits which people outside the Canary Islands think of as purely sweet, but which in the Islands themselves, or at least in my house, are considered a fair accompaniment to the main course: we eat them with fried eggs, with rice, with *gofio*. My mother would mix bananas with *gofio garujado* (that is, *gofio* and water), and the resultant ball would be waiting for me when I got back from school. It wasn't a sweet or anything with a proper name: it was just what I ate after school, and for many years I thought that this was what everyone ate in the afternoons, bananas mixed with *gofio*.

Getting the *gofio* from the mill was one of the activities of my house, of my neighbourhood; all the children of all the families would go to the mill to collect it, and then we would go down, or up, to our houses carrying what would later be an essential part of our diet, in our house, in every house. Families in the Canary Islands have lived for centuries, or at least dozens upon dozens of years, depending on the mill and what it produced: this product which went with everything, which could be used for everything.

Gofio is the universal substrate.

And it has been one of the strange things that the Canary Islands have exported, to Cuba, to Argentina, to Venezuela, to Uruguay—wherever a Canary Islander has gone, in successive waves of emigration throughout the nineteenth and twentieth centuries, *gofio* has travelled with him, to add flavour to his life and those of others: an ID card—racial, rural, concrete—for Islanders all over the world.

A few years ago, in Montevideo, the capital of Uruguay, founded by thirteen families of expatriate Canary Islanders, a young man of Island descent offered me cheese with *gofio*, a fairly common version of our standard fare, and offered it to me saying that it was a genuinely Uruguayan dish. I corrected him, but he did not correct me: *gofio* cannot be as ethnically Canarian, as prehistoric, as I thought, if it is made of millet and millet came to us from abroad, from the America discovered by Columbus.

It is true that before the arrival of *gofio*, the Canary Islanders ate the roots of ferns in a paste which, after being milled, tastes similar to *gofio*.

But that is another story.

So, BACK ON THE LITTLE MOUND WHERE THE GOAT GRAZED THAT MY mother milked, and whose milk my father used for his early morning breakfast; *gofio* was the food which gave him the strength to shave and set off on a day's work which, for him and people like him, was a continuation of the dark days of the post-war period and the economic misery which seemed another tradition: the tradition of scarcity, the custom of hunger.

The essence of our family's economic survival lived on this little mound: in front of the goat, who was calm through the night and who bleated as though being tortured as soon as the cocks started crowing, was the farm where the animals lived who assured the future of the house. We drank goat's milk; we sold cow's milk, which was more expensive: it went into large metal receptacles, men came and hoisted them up onto their shoulders, and the cows stood there, their sad eyes on the ground. My mother used to recite a little bit of doggerel: 'The cows are standing there, their sad eyes on the ground, because they know their milk is going to be watered down . . .'

My parents sold the milk from the cows, which was much more valued for some reason, perhaps for its nutritional value or else simply because there was much more of it, and kept goat's milk for family use, relying on that nervous animal which started bleating at dawn. I would hear from my cot, and later from my bed, the noise of the streams of milk falling into the bowls my mother used for this task. The sound was always the same, as if it came from a dream, or were the extension of a dream, but also it was different every day: it was the noise of something being born, a novelty in spite of the fact that it was always the same milk, the monotonous sound coming from the goat's udders.

MY CONCENTRATION ON NOISES, ON THE SOUNDS THAT SURROUNDED me, marked out the universe that made up my childhood. Every noise had a meaning, always more metaphorical than real. I remember going out with my father to find some parts he needed for his van and racking my childish brain to come up with reasons to explain the different noises that came from the various workshops he went into to try to find ways to fix his means of transport, which was also his livelihood; when I heard the noises that were the backdrop to the conversations he conducted at the top of his voice I thought that they were inventing some new torture technique to hurt my father, until he came out, safe and sound, and I could go back to pretending to be asleep in the cabin of the van. The first book I read in my life, by Jules Verne, I read next to the pipes in our house, listening to the whistle of the water rising (or falling), and since then I have associated reading with the noise of water rising (or falling).

The goat was the creature that ruled the house. Its milk, the noise of it being milked, its bleating.

My mother told me many stories, and there was a goat in nearly all of them. She used one very famous story, the tale of Genevieve of Brabant, who saved her son's life thanks to the milk of a goat, as a thread on which to hang a number of other stories, in which goats saved children in imminent danger of disaster.

How could I not drink goat's milk, she seemed to be saying, when goats were the saviours of humanity?

Even the animals with Jesus in the manger were goats, as she told the story.

MANY YEARS LATER, HERE IN LA GOMERA, WHERE I WAS STARTING OFF on this sentimental journey through my own land, I heard an abrupt bleating, almost desperate: it was a solitary goat on a hillside which I remember, very close to where Juana served us on that wintery August day the *gofio* which has unleashed all these memories; the goat must have been lost, left behind by a peasant and out of earshot of the whistles that could have brought it back to the fold.

I was high up on the mountain, and I heard this bleating as though it were a human voice calling to me, but of course the goat was calling out for other hands and for other whistles, looking for a familiar smell or else its master, the man who could save it from this loneliness; the goat bleated as though it were the most abandoned creature on the earth, using that earthy yet animal voice that sounded like the voice of a wound. And then the sound of its master's whistle came, and the goat bleated again, as though it had just been saved from an earthquake. And then it fell silent, calm, on the way back to the enclosure where it felt safe.

I associate the Islands, or those areas of them where goats still live out their dramas of loneliness and bleating, with the sound of silence: it is as though everything is asleep, until the sky suddenly cracks open because something has called out, or else the constant beat of a cricket sounds out like a hammer blow. A precise silence, somehow special, which in La Gomera may also be broken by someone whistling for their flock or calling to a neighbour across one of the many gullies here.

Whistling. The word is out now. La Gomera is a place with many peculiarities, and Garajonay is only one of them, perhaps the greatest one, or in any event the most beautiful, the most faithful metaphor for the contradictions of geography: the mountain is covered in vegetation, and where the mountain ends are vast openings, dull-coloured land, immobile gullies, steep crags that can only be climbed (or descended) by powerful giants or very brave men.

These giants don't exist, but very brave men do, and over the course of the centuries they have ascended and descended the cliffs using walking sticks which have evolved with time: from rustic poles to sophisticated staffs which cling to the ground as though they were the claws of leopards or tigers. And these men have gone up and down the cliffs with their flocks since prehistoric times, fighting to survive on terrain that is sometimes barren and sometimes extraordinarily fertile, but always as hard to deal with as life itself.

And so that goat reminded me of the goat we had at home, its bleating and its evening loneliness, when it dozed as domesticated dogs do when they are left alone. The goat was the queen of the house: as it was the most secure means of subsistence (a kind of privileged being which would never dry up, which would always have milk to provide for the family), it also had its survival assured.

The pigs and the cocks and the hens did not have their survival assured. The goat and the little chickens were the only ones who knew, as if animals knew about things like this, that we needed them, that they would stay with us. The goat reacted to my mother's appearance as though a party were getting started, and the little chickens followed the sound of her feet as if they were playing hide and seek with her. If anyone were to ask me what happiness is, I should say that it is remembering my mother running after the chickens.

While it gave milk, the goat would only ever die a natural death; the chickens would die whenever it was their destiny as cocks or hens to be useful for soup or a stew or a roast. It was a tough life, but we children knew nothing about the suffering of the chickens.

The goat was in its rightful place: on the islands of Fuerteventura and El Hierro above all the goat served as a kind of totemic animal, or at least quasi-totemic, and now you can see why: the same thing happened on those islands as happened in my house. Because it was necessary, the goat was untouchable; it held the household together; it was like the cow in India or the llama in Peru. An inevitable presence, a decisive need.

As well as this, it was also a legendary animal. My mother used to tell us about how at the end of the nineteenth century (there are photos of this in the house: my mother's parents' house was like a house in a South American colony, filled with photographs of strange places, like the American rainforests, and in the midst of these forests that were not forests I lived out my childhood, as though I myself were inside a photograph) a step-brother of hers had travelled to Cuba in search of a treasure which, according to a dream he had had, was hidden under a little mound where a goat grazed. It was a dream and nothing more, but he believed it: one day he caught a boat across the ocean and landed in Cuba. She told us all this in great detail.

She told me this story as she told me others, simply to keep me entertained. But this one in particular seemed almost convincing. It seemed plausible that in the years when she set this story she might have had a step-brother who travelled to Cuba; the first great wave of emigration from the Canary Islands was to Cuba, and the emigrants all travelled, like this stepbrother, following the lure of a new world filled with treasure, with food and work. Cuba was like another part of the Islands—not simply a mental extension of them, a space in which we could live other lives while still believing ourselves to be in the same land, but also a physical space to which we Islanders could travel without any pain or melancholy. Our place.

There were other destinations, such as Argentina or Uruguay, where immigration from the Canary Islands contributed decisively to their development, or else the United States, where the city of San Antonio in Texas was built mainly with Canary Island labour. But Cuba was the most mythical of all destinations for us, and almost the most natural. In the waves of emigration which took place in the 1950s, it was said that there was a natural compass: in certain months of the year, a boat leaving the Islands would head directly to Cuba; at other times, it would head to Venezuela. This was the natural law which had controlled the emigrations of the nineteenth century as well. Some to Cuba; some to Venezuela. Or Argentina.

Cuba is an island; it has a climate similar to that of the Islands themselves. It has the same damp which us asthmatics fled from, but it also has the same desert zones we fled to: above all, it has our language, which is still, as it was then, spoken with an accent so close to that of the Canary Islands. Smooth, cadenced, filled with strange turns of phrase, words which come from here and there, or else which are born in one place or the other and have not yet spread their wings.

And so there was nothing strange in the fact that an Islander from Tenerife, from the La Orotava valley—a site which had, like Cuba, deeply impressed Alexander von Humboldt—should want to travel in search of the common dream: the dream that Cuba was filled with treasures which could make the fortune of any outcast or adventurer or anyone willing to risk checking for himself the truth of Calderón de la Barca's phrase, that dreams are nothing but dreams.

GUILLERMO CABRERA INFANTE, THE CUBAN WRITER, SON OF A WOMAN from Tenerife, from San Juan de la Rambla, once told me that he had heard many stories about Canary Islanders who had believed the story (which they had dreamt, or had told to them) of treasures hidden in insignificant mounds where goats grazed.

If there really had been so many hidden treasures, then today the Islands would be the richest place on earth.

And they are not. They were very poor, and now they are not rich: far from it. But they used to be astonishingly poor; not even rich in their dreams.

And so this relative of mine, Domingo, went to Cuba, to Santiago de Cuba, I think.

'And then what happened, mother?'

This question, which I asked every time she told me the story, always produced an evasive reply from my mother, as if she had no real answer, or as if the real answer would be a painful disappointment for a child.

And so throughout my whole life I have been ignorant of what happened to my mother's step-brother who went to Cuba to look for a treasure guarded by a goat on the curved hump of its hillock. My mother did not know: the man had evaporated; she never knew if he had found the treasure or if someone else had found it; no one ever knew anything, and she knew nothing. And neither did I, of course.

Until very recently.

Recently, writing a book about my father and the post-war period in Spain, which was something he suffered through even though he had not gone to war, I was able to work out what had really happened to the man and his dream.

I think that my deduction, although it may destroy that beautiful dream whose resolution I never knew, is probably closer to reality than the legend in which my mother wrapped things up. Every time I asked her about her step-brother's whereabouts, and the treasure hidden under the goat, she changed the subject.

The hillock she told me about, and the goat she spoke of, were in fact the very same hillock and goat that were in front of our house. She had made the story up, made it up just as my father made up other lives as he looked in the mirror in the morning, imagining that he was another person, one who had received the letter that would save him from his poverty. Canary Islanders always make sure to keep a dream at hand. The poet José Luis Pernas, who comes from Las Palmas de Gran Canaria, the capital of Gran Canaria, has a line which runs as follows: 'Then I knew that one has to look for hope in order to keep on living.' This hope was not based on any reality in particular; it was made of words, castles in the air; my parents made up things in order to hide for a little longer the evidence that the horizon was not their future, but rather a wall, a wall that only dreams could knock down . . .

My mother's tale must have been this, oral literature, inventions to keep an asthmatic son entertained, and its elements were all very close, within touching distance: all one had to do was step out into the street and see that the goat was our goat, the hillock was the place where the goat grazed, with the craggy soil beneath it, the pure lava of the valley. This was not the soil of Cuba; she was inventing everything.

The step-brother was probably also an invention: the image in my mind of the peasant stepping onto the boat as my mother told me about this man Domingo was just one more legend out of the many she invented as she thought about how to answer me when I bombarded her with questions.

And so all of this is as close by as she is now to me as I eat my lunch here in beautiful Garajonay, a meal just like the ones she used to make on Sundays, and the very same stewed cress that she made in winter, almost every winter. And now they serve us *gofio* and I add water, mix it slightly, aware that I am doing something that has been done here for centuries, a fact which makes the pleasurable sensation of the *gofio* and the water in my hands impossible to hold back: I am mixing together a flavour, like listening to an old song. A *folía*, for example. Yes, a *folía*, one of those folk songs popular throughout Europe, with its own Canary Islands version as well, *la folía canaria*. 'Ay, *folías*, you want to hear one, you want me to sing, the *folías* of my country are happy and very sad to sing . . .' This is how it runs in the version sung by Los Sabandeños, a group from La Laguna, Tenerife which sprang up almost half a century ago and which embodies all the melancholy of the folklore of the Islands, all the melancholy which centres around this melody that derives from the fundamental sadness of the Portuguese and Galicians who, on their journey towards America, left in these islands the sensation that everything is both sad and joyful at the same time, like everything that remains from our memories in life.

ALL OF THESE FEELINGS, THE FEELINGS THAT THE *FOLÍA* PROVOKES, SENTIments sad and joyous at the same time, all of this memory that is both personal and collective—the memory of an Islander is the memory of all the Islanders—awoke in me when I entered La Vista, Juana from La Gomera's inn. Juana from La Gomera, who reminded me so much of another Juana, from Tenerife: my mother . . .

AND WHERE DO WE COME FROM?

WHAT I WANT TO SAY IS THAT UP THERE, AT THAT GARAJONAY INN high up in the mountains, I felt that if there is anything that defines my country then it is food, the way we eat it, the way we make it, the way in which the ritual of its use to keep us alive takes place. And of course, this food, the customs connected with it, with making it, with sharing it—food in the Canary Islands is collective, just as the *gofio* bag is, or the wine flagon, or the pot of stewed meat and potatoes, or fish soup, or *gofio* itself—all of this comes from our ancestors, although we've never been too clear about where our ancestors came from. Where are we from? Are we *from* here? It's clear that the answer to that must be no: we are born here, but our history starts a long way away; or perhaps it starts from nearby, from the mountains of Africa, from crossroads, from different races, from the journeys of the Portuguese and the Galicians, from the Spanish emigrations to America. We are Canary Islanders, there's no doubt about that, but there are as many races in our identity as there are kinds of bitterness, or joy. We are like *folías*, a crossing point for many sounds, a poetry filled with many different kinds of poetry or sound; we are like the Islands, identical in our melancholy but different in our spelling. A single island (Tenerife, for example) is many islands at once; one never knows at which bend in the road one island ends and the next begins. In Icod de los Vinos, on Tenerife, the sun might burst brightly over the thousand-year-old Drago tree, and a few kilometres further on, on the summit of Erjos, one might pass through a sea of clouds that eventually give way to what seems to be a clean and permanent sky, the sky of the south, like an eternal summer hidden above the northern peaks. Where are we from? From life itself, with all its journeys and sudden reverses . . .

In order to write this book I have needed to investigate what Spanish historians have written, both Islanders and mainlanders, both in this century and in all the centuries that have gone by, practically everything written since the Castilians led by Alonso Fernández de Lugo (amongst others) won their sometimes extremely bloody battles against the primitive inhabitants of the Islands, and no one can agree at all about the origins of the Canary Islanders, who right back at the start of things were known as Guanches (at least the ones in the western islands; those from La Palma were called Benahoares), and who came, according to the most authoritative studies, from the Atlas mountains in the north of Africa.

Antonio Tejera Gaspar, a man whom I trust because he was a school-friend of mine and I saw him study and start to learn how to think, says in his book *The Guanches of Tenerife* that people have claimed 'different and sometimes exotic origins for the Islanders, such as mythical Atlantis, or Germany, and there has been no less polemic about their cultural identity'.

The Guanches (and the inhabitants of the other islands) have been related to 'Palaeolithic European populations, or else the inhabitants of the Mesolithic Capsian culture in Northern Africa'.

What is without any doubt is that we were always told that the Guanches (and, I say again, the inhabitants of the other islands as well) were of Berber origin, and this was the specific family grouping which we, like Tejera Gaspar, started to study when it was tacitly forbidden from saying (in Franco-era Spain) that the Canaries were an island offshoot of the African continent. Yesterday's racism, and everyday xenophobia: the Francoist bourgeoisie of the Islands preferred to feel part of Europe than of Africa, as if it were possible for

the continents to shift on their axes simply by denying obvious proximity. Geographically, the Canary Islands are a part of Africa; it is another thing to acknowledge that because of their cultivation, their
history and their culture they are the point where the paths between
Europe and America meet and cross. And in order to understand who
we are, the interested reader might care to look at *Nature and Culture
of the Canary Islands*, the first large-scale compilation of geographical, historical and cultural information to be assembled in the Canary
Islands, which has gone through a large number of editions since first
being published in the nineteen seventies. It can also now be found
online at http://www.gevic.net.

But the Islands were always a part of Africa, and still are to all
intents and purposes, even though Franco and the conservatives of
the Franco era did not like to think about this proximity. It was a land
of exile and a land of conquest (or vice-versa), and it was conquered
by the Spaniards on the way to America when sources of Spanish
funding dried up and the Catholic kings had to fund conquistador ex-
peditions in order to enlarge their empire.

THE CANARY ISLANDS WERE A TEMPTING MORSEL ONLY BECAUSE THEY
were *en route* to the land of the infidel, but their position was what
would nowadays be called geostrategic: they have political importance
now, and used to be economically vital, or else simply influential both
religiously and culturally.

The Spaniards were keen to sample the Canary Islands, but they
had also been tasted by others. According to Antonio Tejera Gaspar's
book, the Islands had claim laid to them (back when it was not clear
if there were seven of them, or five, or three) by the Romans, and then
the French, and so on and so forth until the Spanish took them under
control. And Nelson's Englishmen also passed by to 'take' Tenerife:
they didn't manage it, and this gave rise to a handsome military spectacle, that of the invader being pardoned.

There was also a time when the Islands were the focus of Plato's idealism, as he situated his notion of Eden in them. For an Islander of today, or even yesterday, it is fascinating to imagine oneself as a part of that idyllic Atlantis conjured into being by Plato and which Pliny himself later claimed to have seen, but from a distance, because neither he nor Plato ever visited the Islands. Or did they? The fogs of the past allow us to say both one thing and its opposite.

Let us see what my friend Tejera Gaspar has to say about the impenetrable night of history. According to Tejera Gaspar's historical summary, what José de Viera y Clavijo (an enlightened eighteenth-century priest, responsible among other things for helping Enlightenment ideas reach the Islands and for compelling them to abandon the Inquisition) said was that 'the idea that the Canary Islanders were the descendants of Plato's vanished Atlantis transformed in a radical fashion what had until that moment been considered the truth.'

Until that moment, 'the Canary Islands had mainly been connected with the mythical islands of Greco-Roman civilisation, out in the open ocean in a distant place where the sun set and the souls of the Fortunate lived.'

And we Islanders, whether we were descendants of the Guanches or of their fellows, believed it and have continued to believe it: we have believed ourselves to be part of an archipelago which had in its day—and why not still?—been 'the garden of the Hesperides, the peaceful Fortunate islands which the Romans first of all invented and then later identified in a very specific way, connecting them always with the constantly disappearing and reappearing island of San Borondón, the finest example of medieval beliefs about islands.'

Medieval beliefs filtered into children's stories: I was lulled to sleep by being told that I had come from San Borondón; it was a part of Canary Island mythology, this island, and, like all mythology, it was based on hope: the idea that there is a beautiful place, probably imaginary, where men are as it was imagined they used to be, living their happy life on the Fortunate Isles.

Pliny had said as much at the beginning of the Christian era: the Fortunate Isles were there, close to the province of Africa which used to be called Mauritania, and which then became Algeria and Morocco, and near to Cádiz, on the southern corner of the Iberian peninsula. Pliny gave their names: Ombrios, the two Junonias (Junonia the Greater and Junonia the Less), Capraria, Ninguaria and Canaria, which later history would name as La Palma, La Gomera, El Hierro, Gran Canaria and Tenerife, which are (according to Pliny) beyond the Purpurarias, little islands off the coast of Essaouria in Morocco.

And so they came from the north of Africa. How did they get here? Some people say that the first inhabitants of the Islands did not know about navigation techniques and for this reason they preferred to live in opposition to the sea, safe in the mountains and caves, which was where they came from. And from this comes the deduction of many historians, both from the Islands and elsewhere, that the initial islanders were abandoned there as a cruel punishment by the Romans who were upset by the refusal of the Berbers (if they were Berbers) to render themselves to the civilisation of Rome.

So they were abandoned on this wasteland, and then spread out over the wasteland that was later to become the archipelago and adapted themselves to conditions which they survived, one now imagines, because of some supernatural resilience.

Is this so?

They came like Noah with his ark. Among the things they brought with them, history says, were 'pairs of goats, sheep, pigs, dogs, seeds', and if this is so, Tejera Gaspar concludes, then their exile 'became a true colonisation', carried out by individuals who, in contrast to other hypotheses as to their skills, actually knew what they were doing: to put it more bluntly, they knew how to swim and keep livestock.

They kept livestock. And if what they brought with them in their probable (or improbable) voyages was what the historians tell us, then their choice of provisions was a decisive influence on what we, centuries later, much more enlightened gastronomically, keep on serving up at mealtimes, in Garajonay or anywhere else—in my own house, for example, not just back in the days when my mother looked after us, but right now, when her great-grandchildren lift the lids of the pots on the stove to see what their parents are making for them . . .

But what if they came by force, thrown into the arms of an uncertain fate, cast into the sea as a punishment? Another Canary Island historian, and priest, Abreu Galindo, writing in the sixteenth century, described in a horrifying way the likelihood of this sequence of events: 'Rome held the province of Africa and sent there its legates and its officials, and the Africans rebelled and killed the legates and officials who were in the province of Mauritania; hearing of the news of the rebellion and the death of the legates and officials in Rome, the Senate, with the intention of taking revenge and of punishing the crimes and injuries committed, sent against the criminals a great and powerful army, and charged it with bringing the criminals to obedience. And in order that the crime committed not remain unpunished, and to give a lesson to the generations to come, they took those who had been the chief leaders of the rebellion and cut off their heads, and other cruel punishments; and for the others, in whom they found no other fault than that of following the common crowd, in order not to destroy them, but to remove their influence in all their generation and ensure that such another rebellion would not happen again, they cut out their tongues, from a desire that they would neither refer to the fact nor boast that they at one time had stood up against the Roman people. And so, with their tongues cut out, they put men and women in boats with certain provisions and sent them to these islands, leaving them some goats and sheep for their sustenance. And so these charming Africans were sent to these seven islands, providing them with their population.'

THE GOATS AGAIN, THE BLEATING AGAINST WHICH WE LIVED OUT OUR childhood and the childhood of the Islands. A terrible history. If what Abreu Galindo says is the truth (and it is just as true as many other interpretations, because historians, as Tejera Gaspar puts it, in this case only have questions), then the first inhabitants of the Canary Islands were cast away here, decimated and wounded, the amputees of a rebellion which could only be quashed with cruel and obstinate violence. They came to the Islands with their tongues cut out. For any civilisation, this would be a barbaric foundation, which would set out attitudes towards the future and which perhaps has done so in this instance. But Antonio Tejera Gaspar puts it well when he says that 'a culture is not what it once was at some long-lost moment of origin: more important is what they have developed into over time.'

That the first settlers came from the north of Africa is obvious, says Tejera, 'but two thousand years turned them into the culture of the Canary Islands'.

There is no debate about this now: all there is, is the past. The twentieth century has been for the Canary Islands a series of events which have shaped, almost as if they were being discovered for a second time, the future of the Islands: they lived through the famines of the start of the century; they dealt with emigration, with provincial divisions which created a great deal of conflict, both political and emotional, among the larger islands, Tenerife and Gran Canaria; they witnessed the Fascist rise of Franco: the future long-term dictator of the country started plotting here, spent time on the splendid Monte de la Esperanza; the Islands lived through the innumerable difficulties caused by the post-war period, which led to new waves of emigration, to Venezuela above all; they had to deal with an ever-increasing wave of tourism which saved the Islands from their agricultural decline given the competition faced from Caribbean banana plantations; and, in the democratic period, they started to build their identity as a group of seven islands which had always been difficult to bring together, not simply because of the sea that separated them, but also because each island is a universe of its own which lives its own life. And while all this was going on, on the cultural side of things, the Islands lived through a peak of success that revolved around André Breton's surrealism and the magazine *Gaceta del Arte*: this was a peak reached in the 1930s, before the Civil War (which the Islander historian and essayist Juan Marichal, in exile in America and teaching at Harvard, called the 'Uncivil War') and the Second World War. This was a spectacular time in Canary Island cultural life, and it was at this point that people began to see the Islands as a crossroads of avant-garde culture, at least until the war among the Spanish began: the Civil War brought some of the protagonists of this precious moment either to death or to prison, and although it could not cut out avant-garde culture by the roots—it was too well established for that—the Civil War did sink the Islands into the same kind of wretched state as other regions of Spain, racked by fear and the threat of Fascist barbarism. In the 1960s, thanks to tourism, the Canary Islands recovered a certain degree of cosmopolitanism, and then the return of democracy opened the floodgates to a new intellectual adventurousness. History was remade; history is remaking itself once again.

But the arrival of democracy has not resolved the sense of mistreatment and abandonment many Canary Islanders hold with respect to the metropolis. Under cover of their sense of being treated as second-class Spanish citizens, a degree of nationalism had set in, especially among Canary Islander emigrants to Cuba at the end of the nineteenth century, and the excessive centralism of the Francoist regime did nothing to lessen it. And so, over the last thirty years, even up to the present day, the regional government of the Islands has been dominated by a single party, the Coalición Canaria, which, without having independence as its aim, has focussed on identity politics and on developing a certain negative attitude towards Spain. Within the confines of its idea of the 'new identity' are contained several ideas: a new pride in being an Islander; an insistence on our individuality as a form of strength that allows us to govern ourselves, and a lachrymose sense of victimhood which blames Spain for all our failings.

COLUMBUS'S ISLAND

AND SO, HERE WE ARE: THIS IS OUR SPACE. A SPACE OCCUPIED BY Romans, by Africans, by Spaniards, by Genovese, by the French . . . Even so, are we a special people, a race apart?

I said above that in the Franco period it was frowned on for the Canary Islanders to say that they came from Africa, at least insofar as their geography was concerned. Out of a still-existing imperialist atavism, the Islands, even the easternmost ones, the ones closest to the neighbouring continent, have looked in the other direction, most likely for economic reasons, but also, at least in the most immediate past, for cultural and political ones as well. Africa has not provided a solution in the past, but now people believe that its market will increase in size and that what was once treated with disdain and ignored will have to be seen at some point as the necessary future.

The Canary Islands have been (to use an expression very much along the lines of those current in the Franco era) a 'Spanish beachhead in Latin America', a site which travels in the Atlantic like that stone raft thought up by the Portuguese writer and Nobel Prize winner José Saramago, a man who lived in Lanzarote for the last twenty years of his life, and who had many visitors—among them Susan Sontag, Günter Grass, Álvaro Siza, Mario Vargas Llosa, Carlos Fuentes—who came to see why he had chosen this site to carry on writing his oeuvre after he had been expelled by his country's politicians and also by its public opinion, having had the gall to write, to the shock of many of his backward-thinking compatriots, a *Gospel According to Jesus Christ*. To a degree, Saramago was a part of this beachhead that the Canary Islands is on the way to America, himself embodying this crossing of paths and visions.

But this idea of the Islands was one which first came into existence in 1492. Right here, where I stand at this very moment, and where Juana stands, and the French tourists stand, putting their boots and anoraks on in order to face up to the persistent rain which offers so great a contrast to the torrid sun of San Sebastián. And it was in San Sebastián, in this peaceful stop on the way, under the shade of the peak which is so like Rio de Janeiro's Sugarloaf Mountain, on a beach with grey sand and prehistoric pebbles, that Columbus dropped anchor when he set off with his sailors and other scoundrels and delinquents whom his voyage was eventually to redeem on the way to the Indies dreamt of by the Catholic Kings of Spain, in their desire to become even richer and more powerful.

COLUMBUS CAME TO SAN SEBASTIÁN DE LA GOMERA, TO THIS CALM AND self-contained port which is close to where I am writing at this very moment, and to which tourists come from all over the world, especially Germans—like Madame Merkel—and other Islanders—mostly from Tenerife, an island which is an economic and sentimental extension of La Gomera. Here people see the same plants Columbus saw, and for years they were able to walk the same packed-earth roads (I walked them myself); here is to be found the same small castle where the few relics of that past time are still kept, and the sea is the same, of course, a sea which wrinkles with waves as soon as you are past the harbour but which here is a smooth harbour where boats from all over the world jostle for position. One of these, the *Never Ready*, holds in its ironic name a concise definition of the character of the Islanders: we are industrious, yes, but always only nearly about to fulfil our aims, never entirely ready . . .

The port of San Sebastián de La Gomera is a quiet one, gathered into a bay which, like many of the natural harbours on the Islands, is protected by a large rocky outcrop, which, like that of Rio de Janeiro, is surmounted by an image of Jesus Christ.

Columbus came here, as did the Virgin of Guadalupe, the patron saint of the island, with his group of adventurers, and it was here that he met Beatriz de Bobadilla, the wife of Hernán Peraza El Joven, the lord of the island; she, and the water and other provisions which La Gomera was able to provide, were the reasons why he would continue to return to La Gomera on his future journeys. On one of these journeys, Gran Canaria was also a stopping point for the great navigator. The Islands all quarrel among one another, and this perceived division in Columbus's affections between La Gomera and Gran Canaria has been a source of discussion for centuries, although over recent years the increasing consensus among historians and the lack of any new polemical materials has led to the debate moving on to other topics which are equally tiring but perhaps more succulent in political or journalistic terms; it is odd that the Islands have spent so much time disputing this strange version of primacy when it would have been good for both of them, for all the Islands, to have acknowledged Columbus's presence and transformed themselves into privileged protagonists of the most famous expedition in history. But that is how things are between us, or at least how they have been: it has always been seen as better to take away rather than add together, and perhaps this has made the Islands smaller than they are, sunk into their own pettiness and diminishing their actual glories.

But Columbus was here. One afternoon I followed the Columbus path from Beatriz de Bobadilla's house (now known as Columbus House) to the Torre del Conde, which was where Beatriz was imprisoned once her infidelities and other unpleasant aspects of her character (at least, those considered unpleasant by other people) were discovered.

I did not find, in any of these sites connected with Columbus, any particular enthusiasm to make the record of the navigator anything more than the kind of memory found in tourist guides: at the

Torre del Conde there were on display some inadequate maps of La
Gomera at different periods, from antiquity to the present day, and
the so-called Columbus House was exhibiting a few pre-Columbian
relics and some abstract art.

Even so, the island does seem to have been deliberately made,
with its peaks and exuberant greenery, its extraordinary, beatific
Mount Garajonay, the Islands' version of the Iguazú Falls, as a door-
way to the exuberant America which Columbus discovered, given
strength by the waters of La Gomera and the caresses of Beatriz, the
woman who bade him farewell as he set off for adventure. It is as if
a kind of Macondo *avant la lettre* were created here, a forest surrounded by incomparable sheer cliffs, as if the damp and shady solitude of America were being thought up already here; La Gomera
established itself, still establishes itself, as a kind of reverse beachhead.
It is as though destiny had been plucked from this spot, from this
South American island, both tropical and peaceful, instead of from
the south of Spain (Huelva, Palos de la Frontera, the Andalucian
Atlantic coast) which was Columbus's true origin on his quest to stir
up the waters of geography and history. The island is like a single
point in space, a point in the middle of the sea, a suggestive and powerful rock surrounded with greenery, spread out like a hand into cliffs
like fingers, a place as immensely rocky as the depths of the sea. An
island which is like the bottom of the sea; there is a clump of rocks
on one side of it, vast and shaped like an organ, and if you pass round
the island at midday, looking at how the shadows outline the organ
pipes, then you will most likely see at one and the same time the island
and her dreams.

SITTING IN FRONT OF THE SEA AT HERMIGUA, WHICH COLUMBUS PROBA-
bly never saw as it is to the north of the island, covered by the fog
drifting down from Garajonay, I wrote down some of these reflections
on Columbus and his journey and what he might have found (or
missed) if he had not come on his journey to the slow, almost domestic

port, where the waters come quietly as though the sea had lost its vivacity and gained nothing but melancholy. As if the sea were the very essence of the *folía*, rising and falling as the feelings rise and fall with arrivals and departures . . . Columbus never came to Hermigua: he couldn't have. Hermigua, with this high and wrinkled sea, would have been a place to stop, not to pass through. He would have halted here, his ships would not have been able to fight against the buffetings of the sea, I imagine, looking at how the tide rises and falls with un-tamed intensity.

If Columbus had come through Hermigua . . . First of all, he would not have come, because he came in particular to see Beatriz de Bobadilla, and this was a powerful reason for him to travel by the course he did (although, Tejera Gaspar informs me, Beatriz was not on the island when he arrived. Legends are like that). Secondly, he could not have dropped anchor without putting his three ships in serious danger.

The sea is still today as it was back then: of course, the sea is eternal just as the landscape is eternal, and if mankind does not dis-figure it, then it should remain the same for many centuries to come. We come down to Hermigua from Garajonay because the landscape compels us. When you are up on top, high on this magnificent moun-tain that seems to be a metaphor for a mountain, after having crossed the paths cut by water and the woods and the laurisilva (a word that comes from Latin, *laurus* + *silva*, 'laurel forest', and which is used to mean a kind of subtropical forest which is found in warm, damp areas), and when your gaze is sated with the recurrent vision of the huge trunks of prehistoric trees and fog, then the road offers you two options. If you turn back, then you will make the same journey through the scrubland, down into a dry south which it appears im-possible could ever have come from such a vast, exquisite, unusual forest; or else you will travel into a soft north, filled with banana plan-tations and old houses done up by the Germans or the Islanders them-selves, the path moving sheer down to the sea, as if a green hand were stretched out to inform you what La Gomera lived through for so many years: to tell you what it was going to become, to tell you about the nearby Cedro, the mountain down whose sides run streams of clean water which irrigated the fields and made these gardens a mystery of tree-filled silence. And, from time to time, you will see a palm tree, arrogant as a mountain peak.

And we decided to travel to the north, towards green Hermigua, presided over by a silence which is given life by the sheer cliffs which lead to the peak from which there emanates an unending air of mystery. From above, Hermigua is nothing more than this singular, absolute, almost vertiginous green, and then the sea. The sea is the counterpoint; one senses its waves—the strength of its waves—and how they come in like nothing but the sea, majestic but inaudible until you reach the edge of the cultivated lands and the planted terraces, the fertile banana plantations, the tomato fields, the vineyards which are not simply fertile but which used to be the main element of the commercial life of the town. Wine always rising up like a light from the ground; the humble vineyards alongside the roads of the Islands.

IT GOES WITHOUT SAYING THAT, AS HAPPENS SO OFTEN IN THIS LAND, AND in so many other lands as well, Hermigua is, with respect to San Sebastián, the yin (or the yang, if San Sebastián is the yin), and this is so not simply for logical reasons of local rivalry, but also because here, between the southern capital and the northern territory, we see the divisions within the Islands themselves, an archipelago which has its north and its south almost as though it had two souls, two sets of customs, two ways of being. The splendid north, filled with the colourful farms, the bright paths and damp lanes, and the dour south, where the touch of the sea gives scarcely any water and the interior is a parched land where, on the larger islands, avarice has built apartment blocks, hotels, chalets and motorways in order to transform what was once a kind of desert into a continuous and largely disorganised urbanisation. Here, where I am now, under the Garajonay fog, in Hermigua, a stimulating equilibrium has been preserved: the sea and the cultivated land, and the old houses, and the silence where even the softest voice sounds like an attack on the crickets and the chickens.

And the soul of Hermigua is in the sea; that sea which Columbus could never cross, because it would have stopped his journey; the sea is much stronger than Columbus.

IT IS THE SEA WHICH TRANSFORMS THIS TINY PARADISE—A SIGN ON THE way into the town says 'Hermigua: the best climate in the world'—into a natural halt in the world; you look towards the sea, and it is there, unsettling and majestic, epic; the sea raises itself up against the tallest rocks—and it may be that the rocks at Hermigua are the tallest in the whole archipelago—and then it falls as wild foam, the foam of a giant or a prehistoric animal, and this process transforms into a kind of lyric spectacle, vast and overwhelming.

This is an island, like others in the archipelago, like La Palma, like Gran Canaria, like Tenerife, built up out of deep ravines, of cliffs falling into the sea, but it is here, in La Gomera, where the ravines are deepest, where the division between the north and the south, the yin and yang of the Islands, is most profound. The hellish topology which the aboriginal inhabitants of the Islands dealt with as best they could and the descendants of the Islands' conquerors dealt with in Christian humility. At least, this was the case until mechanical shovels and great digging machines gave the Islands more control over their north, or their south: the island of great drops and sheer ravines has been diminished somehow.

IT WAS THIS TOPOLOGY THAT FORCED THE INHABITANTS OF LA GOMERA to learn to communicate by whistling, a strange custom which still survives despite telephone lines and mobile phones, despite greater mobility and better means of transport. The whistling language of La Gomera, which was declared part of humankind's cultural heritage by UNESCO and which is now taught in schools so as not to be lost for ever, is an ancient tradition that dates back to the African ancestors of the Islands, but it is also a necessity; rather than being a fascinating gizmo or contraption of little use, it was a natural invention of the inhabitants of La Gomera in order to overcome the distances which the make-up of the Islands imposed on them, and it has survived not simply because of local stubbornness, but because it was, until the arrival of mobile phones and other portable means of communication, the only way for individuals to be in touch regarding questions of livestock and other elements of daily life. In these wildernesses crisscrossed with ravines of all sizes, to hear the whistling language is not simply an alert, but also makes one shudder with recognition: it is a signal of life which comes from the depths of earth's history. Women and men, fingers in their mouths, producing a sound from prehistory, the voice of essential help and assistance—a way of communicating from out of time that has come to us right up to the present day.

I have said that the boundaries between the north and the south are being eroded: water, highways, bridges have all turned the landscape into a continuum. But the evidence that things were not always this way, that the north and the south were geographically irreconcilable both here and in many other islands, finds in Hermigua and its surrounding villages its clearest metaphor. One had to approach this area from San Sebastian and the other islands by crossing this boisterous sea which sounds as though it is snoring on the August afternoon where I write, just having come from eating in the friendly surroundings of Doña Juana's refuge. Ferries carried travellers from one side of the island to the other, from San Sebastián to Hermigua, over rough and calm seas: a form of transportation which to us might now seem primitive, but which was all there was right up until the day before yesterday, if I can put it that way.

In order to be able to establish connections with Hermigua, people built a spit, a kind of artificial port, stealing space from the sea and her rages, building around a natural pool among the crags. Another time, when I was watching the angry salt water, the sky above me was, as it often is in this melancholic and cloudy north, a firmament of brick and mud over our heads, and the clouds helped give the scene the air of an illusion; we were the subjects of the sea and the fog, and we were being overwhelmed by a perpetual invasion of sounds both indifferent and powerful: the all-encompassing, pitiless sound of the sea.

As if the northern sea wanted to make its victory even more visible, the waves beat against and climbed over what remained of the spit, a few powerful but ancient columns from which sprouted the pointless iron bars that had been used to make them. A boy pointed out to me the point the waves could reach when the sea was really wild, and I felt even more fearful, because on the rocky outcrop where we sat we were more than six metres above the endless waves. And down below us, the boy said, people still go swimming, in spite of the immense violence of the waves, in spite of the pitiless, predatory willpower of the sea which Columbus would not have dared to brave, at least not here.

OLD HOUSES, SILENCE, BANANA TREES, THE SPIT REACHING INTO THE SEA. Hermigua is a series of symbols, both of La Gomera and of the islands in general, perhaps because, who knows, La Gomera is a metaphor for all the islands. It is said—and I imagine that this is said of every island in the world; it is definitely said of the British Isles, for example—that the Canary Islands are like continents in miniature; and if the Canary Islands is a continent in miniature, then La Gomera is a continent in itself: it may be miniature in terms of its size (142.76 square miles), but it has to be a continent because of its ravines, its eternal ravines, which have never been broken by the bridges cast by the hand of man. A self-sufficient, self-sustaining island, just as back then, in the post-war period, was the yard of the house where I was born. Poor but self-sufficient, standing firm against hunger, protected by the forest of beauty.

So, here is Hermigua, the central metaphorical element of the physical presence of the soul of the north of the Islands. Nervous when faced by the island gorges, I made a note in my book: 'the milky water violently caressing perfect rocks, almost prehistoric'. Rocks like the stones which García Márquez examined next to the ice factory in Aracataca. But then my eyes grew accustomed to the situation and I saw the uniform terraces, designed by the imperious randomness of perfection, like the ones that you see to the south in the Gran Rey Valley, or like the ones that Humboldt saw when he climbed into the La Orotava Valley on Tenerife, a much more friendly landscape, one that almost caresses the eye itself, or like the ones on Gran Canaria, near Bandama or Tejeda . . . Mankind, ever since he started to cultivate the Islands, has made common cause with nature as though he were blending into nature itself, or as though he were its accomplice, its way of clawing at hunger, the violent wound of misery.

But man has not been able to tame the sea, not at all, and here you can see (as my notebook says), 'black rocks and the white dew covering the violent sea all the way into infinity'. When I left I went back to see the spit, which nowadays is like a sculpture by Eduardo Chillida or Tony Gallardo, or Martín Chirino or José Abad (the last three of these artists are themselves from the Islands): a violent sculpture, or one which has had violence done to it; four enormous columns resisting an assault which still, even in my memory, is overwhelming. And I saw, perched on one of these pillars of Hercules, a single seagull, picking its way through the wild remnants of the spit, like a dove on the shoulder of a demigod.

Ignacio Aldecoa was unable to go to La Gomera: the seas were too high for his baot, and he writes in his incomparable *A Tourist's Notebook* that 'La Gomera is a strange fantasy of valleys for this tourist who wanted to see them and could not, because of problems with the motor of the ferry that was to carry him. He saw it at a distance and heard tell of its magnificent valleys.' The word he uses for 'tourist' is a specific one: *godo*. A *godo* is a Spaniard from the mainland who is not yet used to the customs of the Islands, who is not yet an adapted citizen. It's a slightly derogatory term. When they say 'mainlander' they are not trying to be derogatory; they only hope that the visitor knows whose land he's walking on: Aldecoa called himself a *godo*, and that is the vantage point from which he looks at the Islands. But he cannot enter La Gomera; the sea won't let him: it is treating him as though he were still a *godo*. The Basque writer also says the following about his observation of the island at a distance: 'The traveller had to return to Guía de Isora-Alcalá, where the old men of the sea were waiting for him, the seven old men from the Tenerife legend who fish for tuna alone. They row out to the horizon and beyond, into the open sea. They seek the huge tuna which swim in the sea round La Gomera. They navigate by Mount Teide, the silver head of the mountain which starts to shine in the early sun. The old men set out to sea at the mountain's first light and come home with its last. The old men belong to the sea; they might die with their oars in their hands, their tackle pulled down into the deeps by some great fish, their prows spun round like a candlewick by some sharp gust of wind; but the seven of them are there now, to the south of Tenerife, facing La Gomera, ready to be counted.'

The sea welcomes them; the sea throws them out. And to think that I came from this land, and here everything is sea, an intrusive sea which travels like a seagull towards the America sought by Columbus.

ABOVE ME WAS THE LAND, WITH ALL ITS FAIRY-TALE MYSTERY, STRANGE nooks where men and birds made the nests they dreamt of, nature calm and under control, shaded from the rain in summer; down here at this singular sea, infinite, it is as though the noise the trees make is torn from its depths.

I haven't been able to forget Hermigua, although I do not know if I can explain why.

AND NOW THAT HERMIGUA IS NO MORE THAN A DAMP MEMORY, THE evidence of its high tides, the green paths through its cultivated terrain feeling almost like courtyards or gardens, I have travelled over the

southwest of the island, I have climbed down the great cliffs that separate San Sebastián de La Gomera from the next valley, just one of
many, but perhaps the most exotic of them all, the valley which shelters Santiago beach at the end of a steep path lined with palm trees
and thistles, where every now and then one hears the lonely bleating
of a goat separated from its flock. And after this bleating, as though
all it were waiting for were someone to throw a rock at it to wake it
up, there is a calm ocean which dozes and makes a noise as though of
underwater trees or crickets who dare not make too much noise.

It is a desert, but its dunes are infinite and tall and made of stone
as though carved by the hand of a mighty sculptor trying to divide
the island into pieces, as though he had broken it up in fury simply in
order to create articles of beauty out of the wreckage. These huge
stones, rocks which are sometimes in the shape of houses, or lions, or
arms, give the spectator the idea that he is in an empty forest, inhabited only by ghosts which will then visit him in dreams or nightmares.
People who suffer from vertigo should think twice before entering
into this indescribable phenomenon of curves and surprises. Palm
trees, or pines, or the cacti that line the winding path are only halts
on a path that at times appears to be an allegory of thirst.

THIS IS A LAND DESIGNED FOR LONELINESS, A DESERT INHABITED BY THE
sound of the lonely, by whistling and by melancholia. I haven't heard the
whistling over the last few days, but it is there, like an ancestral language invented by man in order to eliminate all kinds of distance, to allow
him to be understood both by other men and by animals. The whistling
has not been heard, or I have not heard it, but the cliffs which made
it necessary are still there. They have made tunnels through them, but
it has been impossible to deal with these crags upon crags upon crags.
I hope they never do, because they are where the changing appearance
lies of an island which, simply because it had and has these ravines
and cliffs, is still a miracle which can be pointed out to show men
how the intact physiognomy of the planet once was.

BUT MAN HAS NOT BEEN ABLE TO REFRAIN FROM ACTING; HE HAS HAD TO take from this island even the symbols preserved in the desert of enormous and incessant rocks, and has done so to such an extent that the sea has been substituted for the air: he has built an airport. Was it necessary?

In the area that was perhaps the least sheer of this island of huge precipices, man decided, then, to lay down a runway and establish an airport which looks more like a refuge in the midst of the most gentle calamities of the desert. The cliffs might have protested, but the steamrollers eventually found a way.

But this is no refuge; it is an airport like many others, open from dawn until mid-afternoon for inter-island flights; people come to see it as though it were a symbol of the future, but they also see it, as do I, as a relic of the past, the final attempt, the most modern and riskiest attempt, to make La Gomera bring into itself, from its ancestral silence, all the noises of the modern world, including the sound of aeroplanes.

The airport, built eleven years ago, was installed in order to break the large distance that separates this island from the other islands; since 1974 this is a distance which has been made shorter by ever more frequent and faster boats: today one can travel from Los Cristianos in Tenerife to San Sebastián de La Gomera in half an hour; in the past, the boats used to go to the spit at Hermigua, that relic whose remains —now guarded by seagulls—symbolised the absolute, almost stellar, distance between La Gomera and the other islands; more recently, boats have connected Tenerife and San Sebastián de Le Gomera from Santa Cruz, the capital of Tenerife. Travellers would journey in re-purposed post-boats, and the journey would take the whole night: they would sleep surrounded by the food and utensils which were being delivered to what was then the most distant of the islands, in spite of its role as the compass needle or key to Columbus's American journey.

I travelled in one of these post-boats, first of all in 1968, when the Olympic torch came through La Gomera on its way to Mexico, pausing first of all at the Olympic Games and then heading to

Tlatelolco, where the Mexican government ordered troops to fire on students who were protesting in the run up to the Olympics: 1968, a year when the foundations of the world trembled, from Paris to Peking as well as in Tlatelolco . . .

But the Olympics and Tlatelolco hadn't happened yet. The torch was brought in the Juan Sebastián Elcano, a Spanish teaching boat commanded by a descendant of Christopher Columbus, himself called Christopher Columbus, and the vessel stopped in San Sebastián de La Gomera as a memory of the vital journey of the admiral who discovered America.

We saw them carry the burning torch out of the boat, and we saw some local athletes climb up to the ceremonial urn which had been built on one of the lower rises of the La Cueva beach, where the Nautical Club of San Sebastián de La Gomera is now situated. The local authorities, all of them back then appointed by Franco, came to welcome us, and the island was decorated for what was the most important event since the earlier Christopher Columbus has passed through on a mission which at one level appeared similar: to discover the world, to cross the sea to bring a new light—a light that was no better or worse than others, merely distinct. The torch seemed to be a metaphor of that past.

They lit the torch and put La Gomera on the map, once again, and then they played floral games, read poems in homage to the New World, and the Juan Sebastián Elcano (a ship of the Spanish navy) sailed on, leaving the ceremonial urn still warm from the flames of the torch, and leaving behind also the square with its large trees, the main square of La Gomera, where people still live their life in common, where people gather to give each other the news and gossip, and where the artisans and farmers of the island, many of them married to foreigners, until recently sold their products or merely gathered to talk.

I have gone to see the urn now, I have seen it there, standing upright, its iron cold now: the American flame still burns in the soul of La Gomera (how could it not?), but the fire is no longer visible, or rather I have not seen it, the torch is not lit and people don't remember the last time they saw the flame.

And so La Gomera, which was the most important staging post of modern exploration, sanctioned by Columbus as the point from which one had to set off (like the torch) in order to head into the unknown, was even in times of absolute violent contemporaneity, until the twentieth century, entirely inaccessible by air, and even today the connection is uncertain, because it is not clear that it is either affordable or desirable for such a precipitous land, so many islands within a single island, to have a landing strip for transitory visitors.

BACK THEN, WHEN WE TRAVELLED IN POST-BOATS, LANDING WAS AN EVENT in itself; the inhabitants of the Islands, people of all ages, gathered on the old pier (later to be rejuvenated), and the island, which seemed almost like a film set, was set in motion; this liveliness which entered into the island when the boats arrived is in some ways similar to that which takes place in the Colombian city of Cartagena de Indias—which also looks like a film set—when the aeroplanes arrive: in both cases, people seem to burst into life before shortly sinking back into lethargy until a new boat arrives, and the cycle repeats itself. It is not like Cartagena, but sometimes it appears to be like Macondo, with the old people waiting for time to pass, looking at the calm sea, greeting and bidding farewell to the boats that come with passengers and goods.

THERE WAS ONE OLD MAN IN THE SQUARE WITH THE BIG TREES, THE ONE known as the Square of the Discoverers, who sat there and told old stories about the old islanders, and also recited proverbs and told jokes, and was like one of those old men who name things in *A Hundred Years of Solitude*, whose author, Gabriel García Márquez, was born in Aracataca, a tiny village in the north of Colombia which reminded me, with its sweat and wind and inclement yet fruitful climate, of some of the hidden areas of this island—another mythological place.

Back then, the people who came to San Sebastián and listened to this man giving names to things were not tourists; they were travellers, and they came bringing things that the island needed; they would stay for a few days; they were civil servants or messengers; they were known to the islanders; they were not *godos*, as Aldecoa said he was; they did not come to sunbathe on the isolated or beautiful beaches, or to smoke cannabis, or to grow cannabis, or to meet in hotels or tour groups. They were travellers, but they were a part of the island. La Gomera produces a complicated and delectable variety of food; its fruits (mangoes and bananas in particular) are always sought-after; its livestock is rough but fertile; its cheeses are good (Columbus mentions this: 'We took on board water and firewood and other provisions, cheese in particular, of which there are many and all of good quality'); you could sever all connections between La Gomera and the rest of the world and the island would carry on working, up to a point, because the inhabitants of La Gomera had learnt, within the islands that make up the island, on this wrinkled sheet of cliffs which divides the island into many islands, to survive without any external assistance. And this had been the case for centuries.

But here is the airport; people who live in this part of the island (for example, the people who work at or who visit the Tecina hotel, the most important element of the La Gomera hospitality industry) now save themselves the trouble of travelling round the cliffs from San Sebastián; however, the other inhabitants of the island prefer to rely on the boats, a tradition which is also a sign of identity for La Gomera, and an extremely resilient one.

As well as all this, the economic contributions it brings, the ease it brings to travel, the airport appears to me now that I see it for a second time an island palace, a symbol which accentuates the image of this tiny island which embodies so much history and—perhaps because of this—so much melancholy.

The airport underlines the distance inherent in the island, a distance which is already under the skins and in the souls of the people who live on La Gomera, a distance that can be touched, that can be felt in the air.

La Gomera is distance. This much is emphasised by its cliffs and by the line of palm trees which seem to mark the beginning or the end of a desert.

AS I WAS WALKING DOWN THESE SLOPES WHICH THE SUN TRANSFORMS into the physical manifestation of thirst, I was looking at the ground and the rocky distances; and there in the distance, under Mount Teide—the volcano which, at 12,198 feet above sea level, is the tallest mountain in the archipelago, and which can be seen from this point better than from anywhere else in the Canary Islands—the range of Tenerife seemed like a natural extension of La Gomera, as if the two islands were connected and formed a single continent without an obstinate sea between them.

But the sea was there, down by our feet, like a dull witness to so much melancholy.

MELANCHOLY IS BORN UP THERE, UP IN GARAJONAY, AND IT TRICKLES down. Geologists say that the volcano that is the island is dormant, that the immense burst of greenery on the top of the mountain hides underneath itself a fire which went out three million years ago, but only provisionally, and which could in theory spark up again at any moment. It is difficult to imagine a rude awakening in the middle of these beds of water and moss, and it is difficult in general to imagine fire among the fog, even though these mountains have shamefully been the scene of terrifying fires, mostly caused by the negligence of people who set a fire without wanting or needing to, and then terrible things happen, like the fire that thirty years ago devastated a huge tract of Garajonay and led to the deaths of twenty people, among them the civil governor of Tenerife, Paco Afonso, a friend of mine from childhood.

THE DISCOVERY OF FOG

IT IS DIFFICULT TO IMAGINE SUCH FIRES IN THE MIDST OF SO MUCH FOG. Fog is a factor in the mountain, and I think that when historians talk about the character of the people of La Gomera (and that of many of the inhabitants of the Canary Islands as well) as being turned in on itself and melancholy, then they need to bear in mind the effect which this fog has on the soul of the island. The director of the Garajonay National Park has studied the phenomenon of the fog and summarises his conclusions as follows: 'Throughout a large portion of the year, especially in spring and summer, the islands are affected by the trade winds which come from the Azores anticyclone: these are superficial northeasterly winds which are filled with moisture by their passage over the relatively cool waters surrounding the archipelago, and which bring freshness and good weather.'

Good weather and melancholy, the pleasure that each inhabitant of the Canary Islands has in imagining that his is the best climate in the world.

According to a chronology of Canary Island history which I have been using to tell myself the history of the Islands, the Islanders have always referred to the place where they live—even when there were no maps, even when it was believed that there were more islands than the ones people knew of, when people thought that there was an undiscovered island, San Borondón, an island which was never discovered because it does not exist—as the Fortunate Islands, because of their situation, because of their climate, just because. And the first time they were referred to as such was in the year 188 or 186 BC; Plautus referred to them in his work *The Three Coins* and then, with Christ already walking among us, the Greek geographer Strabo 'refers [I'm quoting from the chronology here] to some islands in his *Geography* as the Fortunate Islands, and he is doubtless referring to the Canary Islands.' And it was in the second century AD that Pliny the Elder 'wrote the first more or less faithful description of the Canary Islands in Book VI of his *Natural History*', which must have been written, according to the same chronology, round about thirty years after the death of Christ.

So, ever since then the Canary Islands have not been a matter of merely fiction or history, but they have been identified with this 'fortunate climate' which is the foundation and the surface of their value to tourists.

If their climate is so fortunate, if they are themselves the Fortunate Islands, then where does the melancholy come from?

The truth is that the melancholy which is attributed to La Gomera as one of the key elements in the islanders' character is distributed throughout the Islands, and has taken root in almost all of them, like grief, like hopelessness. This was something which Alexander von Humboldt noted in 1799 when he reached Santa Cruz and then looked for the topographical essence of so much beauty in the valley of La Orotava; it was noted with a deal more humour by the Canary Islander Viera y Clavijo (1731-1813), when he recounted the self-obsessed and confused story of how the Guanches were shaken out of their ingenious laziness by well-equipped conquistadors, and it was also noted by Miguel de Unamuno (1864-1936), the philosopher and poet, when Primo de Rivera, the dictator who first showed Franco the way, chose Fuerteventura as the site of Unamuno's exile for his disobedient behaviour.

What Unamuno saw in Fuerteventura was an extension of the African desert, an Unfortunate Isle, an island without any fortune whatsoever, assaulted by the sun and the wind, on which a decimated population looked to the sea as though it could provide them with a miracle. In the poems which Unamuno wrote about his experience in this prison without any walls, an experience which he transformed into a seminar on poetry and philosophy, the great Basque writer went deep into the soul of Fuerteventura, the soul of the *majoreros* (Fuerteventura used to be called Maxorata, and its inhabitants are called *majoreros*), and discovered within it the identity of the island: 'this mountain a ruined volcano | corroded by thirst and so naked | that desolation itself looks out in silence | from this suffering and hermit island.'

One need do no more than step onto the island and walk across its barren plains without even a single shrub rising from them, in order to imagine this desolation as always having existed, right up until the present day; and when desolation itself did not look out to sea, Fuerteventura appeared to be the dry abyss of a ravine. People say that to a degree Unamuno was the first person to discover the happiness of the sun and the extraordinary possibilities of the sea in Fuerteventura. But this is, of course, a legend based on a number of anecdotes.

They say that Unamuno, that sullen Christian philosopher, who was to some extent as gaunt and desolate as the spirit of the island itself, was the inventor of public nudism, both in Fuerteventura and in the whole of Spain, back in the 1920s when Spain had not yet decided to be modern; at midday he would leave his friends in the intellectual discussion group which he had put together in Fuerteventura, and go up to the terraced roof of the apartment block where he lived in order to enjoy the sun naked as God intended. Without any scandal attached to his actions or any attempt at provocation, as though it were nothing more than a poetic gesture and to that extent necessarily healthy, the author of *Through the Lands of Portugal And Spain* defied gossip and also the perception that the sun was the single element of the curse that separated the island from the possibility of any dampness, of any life, and instead claimed it as a force of life itself. The sun as an emblem of the future, a sign of the health of the island; the sun became, with the passage of years, perceived as the guarantor of the island's survival; if not for the sun, what would have happened to the beaches of Fuerteventura?

Unamuno was also the discoverer of one of the best and most sought-after kinds of seafood, gooseneck barnacles, which on the island are large and tasty, and as difficult to gather as the gooseneck barnacles from the Atlantic coast of the north of Spain. Unamuno, as a Basque from Bilbao, knew well that the taste of the sea, its smell, is concentrated in these molluscs which look as though they are made of moss, and that are the size of a non-tumescent penis (that is the technical term, at least in Galician, the language spoken in the northwest of Spain: *do carallo de home*), and Unamuno found out that here, on the Fuerteventura coast, just as on the Basque Atlantic coast, these delicacies could be found in abundance. And he convinced the local fishermen not to ignore these barnacles, called by the unflattering nickname (until Unamuno gave them another name) of 'goatsfeet': the Fuerteventura fishermen used to throw them back into the sea, they felt disgusted or superstitiously fearful about them, they thought that they were rubbish which the sea tossed out to them along with the other trash it occasionally sent back.

I ate some of these 'goatsfeet' in Gran Tarajal, one of the black sand beaches of Fuerteventura, sitting and facing the ocean which here, in Gran Tarajal, comes in high and almost frowning, perhaps annoyed at having had to travel such a great distance, dark as the memory of stones. They were larger than Basque or Galician goosenecks, and our hosts said that this was because they came from Africa; a few years later I ate them again, in Madrid and elsewhere, ones that really came from Africa this time (they all come from Africa, perhaps, and this is no contradiction to what I am saying, because we are talking about Africa when we talk about Fuerteventura).

And so, in discovering the sun and gooseneck barnacles, Unamuno discovered the soul of Fuerteventura for his poetry, the soul of this island right at the other end of the archipelago from La Gomera, in the part of the Islands closest to Africa, both of them distant from everything (from Europe, from America, from the world, if I am to speak with the sense of drama which we islanders regularly deploy when we talk about our isolation), and both of them sharing this kind of melancholy which comes on the one hand from the fog, and on the other hand from its absence; it is here, in this desert which the sun has made just about habitable, that one sees the other side of the Islands: La Gomera is where the greenery is to be found, and here is where drought dwells, the yin and yang of a fragmented territory, an archipelago with its light and its shade, and the light is not fully light and the shade is not fully dark.

In this poem, the sixteenth of his collection *From Fuerteventura to Paris*, Miguel de Unamuno describes the island as 'suffering and hermit': 'The merciful sea bathes with its foam | its feet, and its sharp-edged | camel chews on the rough gorse, | spreading out four colossal legs to scratch. | Balls of *gofio*, the skeleton of bread | form these men— the rest is *conduto*— | and on this slag-heap ground, simple | and rooted into the stones, grey and scrawny, | the grandson walks by like the grandfather | without any leaves, giving only fruit and flower.'

This essential landscape described by Unamuno (who was Basque, and Castilian to an extent, a scrawny fellow himself) is almost the landscape of himself, because he was like this, a pure skeleton, as though he were the very definition of a struggling man, a man agonising, as he liked to call himself when discussing his life, using this word, originally Greek, agony, a word from one of the languages that animates his culture. In the notes that accompany the edition I have of these poems, all of them beautiful and hard as a ball of *gofio*, there are a few explanations which make the description given above not simply a journey through the landscape of Fuerteventura, so far away from La Gomera, but so close to its soul.

The note that explains this song to Fuerteventura, poem number XVI, reads as follows: 'The Fuerteventura peasants principally live off *gofio*, wheat or maize flour—or a mixture of the two—which is first of all toasted and then milled in a windmill. They call *conduto*— in Castilian it used to be *conducho*—everything that accompanies this fundamental basis to the dish: dried fish, dried figs, cheese, etcetera. *Conduto*, from the same root as *conduct*: that which makes something pass. Gorse is practically a skeleton of a plant, the camel is almost a skeleton, and Fuerteventura is practically a skeleton of an island.'

The description given in the poem and the note corresponds to the past, but the precision with which Unamuno develops his own desolate impression scratches into the soul what still today is the essence of the island, its deep melancholic root, growing from its own history, a physical history, scorched by the sun even on the summits.

I have been up on these peaks, and from above the sun casts the shadows of the cliffs as though it were opening them up for the first time, breaking them gently to allow the sea to observe them.

AND MEANWHILE, WHILE THE SUN AND THE SEA ARE YET TO BE SEEN, when it is night and all that can be heard on the peaks is the desolate clonk of goat bells, Fuerteventura seems like a camel lost in total solitude, without any light to show it the way in the desert.

I want to lose myself mounted on this camel, following the path of Ignacio Aldecoa, who in the 1950s, as I have already told you, travelled all over the Islands looking for refuge; Aldecoa found his harbour in La Graciosa, a unique island, a beautiful little island isolated from the world by a powerful and boisterous arm of the sea. On his journey Aldecoa wrote as follows about Fuerteventura: 'Over gorges and gullies, over the beds of pools which once were and which are now nothing but crystallizations, like snowflakes, the seagulls sail and hunt. Sometimes there is an oasis, a green point. The violent red of the earth fires the green up to the sky.'

And Aldecoa continues on the journey which it is my aim to imitate: 'In Puerto del Rosario—called until just the day before yesterday Puerto Cabras—wind and red dust. An ancestral landscape. Ancestral Castile, where Miguel de Unamuno spent his exile, rediscovering his Castilian love, his love for the land of the plains of the peninsula in the barren and thirsty lands of Fuerteventura.'

I walked through these godforsaken places, searching for the monument that commemorates the exile of the Castilian philosopher. His statue has now turned the colour of Mount Quemada where they set it up years ago, his image back then a pure white. You reach Mount Quemada, at whose feet the agonising poet now rests, by crossing over the twisting folds of this sensual island, perhaps the most sensual of all the Islands; it is the island of loneliness and echoes; above, in the village of Betancuria, set among terrible statues of unlikely Guanches, huge, powerful as mythology demands, one hears the insistent bleat of grazing goats, feeding indifferently on the dry grass in front of an abandoned sixteenth-century church on whose portico one can still read 'Diego García Herrera (Conquistador), 1485'. It is a church that is now useless, Spartan, in an architectural landscape which evokes that of Castile, just as Aldecoa said: that is to say, that it is an empty church, filled on the off-chance with a humble light which fades as the day fades, the light of the sun, which to a certain extent is the light of the wind: I have seen film footage of this church: there was something a little like terror in that light, distance and fear, the accumulation of the sentiments formed in Betancuria, hanging from the light of the world.

On the journey that takes me to see Miguel de Unamuno, or at least his statue, there are trees that have been knocked down by the wind, fig trees that give this desert space the appearance of an ancient Greek city, tormented and white; inside the empty church I have seen a mysterious alcove which seems, from its colour and from the sense of mutilated space which it gives to the religious image it shelters, to be a painting by Antonio López, the Castilian artist; as if the church had suddenly become a museum. I can see here evocations cast up by chance and nature that make the walls appear fragments of a work by Fontana or Brancusi; here everything looks half-made, and ruination has done its job, as it looks as though time has passed here, a great deal of time.

A green tree suddenly shows that there is life in this spot, and not just buried history. I cling to the tree: it is the shade within which I want to walk.

Aldecoa says, as does Unamuno, that 'Fuerteventura, the fortunate island, is unfortunate. A good land, but no water.' Thirst and
hunger. I feel it, I feel hunger and thirst, and so I eat a sandwich made
of good bread, the good bread of the island, with cheese in it, somewhere between soft and hard, somewhere between salt and dry: this island, owner of one of the best cheeses in Spain. I eat it in front of a
windmill, near the Betancuria palm trees, before I carry on walking.
The road that gave Aldecoa hope leads me in front of the so-called Tefía
Mill; I knock on the door as I pass, but the mill's sleeping sails make
no response and no one comes to the door; of course no one comes to
the door: I knock as though I were calling the past, and the past no
longer exists, makes no echo, mills no grain. The mill is a symbol and
I sit down next to it as though I were visiting an ancestor. The past,
that past of hunger and farming which first Unamuno and then Aldecoa
saw, is a sealed past, the past of those desert stretches at the back of
which one always hears a cock crowing, at any hour of the day, or else
a humble cricket, fighting to escape from the shadow of a pebble.

The sun is like the stones, rugged, obstinate, and while I write
in this humble and ancient air, importunate flies remind me that this
is not simply the idyll of the earth and the sky, but also the place where
the earth stores its detritus. But the noise of the volcanic sand crunching under my feet finally scares the flies away, and there is a moment
at midday when this truly seems like a desert, when the palm trees
are like hands blocking the sun which comes from heaven and hell at
the same time.

The walls of the Tefía Mill seem covered with the earth of centuries: here it is, overlaid on the primitive white skin with which it
was first built to fulfil the role it no longer carries out. It is not strange
for me to feel here that I truly travelled back into a past which also
belongs to these flies that now come back as there is no more noise; I
have stopped walking, and the volcanic *zahorra* sand does not crunch
under my feet any longer, and I am sitting down once again, leaning
against the past of Fuerteventura.

It is odd, on this trip that takes me across this land which both

Unamuno and Aldecoa saw as a land with no hope, no fortune, that I should now think of Mexico, the country from which I have just travelled. Just as there, among those burning Mexican deserts, I sense here the same climate of death and indifference which one feels in the country of the Aztecs, and I sense that perhaps Aldecoa saw here, just as Juan Rulfo saw in the tundra of his own land, the same shadow which pursues people who identify land with nightmare. But it was here that Aldecoa unleashed his loneliness. I am taking his place for an instant. I remember his words about the same crags: 'A good land, but with no water. La Oliva, with its hayricks and its large house—Quinta Roja—is one of the villages of the island that suffers the most from this lack of water. La Oliva is a village from a Gothic landscape. Desperation and misery. Misery which, like the Fuerteventura vulture, threatens us from the stone crenels or the surrounding lava.'

Time has gone by, of course: now it is no longer hunger or misery which are immediate descriptors of this landscape, and water is no longer so dramatically scarce. But there persists a part of both poetic viewpoints (that of Aldecoa; that of Unamuno) the anxiety with which the two Basque writers—one from Bilbao, the other from Vitoria, two Basques accustomed to seeing greenery—looked at the stony ground.

Unamuno was furious, and there is fury here, in this interior and intimate landscape, and Aldecoa wrote in a series of blows and attacks, as though he were swiping with a brush at the grinding stones of a mill; Unamuno was a follower of Kierkegaard, if one can put it that way: he was possessed of a Nordic melancholy, and Aldecoa came from Hemingway, or Camus, and wrote as though he wanted to tear off people's skin, to blind them with the pitiless light of his words. I come from Unamuno and I am headed towards Aldecoa, for Fuerteventura is like that, carrying you from one symbol to another, it moves you around just as the wind of Morro Jable moves you, or as the wind moves the dark sails of windmills that I see on my journey.

'Further south, the desert,' Aldecoa writes. 'From Puerto del Rosario to La Oliva, through La Oliva to the right. You can't miss it.' It is Corralejo. This is what that Basque traveller was looking for, what I am now looking for, by the sea, among the dunes, the lively sea beating against the docile rocks of the shore.

AND NOW I AM NOTING DOWN, AS UNAMUNO DID, PROPER NAMES, places with their unforgettable euphony: Ampuyenta, Almácigo, Tuineje, Tiscamanita, Antigua . . . And I reach Los Palmerales de Gran Tarajal, which appears to be a place of rest from this loneliness. I am in the Tiscamanita desert, in Los Arrablaes. Here are the windmills, dancing among the bright colours of the volcanic sand. A single palm tree gives some kind of meaning to the landscape, which here is nothing more than a metaphor, in its vast loneliness, for the earthy intensity of Fuerteventura.

The landscape which I see in this desert is impressive. In La Gomera one feels this degree of immensity in green, and here the colours are different: sand, *zahorra*, rocks and loneliness. Here, in the face of this immensity, what one feels is that the trace of mankind, although probably visible further on, in Tiscamanita, is nothing more than a scratch on the world, nothing, the trace of a car that passed by decades ago, the buzz of a fly that will die a little further on, of the heat, or else of thirst, or boredom. The flies in Fuerteventura must be astonishingly bored.

What this rocky landscape of Los Arrabales does have is the soul that Unamuno wrote about: volcanic, nothingness, but not a wretched kind of nothingness: this nothingness where the wind has built its metaphors is the air that the Basque poet and thinker identified with the difficult happiness, the search for any kind of fortune, inherent in this island. To be here is to accept that man can fly, or that his ashes can. Or that the island itself can fly, as though this proud and lonely island were never calm.

I AM SURROUNDED BY MOUNTAINS, AS THOUGH I WERE AT THE BOTTOM of a large and tormented crater, surrounded by natural monoliths; but this physical geography is only the visible part of Fuerteventura. In reality, we are sitting on a skeleton that the wind makes dance.

When I descend from the promontory from which I have looked out at the desert which so moved Unamuno and Aldecoa at their different points in the twentieth century, I ask myself which music from that time, or from a time closer to ours, would best fit the memory which they took with them and which I am now taking with me. And I come to the conclusion that The Doors, or Pink Floyd, played at full volume, would sound good, and I walk off humming to myself, after first writing down in my notebook:

'It's the end of the world. Which is to say, the beginning.'

And after writing this, I sat down once again among the crags and wrote the following, as though I were writing down a dream of the air and of the music at the same time:

'Here any noise, even background noise, seems composed, seems to be the result of the natural demands of harmony. Here the wind that takes us seems like a caress, an embrace which makes us small again, just as the birds are made smaller in the air . . .'

AT THE BOTTOM OF THE SLOPE, NEAR TISCAMANITA, BEHIND THE LONELY palm tree, there is a mountain which looks like some kind of maternal hollow, an open hand, and also a face, like a mouth calling for help. The light turns this one vision into multiple successive visions. Nature can speak; I have no doubt of this. And I think that this is the voice of the Canary Islands, nature speaking here in this lonely vastness that the wind bequeaths to the land.

And further behind my back is a black mountain, scratched and scraped by man, straight and upright: in its belly it contains the traces of avarice, because someone thought that there were treasures in the mountains, and cut deep into their hearts: there are lots of these excavated mountains in the Islands; I lived in front of one of them for many years: it was the calm mountain of my childhood, until they gutted it and built a hotel on the top, a hotel which the volcanic sand

tumbled down on more than one occasion, until they laid down concrete foundations which established this impressive building as the
substitute for the landscape with which I grew up.

BUT I AM IN FUERTEVENTURA, LOOKING AT THIS BLACK AND WIDE MOUN-
tain: it is another metaphor for the land. For the presence of man in
the land, and not just the shadow of the wind which falls on the earth.
The wind is kinder; it allows the earth to continue to exist, it sweeps
across it but it respects it. Man digs into the earth in order to wound it.

But man cannot destroy it.

The Canary Islands are a fine example of ancestral survival,
struggling against volcanoes, remade by volcanoes.

And Fuerteventura is the embodiment of this experience.

Here I am on these stones which are like clumps of ice on some
fantastic iceberg, which impress themselves on the memory of your
gaze like a gift from the earth. I sit down here, in Los Arrabales, and
I am happy in the face of this vertigo; it is as though here, in the midst
of all this violent lava, I had discovered the soul of the land where I
was born: it doesn't matter if it is in the shade or in the sun, but this
is the soul of the Canary Islands, I have felt it; what would happen to
mankind if the land did not give him so much?

And the sun.

The sun is mythical, like an animal agonising before its death,
throwing out fire as one of its miracles; here and now it is a setting
sun, and the shadows of the mountains are sinuous black suggestions
of the night.

In the face of such a landscape one can only feel vertigo, as if
the air here were the antechamber that led to nothingness, to fear.

Silence.

Fuerteventura. *Fuerte ventura*. Strong fortune. The wind's fortune.

I made it here. I want to shout this out and let the night make
the sun its final refuge. I touch the rocks which are still warm; it is
possible that they have been here since the beginning of the island's

history, and I imagine that eternity must also be a kind of stone. Like time, like love, perhaps.

I have come from Mexico, as I said; when I was there the Colombian writer Fernando Vallejo said to me that everything would disappear immediately; I said that it might take decades, and he replied:

'No, everything will vanish right now.'

In the tremendous space that lies in front of me, and in the loneliness which is itself a rock, I venture to suggest that places like this will perhaps survive after whatever Fernando Vallejo fears has come to pass: stones that man cannot dominate and which will never be dominated by the wind.

I carry on walking; I feel that I am on an unformed island, Fuerteventura. In the distance I see Lanzarote, which I will visit later. In my memory it is the complete opposite, a fully-formed island; Fuerteventura is like a young and tired donkey, a donkey that has been rubbed down in the evening. Fuerteventura, an island that remains just as it was when it was first made, incomplete, silent, upright yet fearful.

I travel to Lobos from here, the little island that could be San Borondón if it were not for the fact that it actually exists; the water rises and falls, the beaches appear and disappear; you are bathing in the sea and suddenly there is no sea in the pools. But I am still on Fuerteventura; I will get to Lobos later.

Upon reaching Lobos (the 'wild island', as he called it), Aldecoa wrote: 'You reach the island of Lobos in forty minutes by ferry from Corralejo beach in Fuerteventura. Lobos is a wild island in the strait of Bocayna. This is the strait which separates Lanzarote from Fuerteventura, the gap between two headlands: Punta Gorda on Fuerteventura, and Punta del Papagayo on Lanzarote.' It is nearby, just a stone's throw away: the sea is a tiny channel but filled with dangers, and although the distance is not that far one has the impression that between the coast of Fuerteventura and the coast of Lobos there is a whole world and a number of mysteries. The ferry is now made of rubber and travels much faster: it only takes a few minutes to make the journey, to risk the sea, to risk above all the Calafate, a rock that rises and falls from under the sea and is a danger to any unwary traveller. One might almost say that it is like the mysterious island of San Borondón, which does not exist but which in legends appears and disappears in the midst of the fog.

This was the discovery of Fuerteventura, its deserts, the soul which Unamuno saw and the land which Aldecoa discovered. It is odd that such a deserted island should have blended with my experience of La Gomera, the most fertile of all the islands, as though my opinions travelled faster than my body. The yin and yang of the Islands: La Gomera, Fuerteventura.

But my memory is still travelling, and now it reaches Lobos. The lazy seagulls are accustomed to the solitude of the island; there is no one here; half a dozen or a dozen houses built up into the rock, blending with the rock; summer visitors; fishermen who are tired of fishing; a minuscule harbour which welcomes our boat as though it were allowing us to check whether or not the island exists; there used to be a lighthouse—there it is—upright and closed, on the top of the tallest of the island's tiny mountains; we arrived thirsty, and the only restaurant on the island—serving paella and salad—sells us an enormous cold beverage that opens our appetite for walking along the island's paths. This is life stripped of everything, there is nothing here, it is life and nothing more, and this is what Ignacio Aldecoa was looking for; when he set out to search for paradise he began a flight which gave him not only his book about the way in which a *godo* sees the Islands, but also another book, a very special, very strange one, *Part of A Story*, the tale of a shipwreck on an island (La Graciosa) where everything is still to be discovered.

BUT LET US RETURN TO ALDECOA'S DISCOVERY OF LOBOS, WHICH WOULD be a very similar discovery today. I have visited Las Lagunitas and have observed, as though they themselves were immobile, the undaunted seagulls that would move only if there were to be an earthquake; the launch, which moves exactly as the island itself would move if there were an earthquake, has taken us to Las Roques, rocks covered with red crabs and with an eagles' nest somewhere, blending with the darkness of the stone. It is an eagles' nest, but it houses only a solitary eagle; we wait for it, hoping for its arrival as though we were looking for the green ray at sunset, but the eagle and the green ray both disappoint us.

But we can read here what Aldecoa put in his book: 'The island of Lobos has monk seals, known as sea wolves, and it has a lighthouse, as well as dangerous sharp reefs and Technicolor coves and a rock that rises and falls from the sea, known as the Calafate. At the tiny landing point where the whole population of Lobos lives—only over the winter—it is difficult to land a boat if there is a high tide. If there is a high tide, then access to the sea is difficult. And the high tide becomes a lottery, according to the fishermen, and reaching Papagayo or returning to Punta Gorda is no longer difficult but a one-in-a-million chance, with you more likely to drown or faint from fear. Shipwrecks in the Bocayna are less showy than those in other straits, in other latitudes. There is an intense blue sky, and it is as though the appearance of the islands were covering up another sky behind them. You can't trust anything.'

You can't trust anything. I too was scared, sitting right in the bottom of the motorboat, splashed by the lively waters of the Atlantic, following the trail of the sea and seeing the reefs which Aldecoa spoke of showing their teeth like sharks. I saw the Calafate, a threat to all unwary or inexperienced sailors; and yes, I was so scared during the journey that it was as though the fear were a warning, a perception that things were going to go badly for me. And they did. But not yet, I shouldn't tell you that part of the story yet. I was pleased to find out that Aldecoa, who was so intrepid, suffered in the same was as I did. He was scared, and then he described the fear in tranquillity, described the black shadow of Lobos, a forewarning of the island: 'From Playa Blanca, as though shrouded or with an undercurrent, Lobos is no more than a black shadow, a thundercloud in a clear afternoon. The sun shines over the slopes of the ocean, between Punta Pechiguera and Punta Tostón. Over the deserted slopes of the ocean. Calm is born.'

Calm was born for me once I set foot on dry land again, when we bipeds were once again back in the environment for which we were conceived. The sea belongs to the fish, and here, between Fuerteventura and Lobos, the sea is a danger. You can't trust anything; I saw how close the Islands were, but I also saw the nature of our fear of the real and hazardous treachery of the sea. In front of me 'Lobos is no more than a black shadow, a thundercloud in a clear afternoon', but it is also bluntly distant from me, a large black stone which I want to reach simply to be able to hold onto something solid, a long way away from this sea which seems like a caress from a distance and which when you are riding on its back is actually a treacherous and wild stallion.

And so it was a relief for me finally to set foot on Lobos, looking back at Fuerteventura. Then, when I returned to Fuerteventura, I knew that there is danger also on dry land. It was on dry land that this traveller had his belongings stolen, and the computer on which he was writing and all his notes about his trip to the Islands. The sea scared me, but the land took away a part of my memory, and it was not just anywhere that my belongings were stolen, but from the left luggage office at the hotel where I had left these papers and all my materials, which are now nothing more than a part of the trash of the world . . . But at least I was back on Fuerteventura by then, which is luck enough in itself.

THE ISLAND, FUERTEVENTURA, SEEMED IN THE DISTANCE TO BE A SERIES of mountains overlaid one on another, shaded by a sun that at that point was at its zenith, right at midday. Lobos is an animal extension of the land we abandoned. And the trail behind the boat as it crossed the sea was like a handkerchief waved across a void.

Lobos is a series of forking paths; at some point the anatomy of the island turns into a marine biology laboratory, the white sand beaches seem a replica of the beaches to the south of Fuerteventura; but they exist and do not exist at the same time, depending on the frequency of the tides; and so you can swim out of your depth in the sea and then, a few minutes later, a very few minutes, you are not in the sea but on pure white sand, prehistoric sand like that which I saw one day in the Cíes Islands off Galicia, sand that is so white it hurts your eyes, or makes you dream of other visions, things that only appear after nightmares . . .

LA GRACIOSA, WHERE I GO FROM LANZAROTE, IS *TERRA* MUCH MORE *firma* than Lobos, as though Lobos were an island still engaged in its apprenticeship and La Graciosa had already graduated: it has a bakery, a post office, a school. Lobos has nothing. La Graciosa is already heavily populated; it is no longer the desert place where Aldecoa went looking for peace and solitude and nourishment for his melancholy. While we were travelling—not in a small boat as Aldecoa did halfway through the twentieth century, but aboard a much more powerful vessel —I went back over what he wrote about the place. His vision, before he actually travelled there, was an idyllic one: it is as though he were travelling to some place which he imagined as a metaphor of all islands. 'La Graciosa is on the other side of the River. The River is the strait which separates Lanzarote from the first of the three northern islands. Lanzarote has a point which sticks out into the sea and wounds it like a knife, a point called Fariones. The beaches of La Graciosa curve sweetly in front of the keel of Fariones.'

He arrived there in a ferry. When we boarded, in the summer of 2010, sixty years had gone by since Aldecoa's discovery of the island, and the following poster was displayed in the village of Órzola: 'We want to be able to bathe where our grandparents and parents did.' This is because La Graciosa, like Lanzarote, has grown up, has become more popular, and the beaches are being overwhelmed by building works, and people want the appearance of their dwelling places to go back to how it was in the time of their grandparents and parents. The journey there, of course, can be imagined as though it were the journey made by Aldecoa and so many others both before and after him . . . The cliffs are still there, albeit drowned by the white buildings which mark the tip of the island of Lanzarote on the way to La Graciosa. The sea is clear, a little dulled by the dawn clouds. And it is cold on deck, where a drunk enlivens the dawn just as he would have done on one of Aldecoa's boats. The sea is peaceful, or nearly: at least it is nothing like what Aldecoa called 'the disturbed River'. 'Sometimes,' he added, 'there is no way for anyone to cross the River.'

From the sea, as we leave Los Fariones behind us, in the middle of the River, facing towards the beach of Famara on Lanzarote, the island of La Graciosa seems to be an extension, an extra limb added to the island that César Manrique dreamt of in order to recreate it, the island of Lanzarote. But as the boat draws closer, La Graciosa takes on its true dimensions. To my left Lanzarote is a wall, and ahead of me La Graciosa is a single figure, perhaps a woman, lying down. And here we are: when I put my foot on dry land I feel that I am stepping onto an island for the first time, as if I were arriving somewhere whose mysteries always made space for adventures. The sound is different: the music of places is always different when you reach them by boat; it is as though you were treading on dry land for the first time, even though you only stepped onto the boat twenty minutes ago, back in Órzola where the dawn was breaking. People are still queuing here to buy bread, and we get down off the boat just as Paul Bowles and his companions would get off their old vessels when they reached Tangiers, back when everyone dreamed that true adventure was to be found in travelling.

BUT BEFORE I CONTINUE, BEFORE I TURN MY EYES TO THE LAND, LET ME pause for a few minutes on a species of no-man's-land, which would certainly have been the landscape of Bowles if he had come through here: the salt flats, which are a special terrain in Lanzarote. There are at least twenty salt plants on the Canary Islands: some of them abandoned; some of them still in use, and the saltworks of Janubio on Lanzarote are the most beautiful and interesting of the whole Islands. Cipriano Martín and Alberto Luengo, who have seen these saltworks in the light of both architecture and science, write as follows in their book *The Salt Garden*: 'its values both as a landscape and as an ecosystem, added to the original and complex architectural and hydraulic organisation of the whole, allow us to claim, with no room for doubt, that it is one of the most important saltworks in the world. The drying pans and the work sites, the ramps and the windbreaks, are all gathered to form a landscape of extraordinary architectural beauty.'

The preparation of salt requires the four fundamental elements of ancient alchemy: water from the sea to fill the salt beds, the mud needed to keep the water-sheets impermeable, the fire of the sun that crystallises the salt, and the soft warm winds that help the evaporation. 'For Aristotle, this was "burnt earth": a gathering of the four elements: fire, air, earth and water.'

The work involved in the manufacture of salt is closely related to the rhythms of the agricultural world, because 'in all the salt beds on the Canary Islands, the harvest time runs from March to October, and the low season is used for maintenance and expansion.'

The saltworks are a work of art. I can still see in my mind's eye the Janubio works, near Yaiza, looking as though they were a painting by Turner, or Rothko, or Cy Twombly, or else a Brancusi sculpture. Ghostly, spectral, the breath of a cloud laid down on the earth. My friend Eduardo Manrique, the sculptor, the nephew of César Manrique, made a sculpture for his uncle, a door, and this work of art is where my image of this natural marvel now resides, a marvel which is not on any map and which is one of the most beautiful symbols of my land . . .

In the first half of the twentieth century there were thirty saltworks in the Islands (above all in Lanzarote and Gran Canaria). At the end of the 1970s, when tourism started to turn itself into our daily bread, these saltworks started to fade away, and their remains are now a decadent and beautiful symbol of the terrain which the salt of the sea has won back from the land. César Manrique, the man who reinvented Lanzarote, explains his fascination with this in the prologue to Martín and Luengo's book *The Salt Garden*. 'I have always been impressed by the sight of a saltworks. The ones in Lanzarote have always struck me with their rectilinear beauty and their blinding whiteness.' The survival of the saltworks is a blessing that the Islands owe to the blind chance with which beauty works. Lanzarote has other tangible attractions, other miracles which César emphasised with the energy that he used to reinvent the island, changing it from the lava field of previous perception. But among the marvels that I can still see in my mind's eye, when I talk about Lanzarote when I am far away, the saltworks are the spectacle that seems to me to be the most perfect, the most powerful pictorial representation of this island, black and white gifts of the sea.

I HAVE LEFT BEHIND THE HEADLANDS THAT POINT OUT INTO THE SEA, AND here, in these bars which give La Graciosa the air of a Mediterranean village, perhaps on one of the Greek islands, I think that it would not be entirely terrible to spend days and days waiting here for something, anything, to happen. Like Aldecoa, like these fishermen.

But this is no longer a fishing village, which is what its discoverers sought in an earlier time; this is now a tourist village filled with jeeps that carry sleepy travellers along roads that were once dusty paths on which it would be possible to imagine the plots of mystery novels, stories of love or broken hearts, as in *Part of A Story*, Aldecoa's novel. The salt is still there, the seashore, perhaps the memory of the mystery, but it is now becoming just another island. It has lost for good the physiognomy which Aldecoa sketched out. Now La Graciosa is an extension of the coast opposite, a mirror of Lanzarote, with its houses gathered together, showing off that kind of collective air which all contemporary villages have, forcing their inhabitants to breathe at the same time and keep the same hours.

All right, the smell of the pier is the smell of the piers in the smaller islands, its noises are those of solitary islands waiting for adventurers, good entrance points for archipelagos, anthologies of the whole territory.

What can be heard is, if I may put it this way, the noise of the first villages, and when we step onto the island, when we tread on its sand, then everything, or almost everything, is a part of the village, the sand remains in its narrow streets, the hippies are setting up their stalls, the queues in front of the bakery are still there and an old woman gives us the dried fish that she herself was eating in the shade of her house. I took the fish with my own hands and looked at it: in some way it was the embodiment of the mystery of the island, a mystery that she had inherited by cooking, and I felt obliged, in spite of the fact that the morning is the wrong time to eat salty food, to eat it slowly, just as she did, showing my enthusiasm for eating the fish her sons had caught.

Seagulls are privileged inhabitants of La Graciosa; their unpleasant call, like that of a stray, cruel pigeon, must have been the first thing Aldecoa heard as he set foot on the island. Around me, in the café, some keen cyclists from Catalonia are talking, and also a group of teachers from Pamplona, who have just arrived, like me, at the isolation of La Graciosa. There is a school named after Ignacio Aldecoa, and there is a parish church which was consecrated in 1945, and the sun comes out, which is good news because the island has the 'donkey's belly' hanging over it, that accumulation of low clouds which regularly attacks the Canary Islands and which threatens their inhabitants with spending the whole day feeling oppressed by the weather, which can drive you mad, or give you a migraine. When the donkey's belly moves away, the sky is clear, virginal, and makes you want to touch the sea, which has now taken on the same perfect colour as the sky. When we leave the pier and the bars and the bakery and the cyclists having their party, the island sinks into an almost miraculous silence that accompanies me to the cemetery.

There are more tombs here; life turns into more life and more death, and the two graves which Aldecoa described in his book are now dozens. Cemeteries are a visual chronicle of life: the more life there is, the more death there is too; statistics don't lie; La Graciosa grew bigger, so the number of its dead also increased. Aldecoa saw it like this too, back when it was still difficult to die on La Graciosa: 'La Graciosa has a cemetery with only two graves, because the deaths coincided with the high winds and the fishermen could not take the bodies back to bury them in Haría on Lanzarote. This seaside cemetery, this hallowed ground with only two inhabitants, must be almost a holiday resort for the afterlife. The beach at La Graciosa is a great place to await the resurrection of the body, with the sea up against the walls and the noise of the sea in the shells that surrealist nature has scattered all over the sand, with the boats in the port and the wind in the sails, the vast angelical sails which the fishermen's wives make.'

THAT'S HOW IT WAS, THE IDYLLIC VISION ALDECOA HAD IN HIS MIND'S eye, and the one which he gave in his book. The island is not now like this: there are now very many people here even among the dead; but the sand on the beach still has the revivifying and idyllic power which Aldecoa saw and which can also be seen on the other great beaches of the Islands, such as Las Canteras on Gran Canaria, or Famara on Lanzarote, or El Médano on Tenerife, or La Barca on Fuerteventura.

Here I am, stranded on this island, sitting next to a dusty jeep which has driven from the most isolated and softest beach. The driver talks to me:

'They can't build anything anymore here. No one will give permission. It's over.'

And he was quiet for a moment, then spoke again.

'The fishing is done for, of course.'

Then I said:

'If the fishing is done for then La Graciosa will be done for too.'

He replied:

'La Graciosa will live forever. It's a magnet.'

Aldecoa's magnet.

The man who spoke with me was called Orlando: he had been a merchant mariner, and is still young. He was the one who took me to the cemetery. And I wrote in my notebook: 'In the sailors' cemetery. Like that strange cemetery that I saw in the sand at Cofete, Fuerteventura. Ghostly, the colour of the earth, the stones already illegible, like the empty lives to which they lent their names. But in this cemetery, unlike that other cemetery of sand and forgetfulness, life has not stopped; the dead are still coming, marking the natural cycle of La Graciosa, where there are now very many more people living, and more people dying too.'

Orlando points at his jeep, and speaks with nostalgia and arrogance: 'This is my boat now.' He drives me to a little mountain: 'Las Agujas, 876 feet above sea level. It's our Mount Teide,' he says proudly. And then adds: 'It's one of the few national parks of Spain that doesn't have any asphalt in it at all.' From the beach where he takes us ('travelling along the La Graciosa M-30,' he explains, talking about the road we are travelling on, which on this island has the air of a broad highway: he is joking as he refers to it, making a reference to the ring road which goes round Madrid) we can see the little further islands: Alegranza, which is very like a whale, Montaña Clara, Roque del Este; here is one of the most diverse marine reserves in Europe. It is there, in front of us, protected by the clear waters of the Atlantic, which here looks like a backwater. It is a perfect beach; I walk in bare feet across its sands, and it is as though I am travelling on a shifting boat which rolls and seduces me with its movement; I have the same impression here as I did in Famara when I visited it for the first time: a beach which makes you young again, which makes you excited, although I have another sensation as I walk on La Graciosa, as though the beach were also the end of the world, a beach which is the prophet of another universe or another age, the perfect place for a mysterious shipwreck. This is the mysterious place where Aldecoa set his novel *Part of A Story*, in which the shipwreck has such an important role to play.

TO GO, TO RETURN:
THE FATE OF THE TRAVELLER
AMONG ISLANDS

I WENT TOO SOON FROM ONE PLACE TO ANOTHER, AS IF THE ISLANDS were all connected by a great motorway across the sea. As though you could travel from Garajonay to Betancura on the back of a high-speed mule, as though you travelled from La Gomera to La Graciosa, or Lanzarote, throwing stones that stayed in the air alongside you as you travelled at the speed of a flying stone.

In fact, while I saw all these primeval spaces of my Canary Island memory I was travelling from La Gomera, present for one last time at the almost religious expressiveness of its mountains, which in the distance seem to be temples or figures brought over from legends; ahead of me is Tenerife once again, omnipresent as a memory. As I went through Vegaipala on La Gomera, I felt a strange symphony of cliffs, valleys, crags and palm trees, and silence, and in my imagination I recalled a similar feeling in the mountains of Tejeda, on Gran Canaria, or else in Vilaflor on Tenerife, or Betancuria on that yellow and des-olate land that is Fuerteventura, a high plain, an island which is like a donkey or a camel put face to face with a desert, indecisive and lost, listening to the noise of a wind that is like the wind I heard on the south coast of Tenerife, in El Médano.

The wind is an odd topic, diluted, something which adds a melancholic gust to the music of the southern islands, in Gran Canaria, in Fuerteventura, in El Hierro with its juniper trees, in the desert El Médano of Tenerife . . .

Here, higher up, in Antoncojo and Lo del Gato, further on in my voyage through La Gomera, the symphony can be heard which is sometimes the sound of the wind and sometimes the sound of the earth, here is also the almost eternal dun colour which transforms La Gomera into a large and humble dog, stretched out under a persistent and lazy sun; Fuerteventura is a donkey, or a camel nonplussed by the earth; and La Gomera is a dog, howling in rage or from melancholy, lost among the cliffs. A large dog looking at a lizard: because La Gomera is an unquiet dog, and the land that it faces is the southern range of Tenerife, which is like the spine of a sleeping lizard; this is what can be seen at a distance, at the foot of Mount Teide, a mountain range which looks like the risky and angry tail of a giant lizard.

I don't know why I always associate the appearance of my homeland with the subtle elegance of a saurian, creatures of the mountains or the deserts, odd animals which hide from the shadows and which only appear when they can be certain of finding the sun.

I RETURN TO LA GOMERA, I LEAVE LA GOMERA, I AM ALWAYS COMING and going, and La Gomera is like the island-magnet which Lezema saw in Cuba, the island which repels and which attracts, the sweet Gomera of the forests and the terrible Gomera of the cliffs, yin and yang of a perfect island which stretches its limbs under a sun made of fog. I travel by boat, and the ocean is the hand that waves goodbye.

There is an intense sun beating down on my head, I am leaving the island this time, to my right is the ceremonial urn from 1968, empty and dry and forgotten, and a little further on is the Square of the Great Trees where I drank a coffee at midday, my ears assaulted by the almost nautical sounds of the creaking, uneasy trees. People here walk slowly, as if they had made all possible journeys already: to arrive at an island is to see it in motion, to leave one is to see it at peace, as if behind you there stood only individual figures—men, women, children, dogs, lizards—all of them sunk into a lethargy in which you will find them once again when you return. The August sun adds to this sensation that one only gets from the smaller islands, the idea that life is not so urgent, that it is only a passing event which one can get through much better if one allows oneself to be guided by patience.

In the light of a summer afternoon, from the deck of the boat, the island's mountains seem to become softer, and the cultivated (or dried-out) land which runs down to the sea starts to look at this time of day like a series of Mayan temples, magical places which are made perhaps even more mysterious by the loneliness which distance grants them.

The evening light also bids farewell to the sensation that one is beginning a new voyage, a journey towards another kind of melancholia.

Suddenly, after the announcements in English and in Spanish to the passengers, the same warning is repeated as a whistle. It is almost a song, I hear it as a song. For centuries, this was not any kind of music, but rather a real need, which now has developed into a symbol of the solitude for which La Gomera was always destined. I hear the whistling and remember, immediately, one evening in the Valle Gran Rey, seeing a line of perfect palm trees and then a single palm, an open window and the sun that poured through it, as if this memory were suddenly a postcard, a metaphor for the light and trees of this island, which I recommend you come to observe as I would recommend you to feel the touch of paradise . . .

THE BOAT WHERE I FEEL THIS VISION OF THE ISLAND AS A METAPHOR IS taking me back to the island where I was born, Tenerife; I have reached the south, Los Cristianos, the beach of extremely fine sand where I lived through the years where one discovers love via discovering caresses, one's own caresses and those of others, and this sand, the sea stroked by the noble cliffs that are still there, even though surmounted with new buildings that make the place unrecognisable, was the scene of all my discoveries. And here is where I come from La Gomera, which was the first point I visited in this reconstruction of my memory of the Islands, but I don't want to start this return journey here, I don't want to begin this return to my native land after so many years on this beach at Arona, so far to the south, and previously even further to the south, when Tenerife did not have the motorway with which it now is provided.

I want to start where Alexander Humboldt started, an excellent guide, perhaps the man who has best described what it is that the stones of the island tell us.

The first thing that Humboldt saw, without a doubt, was the enormous headland of the Anaga range, right to the east of Tenerife; on this new journey in which we reconstruct Humboldt's vision, the headland is pointed out by the biologist Wolfredo Wildpret, an inhabitant of Tenerife but of Swiss origin, to Hans Magnus Enzensberger, who travels over the island as though he were the reincarnation of Humboldt, getting excited about everything and asking all manner of questions. Back in Germany, Enzensberger is the editor of the complete works of Humboldt in twenty volumes, including the famous (or at least, famous for us) *Journey to the Canary Islands*, which for several years has been one of my key books, the explanation in book form of the genius of the botanist in seeing what it was the landscape was telling him. So here we are, in Santa Cruz de Tenerife, the point where Humboldt landed. Over on this side, Wildpret says to Enzensberger, is the Anaga park, a huge nature reserve; and on this side is the container park. Yes, here they are, the island has evolved and now bears that contemporary ecological burden which so obsessed the Lanzarote naturalist César Manrique, who guessed that one day there would be more containers and cars than trees on the island. This is not yet the case, Wildpret said to his companion, but we are on our way . . . Under the huge Anaga headland are Las Teresitas and San Andrés, the beach and the village, a fishing village with its ruined castle and narrow little streets that remind one of a souk, and its little restaurants (try El Túnel, it's wonderful) where fish is still the clear sign of popular food. And the beach made out of new sand imported from other beaches, strewn there as though it had been there all its life. Behind these are other halts: Benijos, Taganana . . . I did not travel with them, because Wildpret and Enzensberger had another route in mind, but when I was there in the past, among these spaces, I rediscovered the Tenerife that had been hidden behind the mountain ranges, a natural island emerging from its surrealist dreams, open spaces, infinite seas on which the sun lays its enthusiastic hand, just as we do.

Wildpret explains some of Humboldt's discoveries to Enzensberger. For example, Humboldt took note of 460 distinct botanic species on Santa Cruz; in Humboldt's time the poor travelled by donkey and the rich went on horseback; the German naturalist enjoyed the vineyards in the country and appreciated the Mediterranean climate of Tacoronte, where citrus fruit grows so well; the surrealists André Breton and Óscar Domínguez came to the same places that Humboldt had visited many years later and discovered that 'agriculture is a form of silversmithing'. Bréton wrote, when he was back in Paris, the following about his journey to the Islands: 'When I reached Tenerife I washed my hands with common soap that was like lapis lazuli. I washed all Europe off my hands. And first of all, I washed away France, which was where I had come from.' And on his journey, without having washed his hands of Europe, Humboldt discovered the Valley of La Orotava, back when it still contained 'all the shades of green'. The title of one of John Ford's films came to Wildpret's mind: *How Green Was My Valley*. Because this valley, where some people say that Humboldt dropped to his knees (something that he never did), is now not even the shadow of the one that he saw back in the eighteenth century ('I have never found such peace as I have in this valley' is something he demonstrably did say): building works have proliferated, the banana plantations have been decimated by the incessant progress of housing, and not even the vantage point which was set up in Humboldt's honour was in use when Wildpret and Enzensberger made their excursion back in the spring of 2010.

And how would Humboldt himself have spoken of this? In the edition which I have of his now famous book about his journey round the Islands (a journey which lasted only six days, six very productive days) he writes about the impression which he had of the capital of the island: Santa Cruz is 'a great inn, on the road to America and the Indies'. It is place of such strategic importance that 'practically all accounts of any trips taken across the ocean begin by talking about Madeira and Tenerife'; it was here that Humboldt made contact with enlightened Canary Islanders who led him across the island to Mount Teide and even to La Orotava, where, at the end of the eighteenth century, he found an agitated social environment. He wrote that in La Orotava he had met 'people who have a taste for literature and music and who have brought into these distant climes the comforts of European society. In this sense, with the exception of Havana, the Canary Islands are very dissimilar from other Spanish colonies.' And he adds, in another letter to the English nobleman, Baron De Forell: 'What culture there is here, what elegance! One could imagine oneself transported to London, if the banana trees and coconut palms didn't fix us here, in the Fortunate Isles.' He was surprised by what Alonso de Nava y Grimón, the Marquis of Villanueva del Prado, had done over the course of the eighteenth century for La Orotava and, as the editor of the volume I am using, Manuel Hernández González, adds, 'Humboldt was pleasantly struck by the hospitality, friendliness and interest in science shown by the people he met.'

But his enthusiasm, the enthusiasm of a naturalist, was taken to the next level when he saw Mount Teide, as a result of the thick fog which looms over the island; he must surely have seen it from the spot where Gabriel García Márquez's character in *One Hundred Years of Solitude* sees it, or else from where Columbus saw it on his journey to America, but Humboldt found it hard to see the peak which gave him so much work in his dedicatedly scientific investigation. 'On the 19th [19 June 1799], we saw the peak of Naga (Anaga or Nago), but the Peak of Tenerife remained invisible. The landscape was poorly defined; all of its aspects were covered in thick fog. As we approached along the road to Santa Cruz, we saw that the fog, pushed by the wind, was coming closer to us. The sea was highly unruly, as it always is in these areas.' The boat dropped anchor in the middle of the fog, but 'when the time came to start to leave, the fog dissipated completely'. And then 'the peak of Mount Teide showed itself clearly above the clouds and the first rays of the sun, which we had not seen until that point, illuminated the top of the volcano'.

This marvel as described by Humboldt is the chief attraction of the island, and it is a majestic accident of nature which is the pride of all the inhabitants of Tenerife; all the islands can be seen from its peak, and it itself can be seen from many of them (in winter one gets a spectacular view from the top of the sacred mountain of Tindaya on Fuerteventura); snow-covered in winter, clear and dry in the summer, a dormant volcano which at its 12,198 feet above sea level is the highest point of all the Canary Islands as well as of the national park that bears its name and over which it rises with indisputable authority.

Humboldt knew that he was approaching a historic bay in the islands, because it was here, as he records in his detailed account, 'two years before our arrival, in July 1797, a cannonball took off the arm of Admiral Nelson, during the attempted occupation of the islands'. The German scientist arrives at the island and sets himself up in the city like a journalist or a sociologist; he sits down, if you will allow me this anachronistic supposition, in the spot where much later they would build the Atlantic bar, where in 1970 the Chilean poet and Nobel Prize winner Pablo Neruda sat down to drink beers with his friends the Canary Island surrealists, with whom he had entered into correspondence before the Civil War. Neruda did not want to get off the boat that was taking him back to his homeland, to work with Salvador Allende in what would later be the triumph of the Unidad Popular; the poet said that he would never step onto land controlled by the dictator Franco, but some of us, the ones who went to see the boat, reminded him that he had already visited Barcelona, in order to stroll through the town with his friend Gabriel García Márquez; at this, the poet resigned himself to the inevitable, climbed

down from the boat, and chatted and drank in that bar situated exactly where I want to imagine Humboldt as having spent his first
hours in the city of Santa Cruz. It is a bar which contains a huge
painting of Mount Teide by the twentieth-century Canary Island painter
Martín González.

The German naturalist wrote as follows: 'The position of this city
is very similar to that of La Guayra, the most-frequented port in the
province of Caracas. The heat is excessive in both places, and for the
same reasons, but Santa Cruz appears sadder. There are houses, of a
splendid white, built above a narrow sandy beach; they have flat roofs
and no glass in their windows, and are backed up against a wall of
sheer black rocks with no vegetation. An attractive pier built out of
ashlar blocks and the public promenade planted with poplars are the
only things that break the monotony of the landscape.' As they do not
face it, Humboldt continues, the inhabitants of Santa Cruz don't even
have Mount Teide, which can be seen much better from Puerto de la
Cruz, or Puerto de La Orotava, as it was known back then.

Is the German exaggerating? Is Santa Cruz really so sad? It was,
as it is now, a city of merchants, turned in on itself, but open to foreigners, who disembarked here and turned into islanders, like their
hosts; Humboldt himself was received like this, as a most welcome
guest whom the rigors of travelling had led to feel recalcitrant in the
face of the quiet charms of the Tenerife capital. In the streets, the first
thing that drew his attention 'was a very thin woman, extremely at-
tenuated and poorly dressed, who was known as La Capitana. She
was followed by other women who were no better dressed than she;
all of them begged to be allowed to go aboard the *Pizarro*: a request
which, naturally, was refused.' The German is in a bad mood and does
not understand the level of permissiveness displayed here: 'In this port,
so frequented by Europeans, the disarray of general custom takes on
the form of order. La Capitana is a chief chosen by her fellows, over
whom she can exercise great authority. She does the best she can to
prevent any behaviour that stops the ships from fulfilling their sched-
ules: she makes the sailors get back on board their ships at the agreed

time. The officers go to speak with her if they are worried that any members of their crew might be hiding in order to desert.'

And so the impressions which first met Humboldt as he set off on a journey that would be so important for him and for the image of the island itself could not have been worse. But the naturalist got used to the place: 'Santa Cruz is a fairly attractive place.' It is. And now, at the point where he saw La Capitana, there still stands 'that famous monument in Carrera marble, thirty feet high, dedicated to Nuestra Señora de la Candelaria, in memory of the miraculous apparition which she made in 1392 in Chimisay, near Güimar', but it has been joined by a later architectural addition, both polemical and interesting, made by the architects Herzog and de Meuron, who have tried to draw attention away from the monument which the Francoist government set up in front of the Cabildo, the seat of local government, in honour of the fallen on the Nationalist side in the Civil War. Also, it is here that the commercial area of the city begins, then following on down the Calle de Castillo and making a halt in the impressive Plaza de Weyler, in front of what used for many years to be the General Staff Office of the Canary Islands, the seat of the region's military government. Further up is one of the most beautiful promenades in the Islands, the Rambla de Santa Cruz, which used to be called the Rambla del 11 Febrero in the first Republic, and then was renamed Rambla de Franco before attaining its current title. On this street, in the 1960s, in the Parque García Sanabria, which was recently remodelled, there took place a unique exhibition of Sculpture in the Street, which brought together people of the calibre of Martín Chirino, Joan Miró, Óscar Domínguez and Henry Moore. And right here, where Humboldt sat down to contemplate what he called 'the sad city', there passed for years, right up to the present day, the carnival processions of the island, which defied, in the years of dictatorship, the strict moral code of Francoism.

So it might be fair to say that the German scientist jumped the gun a little, or perhaps should have been aware that it is risky to take notes on a topic when one is tired from travelling. In any case, we are left with his adjective, 'an attractive city' which is connected in its layout and its landscape to what Humboldt immediately, with his geographical and geological knowledge, identified to be the case: 'This group of islands is a part of Africa, and, what is more, of the most arid part of that continent.'

But nature had its way of confusing him: when, the next day, he climbed up to La Laguna—the oldest city of the island and the first capital of the archipelago—he saw something that anyone can check for himself if he so desires: that this city, also known as La Laguna de los Adelantados, is the replica, the fundamental model, of the settlements built in Latin America; created with an almost mathematical precision, it houses the university (the only university on the Islands for a very long time) and the middle school; important churches; convents; the archbishop's palace; naturally beautiful streets, such as the Camino Largo; inns; historic buildings in whose damp walls there resides an extraordinary past of men and of legends. A truly fantastic city, perhaps *the* city of the Canary Islands, or even of the entire world; most beloved by the author of this book, by the man who, so many years after Humboldt, is writing this impassioned journey around the Islands . . . The overheated scientist who complained about Santa Cruz found that 'as we entered La Laguna we felt the atmospheric temperature gradually lowering. The sensation felt all the softer given that the air in Santa Cruz was truly suffocating.' In order to understand the heat, Humboldt turned to geology: 'The heat which so affects the traveller when he enters into Santa Cruz de Tenerife or La Guayra must be attributed to the reverberation of the rocks which surround these cities.' But La Laguna . . . ah, La Laguna! 'It is the perpetual freshness which fills La Laguna,' Humboldt concedes, 'that makes it perceived across all the Canary Islands as a delicious and luxurious place.' Now it is something else, of course: La Laguna has grown beyond its perimeters, has spread up into the mountains into the areas known as La Esperanza and Las Mercedes, has covered areas that used to be farmed, has uprooted the forests of 'laurels, myrtles and arbutus' which had benefited from the frequent rain; it is no longer, as might be expected, the city which the contemporaries of Humboldt would have known; but it still, even in summer, has a singular beauty, a beauty appreciated both by its inhabitants and by tourists. Every year, several times each year, many people, myself included, travel to La Laguna almost as pilgrims, as though this urban space were to some extent the ideal city.

Perhaps it is the fact of seeing La Laguna which makes the hitherto-reticent German scientist exclaim at a certain point of his journey: 'Tenerife, situated in a manner of speaking at the entrance to the tropics, although only a few days' sailing from Spain, enjoys all the beauties which Nature has given to its equinoctial regions. And the vegetation grows here in some of its most impressive and beautiful forms, banana trees and palm trees.' And then Humboldt, now fully surrendering, goes on to say: 'Any man who is sensitive to the beauties of Nature will find on this island a delicious medicine for any melancholy he may be suffering. There are no other places which seem more likely to do so and also to return one's agitated soul to a state of peace than Tenerife and Madeira.'

Humboldt also observes one item which back then was a recent innovation and clearly visible, and which now to us seems to hark back to a remote past: 'This effect does not derive from the beauty of the island's position or the purity of the air; they are above all due to the absence of slavery, which has such a shocking appearance in the Indias and anywhere else that European colonialists have taken what they call their enlightenment and industry.'

Humboldt's journey has a particular attractiveness nowadays, because although the island has evolved a great deal ever since he looked at it with eyes that were at one and the same time irritated and admiring, its outlines and its landscapes still clearly reflect his successive discoveries. And it would be no bad thing for someone today to retrace his journey, which is, for the Canary Islanders who come from Tenerife, a sentimental one, a journey which is undertaken with a certain natural degree of patriotic pride.

THE GAZE OF OTHERS

A LEXANDER VON HUMBOLDT HAS LED ME TO THINK OF OTHER TRAV-ellers, those who have seen us while we were making our own discoveries, while the centuries went by and the adventures we had became the background to our lives.

Agatha Christie used us as strategic background for some of her mysteries, as did Jules Verne, seeing this fragmented territory as a broken continent; André Breton transformed us into a surreal landscape; Miguel de Unamuno thought that he could see certain traces of his own Basque homeland here; Daniel Defoe gave up on his idea of coming to the Islands because he could feel the shadow of pirates hanging over the traces of Robinson Crusoe.

The literature, both fiction and non-fiction, in which the Canary Islands appears, above all the two largest islands, Gran Canaria and Tenerife, is large. It is a strategic site: the Islands normally form a stopping-off point in a journey, and such a voyage has usually been a difficult one, threatened by the underhand behaviour of international actors, or sometimes encouraged by colonialist greed.

Shakespeare had heard of our wine; García Márquez knew of our birds, and in the works of both writers, one in the sixteenth century and the other in the twentieth, both birds and wine have been used as the basis for their metaphors. We have seen this, the interest which the Islands inspire in outsiders, as a stimulating factor, because the Islands like to see themselves reflected in all kinds of mirror, just like Narcissus . . .

And I want to compile here a set of fragments of the large variety of mirrors which enfold and embrace us, before continuing along the path set out by Humboldt, down into my own valley, the place where I was born, the Valley of La Orotava.

We have looked into the books in which our islands appear as though we were searching for our own essence, as seen by the eyes of others, as if identity were something that was spilled into texts by people who just happened to be passing through, found that this was an extraordinary environment and told us as much. Some of the books I read surprised me, and others seemed to me, with the benefit of hindsight, to have been written by people who loved the Islands a great deal and who left traces of their exaggerated affection here. Other people didn't love them at all, as certain of the accounts show.

First of all, the birds. There is a pleasant passage in *One Hundred Years of Solitude*, the novel by Gabriel García Márquez which is at one and the same time so Atlantic and so personal to us, in which the Aracataca-born novelist describes the birds that are to repopulate Macondo, his mythical terrain. 'The cage of canaries showed that these were not improvised suggestions. Remembering that his mother had described to him in a letter how the birds had been exterminated, he had delayed his return by several months until he had found a boat that had would call at the Fortunate Isles, and there he bought twenty-five pairs of the finest canaries to repopulate the sky over Macondo. This was the most lamentable of all his frustrated initiatives. As the birds began to reproduce, Amaranta Úrsula started to set them free in pairs, and they took longer to feel themselves at freedom than to leave the village. In vain did he try to make them live in the dovecote that Úrsula had put up in the first restoration of the village. In vain did he make them false nests of straw in the almond trees, and spread canary seed on the roofs and stirred up the remaining prisoners in order that their singing might dissuade their fellows from leaving, but the deserters flew up into the sky at the first opportunity and turned round in the skies just long enough for them to fix on a route and head back to the Fortunate Isles.'

The birds return; the islanders return. They can't deal with captivity; it is their vocation to be free. We Canary Islanders have always connected our name with that of these birds, their light and liberated presence; even though others say that the etymology derives from dogs, *canes* in Latin. García Márquez gives us this honour, and has his birds come from the Islands, but the birds return; they cannot accept any form of captivity . . . a beautiful symbol of our presence on the earth.

Birds and their nests: these childhood obsessions, wherever the birds live, these flocks which Amaranta Úrsula could in no way control. The Islands have always been a peaceful place, with tall trees, and our childhood took place at a time when children still looked after birds in their own nests. Perhaps this is a custom which still exists, but childhood is a period which vanishes forever; I think that the time of nesting is one that passes too.

Birds and Mount Teide. The poet Francisco Brines wrote—as did Rafael Alberti and Vicente Aleixandre, all three of them Spanish poets—about the bird of Mount Teide, a myth which has entered in its strangeness into both poetry and legend, because it is a creature which it is impossible to find. Perhaps because the freest bird is the one which does not exist. To a certain extent, Mount Teide itself, the volcano which presides over the topography of the Islands, as well as their mythology, is a simple bird, an odd bird, a volcano which no longer threatens the Islands and which has drawn in its fiery wings . . . There is a text by the Cuban writer Alejo Carpentier, author of *The Enlightenment*, which describes the mythical character of Mount Teide and the effect it has on his imagination and on ours. It is in his book *The Road to Santiago*: 'That morning, the shadow of Mount Teide had painted itself against the sky like a vast mountain of blue cloud. The bearded man, travelling as a Christian, giving himself airs as though he were a Burgundian who had travelled to the Indies on licence from the King (he has promised to show this on his arrival), knows that his journey will soon come to an end. As Gran Canaria trades with people from England and Flanders, and more than one

Calvinist or Lutheran captain offloads his cargo here, without being asked if he believes in predestination, fasts during Lent or wants to buy Papal bulls on the cheap, it will be easy for him to get lost in the city, and then think how to get off the island and make his way to France. He casts a knowing look at Juan, so as not to talk about what they both are thinking. For the time being, he is happy to have redis-covered, in lentils and *salpicón*, in cheese and in brine, flavours which he had missed a great deal, over there in the stockade where, more in spite than in real grief, Doña Yolofa and Doña Mandinga sit and cry, who used to set themselves up as fine Spanish ladies in front of the other black women, given that they were the concubines of the son of a Squire, whatever that was, it must be something important.'

Mount Teide, the lighthouse that attracts the stranger. Daniel Defoe wanted to come, and in *Robinson Crusoe* he describes what happened: 'I fell into terrible misfortunes. The first was this: our ship making her course towards the Canary Islands, or rather between those islands and the African shore, was surprised in the grey of the morning by a Turkish rover of Sallee, who gave chase to us with all the sail she could make. We crowded also as much canvas as our yards would spread, or our masts carry, to get clear; but finding the pirate gained upon us, and would certainly come up with us in a few hours, we prepared to fight; our ship having twelve guns, and the rogue eighteen.'

A failed attempt, but an attractive and beautiful vision of the mountain which Carpentier saw in his fiction, and about which Defoe says the following: 'Once or twice in the daytime I thought I saw the Pico of Teneriffe, being the high top of the Mountain Teneriffe in the Canaries, and had a great mind to venture out, in hopes of reaching thither; but having tried twice, I was forced in again by contrary winds, the sea also going too high for my little vessel; so, I resolved to pursue my first design, and keep along the shore.'

Paul Bowles did make it to the Islands, as did Lawrence Durrell. Durrell dedicated a poem to Tenerife, an island which he sees as a woman.

Bowles discovered this atmosphere as well and describes it in his story, 'The Fourth Day Out From Santa Cruz'; it is his vision of a landscape which one only travels through, in the middle of the twentieth century, in a city which is both African-American and unclear: 'It is pleasant to walk by night along the pier of an unknown port, with the autumn breeze pushing you softly from behind. Ramón was in no hurry; he stopped in front of a café to hear the guitars and the shouting, without allowing himself in exchange to be importuned by the by the women who called to him from the darker doorways.'

AMONG THE MANY SPANISH VISITORS TO THE ISLANDS, I BELIEVE THAT Miguel de Unamuno is the one who manages to enter the soul of the Islands in the most passionate way. His vision of Tenerife coincides to a degree with the first impression which Humboldt had when he arrived there, when he discovered the unbearable slowness of the Islands. The Basque poet and philosopher writes as follows, adapting to his own purposes a few famous lines of Nicolás Estévanez, the soldier and poet of the Canary Islands who fought, amongst other conflicts, in the War of Cuban Independence: 'There is nothing for me to say to you about Santa Cruz de Tenerife. Except that once I arrived there I started to become impatient with the slowness of the inhabitants of this land. And I started to feel the effects of the somnolence of the Islands, the sweet drowsiness that comes from isolation . . . I hurried up to La Laguna de los Adelantados. On the way I was shown the house of Nicolás Estévanez, and next to it an almond tree which Nicolás had made famous. His lines run as follows: *my fatherland is not the world; my fatherland is not Europe; my fatherland is not Spain: my fatherland is a shack, the shadow of an almond tree . . .* etcetera. Poor man, having no other fatherland than the shadow of an almond tree! He ended up hanging himself from it.'

In La Laguna, Unamuno says, 'there is a silence and a solitude that affects me to the very marrow of my soul. In the sky there is fog, a fog of dreams, a fog of absolute somnolence. Long streets, long as dreams; at the end of them a shattered dark tower. Here and there houses with jutting wooden balconies, and latticework, normally painted green; very typical balconies, behind whose latticework one imagines the lady sitting and waiting, waiting for centuries now, the same lady from back in the days of the conquistadores. Some houses are topped with a *verede*, a little plant like a small palm tree. [. . .] They say that La Laguna is like a Castilian city, and there is something in that: there is also something of Castile, of the mountains of Castile, in the landscape that surrounds it. But there is also a special tone to the place that is not really like that of the old Castilian cities. These wide and straight streets, this clarity, this air that is half romantic quadrille and half ceremony, everything that shows it to be an aristocratic creation of the seventeenth century, all this marks a difference between La Laguna and the rough Castilian streets with unbreakable Roman towers standing over them, where there may be some fragment of a Roman wall, or some air of the Reconquista, something that speaks of a naïve faith brandishing its sword and ready to fight. La Laguna instead wears a dress coat; or a monk's habit, if you will.'

From La Laguna the poet went to Gran Canaria, and searched for the heart of the island. 'The interesting thing here, about this island that is Gran Canaria,' he wrote, 'is to be found in its interior, in the two great bowls of these enormous volcanoes that have been silent for centuries. I climbed up as far as Teror, a village of an almost preternatural calm, which reminded me of the villages of the Miño area in Portugal. If it were not for the palms, that liturgical tree which is like a great green altar candle, if it were not for the bananas, if it were not for the other tropical plants, then this area of the world would remind me a great deal of Galicia. But here, in Teror, almost 2000 feet above sea level, the landscape changes. The extremely leafy chestnut groves in Osorio reminded me of a corner of my native Basque country. And there, in the chestnut groves, I waited for the afternoon to pass until I saw the hills sink into the calm of the night. It is something that is always new, something that seems to lead us to the source of life itself, something that invites us gently to mingle with mother earth.'

And then Unamuno went to Tejeda, in Gran Canaria, a miraculous site where he found the peace in the stones of the island at the same time as other, more Dantesque discoveries: 'And so we started off on horseback to visit the valley or cliff of Tejeda, one of the two great volcanic cauldrons on the island. The path leads between cliffs, where the humble laburnum covers the ground and where the chestnut tree and the walnut lift their fuzzy heads from hollows in the ground, and here and there, from the scorched cliff sides or among the volcanic there sprouts the occasional miserable euphorbia. We made a pause in Valleseco, a tiny village that sits in the lap of the mountain and where the streets were decorated for a party. Continuing along paths that were occasionally cut by sheer and abrupt rock falls, we caught our first view of the Valley of Tejeda. The sight is impressive. All the black walls of the great volcanic cauldron, with their crests that seem to be fortified, with their upright rocks, give an effect that is almost Dantesque.'

Jorge Luis Borges came through Las Palmas in a boat, on his way back to America. And on this voyage he wrote this poem dedicated to the city:

At the noisy point of twenty days' voyage
the night knew, with surprising skill,
how to soothe the seas' relief, that placid reproach
to the upright waves and the harsh storms.

Afterwards there remained engraved in my consciousness
among the sharp jostlings of the covered wagon,
the market and the tower, a calm clasp
linking quiet streets and blue skies.

Some little houses daubed in ochre,
a few little squares, smug as altars,
the palm tree whose top was covered with the soft night,

hills which lift up the mediocre populace . . .
In this spot the soul, broken up by the seas,
received once again the familiar caress of the earth.

Jules Verne saw it in the same way, and in the prose of his novel
The Thompson Agency and Co. describes the same city which Borges
had given us in poetry: 'Built at the end of the Guiniguada cliff, on a
series of extremely uneven patches of land, the city has an entirely ori-
ental aspect. [. . .] Las Palmas is a constructed city, with dark narrow
streets, but one where the nature of the landscape converts every stroll
into a perpetual ascent, followed by a perpetual descent. Apart from
the cathedral in its Spanish Renaissance style, it has few interesting
monuments. As for the Moorish aspect of the city: when seen from
the sea, it provokes unreasonable expectations which disappear as
soon as one looks closely. There is nothing less Moorish than these
streets, these houses, their inhabitants, who offer up to public admi-
rations exclusively European, almost French, refinements.'

And then there is Shakespeare. He did not travel to the Islands,
but he heard the legends attached to malmsey wine. In *Henry IV Part
II*, act II, scene IV, Mistress Quickly speaks as follows:

'I' faith, sweetheart, methinks now you are in an excellent good
temperality: your pulsidge beats as extraordinarily as heart would desire; and your colour, I warrant you, is as red as any rose, in good
truth, la! But, i' faith, you have drunk too much canaries; and that's
a marvellous searching wine, and it perfumes the blood ere one can
say "What's this?" How do you now?'

And Prince Henry says, in *Henry IV Part I*, act II, scene I:

'O villain, thou stolest a cup of sack eighteen years ago, and wert
taken with the manner, and ever since thou hast blushed extempore.
Thou hadst fire and sword on thy side, and yet thou rannest away:
what instinct hadst thou for it?'

Falstaff, in the same scene of the same play, calls out, possessed
by the spirit of dry Canary wine (he calls it 'sack' in the original, referring to malmsey):

'A plague of all cowards, I say, and a vengeance too! marry, and amen! Give me a cup of sack, boy. Ere I lead this life long, I'll sew nether stocks and mend them and foot them too. A plague of all cowards! Give me a cup of sack, rogue. Is there no virtue extant?'

And then, in the stage directions, 'he drinks'. Let us drink, then, let us stop for a moment in the same spot where we left Humboldt, let us look for his tracks, which are not the tracks of his tears but perhaps the tracks of malmsey wine.

THE IMAGE OF THE VALLEY

I AM WRITING THIS SITTING IN FRONT OF THE MOUNTAIN OF MY CHILD-hood, in my village, Puerto de la Cruz, on the coast of the La Orotava valley; here is where they say that Humboldt knelt down when he saw it in his search for the beauties of the world.

Here was where he was overcome, the legend has it.

It would happen again today; he would be scared of what they had done with the valley where he shed his alleged tears of joy.

But here I am, starting to tell another story of Humboldt and the Canary Islands, because I used to live in one of the great beauties of all the Islands, and now I live with the consequences of its development.

Let us leave behind us for the moment the expressions of people who saw these solitary islands for the first time, these islands where Jules Verne thought that he saw the remains of 'a disappeared continent', and where Gabriel García Márquez sought the birds that were to re-populate the mythical land of Macondo.

Those of us who come from here can see this landscape without so much mythologizing, but time and distance have helped us to un-derstand these visions in which the Islands are confused with extraor-dinary apparitions, with firebirds, with surrealist blows struck at the air above Mount Teide.

The La Orotava valley, for example, was for Humboldt the ultimate expression of a virgin territory whose infinite greenness was itself the expression of the volcanic mystery of Teide. But for us it was the land we lived in: neither literature nor legends could in any way transform the daily vision which we had of this place. It was a place where we worked, where we sweated, a place of stale air in a difficult and poverty-stricken time for Spain, the 1950s. You looked at the beauty, but you saw the life.

This was the land we trod on, the place where we breathed, where our memories were kept. If you point out this valley, the place where I was born, then you point out a cradle, a house, a path, a village square, a playground, a bench down by the pier, the silence of my parents, their fight to carry on; you see a path that leads to the school, you remember the remains of a cemetery.

THIS VALLEY, WHICH WAS SHADED AND GREEN AS AN ORCHARD OR A banana plantation, is now a multitudinous gathering of houses. Hotels, old people's homes, flats: life moves on and at some point found its resting place here. And the builders were insatiable: they covered with houses the land that had so affected Humboldt.

When he came, the Hotel Taoro was not there, that spot where Winston Churchill and Agatha Christie both stayed, attracted by the British glamour of the city; since the beginning of the twentieth century Puerto de la Cruz has exercised an enormous attraction for British travellers: after this hotel there came others, and the unchecked building works turned Humboldt's initial admiration into what I imagine would be his present-day lament.

But that is the way things are, and an inhabitant of Puerto del Cruz now sees them with a sense of useless melancholy, because this is the way things are and they are not going to change. They are as they are, and they still have an air of enchantment that is a magnet for tourists and a source of melancholy for those of us who were born here, at this calm pole of the world, the place where one is provided

with the smells that made up a whole childhood: salt, the wind, dampness, the trees in the square, the smell of the pier.

It cannot be changed: Puerto de la Cruz is like this now. Things
are as they are. But they can be described as once they were, or as one
remembers them being, for nothing is as another remembers it; rather
it is as you yourself remember.

In order to get here, along Humboldt's path, and to make things
as they were when I was born, it is not a bad idea to pick up once again
Ignacio Aldecoa's book, *A Tourist's Notebook*. The Basque writer says:
'When travelling from La Laguna to Puerto de la Cruz, one has to pass
famous names, toponyms, names of great battles. The Massacre of
Acentejo, the Victory of Acentejo. And then the La Orotava valley. The
path twists between banana trees and eucalyptus and red poinsettia.
The valley is not strictly speaking a valley, but a slope that leads down
to the sea, covered in terraced banana plantations, which in the midday
sun shine a vivid emerald, and which end in the white garland of the
Atlantic, breaking against the rock and lava of the coast.'

If one compares this succinct description with what has taken
place in the valley now, one would conclude that everything is pretty
much still there, and that what has changed is the highway. Now the
highways are like arrows aiming at Puerto de la Cruz, through the
zones known as Botánico and Las Arenas, which is where my house
was, the place where I was born, next to the ravine. But the highway
has changed everything: now the northern road and the road that goes
through Botánico enable one to travel rapidly, they are speedy solu-
tions which have necessarily diminished the degree of floral beauty
which Aldecoa so admired when he travelled through here. The eucalyptus trees are still there, although not in such great numbers, and
the poinsettia too, but threatened by the fumes from the road. But the
highway has conditioned the landscape: the Lanzarote writer César
Manrique didn't want there to be so many roads on the Islands, because they would change the landscape. The people who contradicted
him and carried on building must have fixed themselves in this landscape so as not to carry out the same vandalism at other sites.

Back then, when Aldecoa came at the beginning of the 1950s, in many of the old houses which I can still see from where I am now sitting there was no electric light, and services were scarce; the Canary Islands were living through the worst moment of the post-war period, and hunger and poverty contrasted with the remains of a feudal baronage which survived here far longer than in the rest of Spain.

Tourism came to save the people, to an extent, from this poverty, and put Spain on the world map, and here, in particular, an era of prosperity began which, with certain ups and downs, has never stopped.

But of course, this spot which surprised Humboldt with its fecundity is no longer the same, and will never be the same again. The mountain which I can see in front of me, for example, was the mountain of my childhood imaginings; it is in a part of the area known as Las Arenas; it stood guard over my dreams and my sentimental landscape; it was crowned with some raggedy palm trees that made it appear to my eyes to be a caricature of a mad philosopher, Miguel de Unamuno for example.

This was the mountain. They started to dig into it to extract *zahorra*, the principal material that makes up the volcanoes of the Islands, and they dug so deep into it that it ended up as a skeleton of what it once was. These bites out of the mountain seemed to be made by the fangs of development and time, and so its progressive deterioration seemed to me to be inevitable, a fateful curse. And because fate does not stop working its wicked way, one day people decided to replace those philosophic trees with a five- or six-storey hotel.

And here the mountain's revenge took place, and after a while it swallowed the hotel into its gut; the first attempt to put the hotel back up was a failure, but because mankind is pig-headed and wicked, a third attempt at building a hotel took place, and there it stands to this day, sticking out over the mountain like a challenge shouted against the calm, stunned beauty that this place once possessed.

And on the other side of this valley of plains, banana plantations, trees and paths, I can see another mountain, the one that stood behind my house, towards the far north of the island of Tenerife, winding and malleable as the sacred mountains which the Basque sculptor Eduardo Chillida loved so much.

EDUARDO CHILLIDA DREAMT OF A MOUNTAIN LIKE THAT. ONE DAY A group of architects, who knew that I was in contact with the Basque artist, asked me to pass an idea on to him in which they thought he might be interested. It involved hollowing out the mountain at Tindaya, a sacred outcrop at Fuerteventura, in the eastern part of the archipelago. I took the idea to Chillida, who wanted to turn the inside of the mountain into a sun room, and the artist drew up a project which scandalised ecologists and other naturalists, because it put the sacred nature of the mountain in danger. Chillida in fact wanted to make the mountain even more sacred. They didn't understand him. He died still feeling the melancholy of the rejection: his dream disappeared with him, and what remained was the hubbub aroused by his supposed sacrilege. Now, several years later, the government of the Canary Islands wants to bring this project to fruition.

The mountains round my village didn't have the luck to generate the same defence of sacredness as Tindaya did. The second mountain that was also a part of the landscape of my childhood now displays on its most visible side a whole building that seems to be made out of slots in a cemetery wall, and up close is undoubtedly a block of flats. Up at the peak, which is still intact, there is still an old white hermitage which connects the present day to a past that evokes a useless melancholy. It was always there, in the distance, like the eye of God, looking down from on high at a part of town that had been through everything that time could throw at it, from poverty to the promise of a life filled with all manner of goods thanks to tourism which had gone and which now returned.

And the rest of the landscape? As a child, at the end of the 1950s, I walked along these paths and through these alleys that ran past banana plantations, drains and bushes, and which now go past building sites and garages. In my part of the town, which is at the foot of both mountains, there was only one telephone, which my father owned, as he was a driver and a builder, and starry-eyed at that, and one single available car, which belonged to a German fleeing his Nazi past. His son, carefree and blond, drove the car, a Volkswagen, over the un-asphalted roads, and on rainy days accelerated when he drove past the local children in order to soak us from head to toe. We didn't know who the Nazis were, but in our infantile and rudimentary way we took notice of his methods; foreigners were normally the suave and generous companions whom we met on our paths, but this Nazi turned our childhood into a torment; even before knowing there was such a thing as fascism, because it was something never mentioned either in our homes or in the press, this man brought it into our homes.

Next to us lived a couple of Swedish bohemians, fantastic people who in their mid-twenties had decided to make the voyage to the south and had stopped in the Canary Islands along with their three-year-old daughter Tamara and a caravan which had already gone through one world war. They rented a house next door, opposite our vegetable plot, behind the cliff down which the dangerous floods would come rushing; he, whom we called Bear, was a painter, and is still alive, at the age of eighty-eight, in Stockholm; she, Anne, who lives in Sweden as well, in Lund, and has not yet reached the age of eighty, is a writer. My mother looked after their daughter, and stared open-mouthed at the spectacle that these bohemians displayed when they came back from the Casino in Taoro every evening: the young painter would empty his pockets and rain down a shower of coins which, in the eyes of my mother, represented surprising wealth; the marriage, which broke up later back in Sweden, gave rise to another child, a son whom we nicknamed Gofio.

The four of them went back to their country, and before they did so they left us some presents and a photograph which at home we always called the Swedish photo; it still exists, and not only that: it provided the title for a book I wrote some years ago about my memories of the place where I grew up, its earthen streets and the cliff.

The first toy we had in our house was a red car, an MG which Bear and Anne gave me, and the first book I remember in our house was by Anne, with photos by Tamara, and was called, in Swedish, *Trulsa ös mormor*. I have never forgotten it, because it was also my first contact with foreigners on the paths round my house, and the first sign of my now ancient vocation of meeting them and understanding them. I needed to understand foreigners, and also the old paths round my house, which I now go back to walk anew.

BUT IT IS IMPOSSIBLE TO WALK THEM AGAIN, ALTHOUGH EVEN SO THIS valley, which I am looking out at as I write, and which I can see from the Taoro Park, where that famous hotel was, still retains some of its special charm, a kind of shaded peace which is surely what the early, primitive tourists—the ones whom we ran after to beg for money— came here to find.

We believed (with the exception of the Nazi and his twisted son; and in spite of the fact that the Swedes were already there, our neighbours) that all tourists were English, because many of them were. They lodged here, in Puerto de la Cruz. We would accost them in the streets and on the footpaths, as they walked past, leaning on their canes or sticks, searching for the occasional rays of the sun, which were often hidden behind the thick white clouds over the valley. We called out to them in English: 'Penny! Penny!', asking for money. I can't remember if they were generous or not, but what is certainly the case is that little by little they started to shift the economy of the valley towards tourism, and what we asked for as children ended up by becoming a demand of adults as well. Penny, penny. We spent all our time on the lookout for the next penny. And that is still the case.

We lived off tourism, and that still is the main crop of the north of the island of Tenerife; of the north, of the south, and of the north and south of all the islands. Tourism has marked the face of the islands; I don't know if it has marked their character.

THIS AREA THAT I AM NOW LOOKING AT, ALL FILLED WITH BUILDINGS AND roads and housing complexes, and where there are still occasional forests, and leafy squares, and every now and then a banana plantation, blocked from view by the building works, still conserves the romantic vigour which it always had for those of us who were born here. This morning, when I woke up, I opened the windows and saw in the sky the clouds of my childhood; I heard the giddy trill of the birds and in the distance the desperate barking of dogs frustrated at their owners' laziness.

But, more than anything else, I saw the stubborn cloud that always turned my village into a vague and grey landscape which only was saved by 'the perfect iodine of the Atlantic', as César Manrique put it. That cloud that sometimes rips a resolute and firm Atlantic sun may be what brought the English here at the end of the nineteenth century, in search of a more peaceful and respectful climate. Perhaps.

The English colony, which has left places and traces here, proper names and legends, even has its own cemetery, which is the best way to define a relationship of dependence: people who allow their dead to stay on foreign ground no longer consider such ground foreign; the cemetery has been there, in my town, since very early in the twentieth century, and is so much a part of life here that the locals even gave it a name, La Chercha, their corruption of the word *church*. La Chercha is here, under my feet, next to the place where I am writing these pages, in the Taoro Park, very close to where I was born; you can see my house from here: it used to be a house that stood by itself in the middle of the banana plantations; in front of it were roads that seemed to me to be leading to a different world, and above was the mountain. Now it is a runway of construction sites, which I look at from here as though I were being watched by the sixty years that have passed between my first childhood and where I am today, sitting here, trying to recover the lost smells of the past in my writing.

DOWN THERE IS ALSO THE ANGLICAN CHURCH, IN WHOSE GROUNDS, LEAFY and calm as those of a tiny English village, they found the corpse of a former member of the OAS, the so-called *armée secrète*, the French far-right terrorist organisation set up in the 1960s, who had fled here after much shooting and many spy games, and a lot of anti-Algerian terrorism. They never found out who killed him. This man, who organised mysterious tourist activities on the Islands, put heavies at the door of the discotheque he owned; I attacked their behaviour in the papers, and he had no better way of attacking me back than by suing me for damages, a claim which luckily enough the judge considered not only excessive but also frivolous.

So, there is La Chercha, a retrospective monument to the respect with which the ideas of outsiders were treated in my town, and to the presence of foreigners here, ever since memory began. Here, through this valley, the ideas of the French Revolution came to the Islands, much earlier than to the rest of Spain, along with the notion of the encyclopaedia and of freedom of thought. It is strange that they should have been brought by a priest, the historian José de Viera y Clavijo, the author of a *History of the Canary Islands* which is the most faithful of all those written here about the past of these islands.

But before I allow Viera, and life itself, to send us down other side-tracks, allow me to continue to describe the spot where I now find myself. Downhill, behind me, completing the panorama as described by Humboldt, is the Atlantic coast, which is called Martiánez on one side and Punta Brava on the other. It is a dark and rocky coast, a savage coast: men have tried to take control over it by putting hotels in unlikely places which they still have not beaten down, like the hotel on the mountain that I could see from my childhood window; however, these hotels have somehow, surprisingly, managed to defy the assaults of the natural world against a landscape that it would have been better for no one to have touched in the first place.

I have swum in these seas, carefully, sometimes with the help of a large black inner tube, like the ones used for the tyres of big lorries,

and I have seen other athletes fighting against the big waves that threw
themselves up in rapid foam onto the dark, almost jet-black sands.
And on the shore I have looked at the waters and the grey skies, even
in the hottest months of the year, and I have let time go by as though
youth were a thing of stone, or of black sand, and would last forever.

This is the site of my childhood and my youth. And the hermitage of San Telmo is still there, and the first public swimming pool
on the island, at whose restaurant there came to eat, in this order, the
elderly Agatha Christie, who used the island for some of her stories,
and the ancient Winston Churchill, already a relic of himself, who
stepped out of his expensive car smoking a cigar which he had surely
had brought to him from La Palma, land of tobacco and sweets. And
there also came to visit, but not to eat, Bertrand Russell, the bright-
eyed philosopher.

THIS AREA OF SAN TELMO WHICH I STILL REMEMBER FROM OLD PHOTO-
graphs of illustrious visitors reaches its peak in what for me is the
finest natural resting-spot in Puerto de la Cruz, my town: La Punta
del Viento, Point of the Wind. The Galician writer Gonzalo Torrente
Ballester wrote a beautiful novel, *Where The Air Turns Round*, which
is part of his trilogy *Joys and Shadows*, about the relations between
the powerful Galician bourgeoisie and the proletariat during the period of tyranny. *Where the Air Turns Round* is a title that came to
him by accident. He was walking along the street and overheard a
conversation between two workers. One of them asked the other for
a piece of material, and the other asked where it was, at which the
first man replied with the beautiful description which now seems to
be a metaphor: 'It's where the air turns round.'

Well, for me, La Punta del Viento is where the air turns round
. . . it is the combination of wind and saltiness that takes me back to
the first days of my adolescence, when one searches within nature for
ways to extend one's desires, and when nature seems, in its vigour
and strength, to be an extension of one's own nature. Wind and salt

are properties of the high sea, and here, in La Punta del Viento, they combine in water and waves and the total purity of the sea: the essence of the smell of the sea.

Also, as man can no longer damage the sea any more than he has already damaged it, the pools and ridges are still here, the same pools and ridges which set this still-savage part of the coast aside from that nearer to my town, here where the air turns round.

I could sit here forever, in this spot whose name chimes exactly—like a line from a poem by Octavio Paz or a metaphor by the great son of my town, the surrealist Agustín Espinosa—with the precise description of the place itself. La Punta del Viento.

Much later, the Basque writer Aldecoa wrote an extension of Humboldt's experiences in my home town. 'Through the Valley one reaches the Port. Through the Port one comes across the two Realejos, the Upper and the Lower. Then a volcanic geography and a road along an overhang. And there is a dragon tree in Icod de los Vinos, which is a perfect place for silence.'

We will come pack to these spots, but first of all let us hear Aldecoa thinking about the climate, the most diverse but most evident wealth of the Islands: 'Tenerife holds the four seasons within itself. It carries winter on Mount Teide, autumn in the large and enclosed woods up on the hillsides, spring in La Orotava and summer in Puerto de la Cruz. It is a land made for discoveries. Whether you discover the moon in its craters or some north pole among its snows does not matter. The discoveries on offer here are more private, more individual. You can discover what is apparently a Malaga fishing village in a cove to the south. But you can't find in all this magic a summary of the island of Tenerife, no one can find the significance of the beauty of the peak of Mount Teide reflected in a cistern in La Orotava, on land that used to belong to Bencomo, former *mencey*, Aboriginal king, of Taoro. Words are not enough to capture something like this.'

We will return, but let us now travel together to the island which is still intact.

THE ISLAND OF THE
SLEEPING LIZARDS

I AM ON EL HIERRO, THE ISLAND WHICH IS STILL INTACT, THE ISLAND OF the sleeping lizards, an abandoned animal, as dark as the desires of the sea, a deep and arrogant island, a small island which is like an unforgettable blow to the face of the fog.

You can think whatever you want about it before you arrive, but as soon as you set foot on the island the very air seems to you to be a metaphor for patience. Everything is possible on the island, but everything takes its time. I saw it from the air, surrounded by the majestic sea, a little stirred up by the wind which drove adventurers like Christopher Columbus and the Islanders who emigrated to America, and it looked to me like the last bastion where a fist had sought refuge, a deformed fist but a fist nonetheless, a fist that fights against the mists and punches through them, turning them into drizzle over the island's capital, Valverde.

People might believe that land is the essence of the Islands: they are made of land surrounded by the sea. But no. The essence of the Islands is the sea, and it is the sea surrounding El Hierro that has made the island what it is, has turned it into this deformed and isolated fist whose own light is blocked out while the sonorous light of the sea still shines on. This is a high sea, invasive, impenitent and impertinent. I have always kept the sea in my mind as the most important constitutive element of El Hierro, perhaps because I first came here by sea

many years ago, when the island had barely any electricity and you
had to wash your hands one by one in the hotels: first one hand, pressing the tap down with the other, then the other. And when I arrived
that time, the boat had to carry out a very difficult manoeuvre (a manoeuvre which it always in the end managed to carry out) in order to
enter Puerto de la Estaca, as if the sea did not want to render up new
inhabitants to the island. It was a manoeuvre which seemed to last a
lifetime, with the captain up on the prow following instructions which
seemed to be coming from the first navigator in history, trying to ver-
ify the first principles of navigation by sea.

Steep and stripped-down, made of lava and of light, the island
greets you like this, by rejecting you, because its true nature is to be
unpopulated, intact. It was much sought-after by Spanish and French
explorers, and fell into the hands of the French adventurer Jean de
Bethéncourt in the fifteenth century, who treated the inhabitants under
his yoke abominably; now it is much sought after by people who are
looking for an island that is still intact.

It has been saved by patience, by the patience of those who live
on it, by that of those who came to enjoy its long silence. Before
landing in the little airport which was my point of entry this time into
El Hierro, I looked down on the cobalt-blue ocean which makes the
island grow or shrink. In other places the sea is a place of transit, a
room without any doors, but here the sea is the journey in itself, and
transforms the island, at every point, into a kind of little boat which
is at its mercy; the day on which I arrived there, 9 August 2009, the
weather report says nothing, but you can see the kindness with which
we are being welcomed if you just look out of the window: the sea is
wrinkled, but there are only a few white crests to the waves, which
look like birds that are also flying to El Hierro, prettifying a surface
which seems at times smooth and at times violent. From the air the
island looks majestic, but monotonous; from below, when I came by
sea, the surface of the sea, the same surface, was powerful and au-

thoritative, like the vast hand of some sea monster that the island pushed away with its imperious cliffs.

Back then I was unable to appreciate it, because I felt the fear of having travelled by sea, but the black cliffs, their reddish colour on sunny mornings, the blunt darkness of the soil, immediately reminded me of Lanzarote, even by night. Lanzarote, César Manrique's island, the island of the artist who reinvented it so that it could stay the same, is a plain; El Hierro is built vertically, it lives by breathing in the air from the clouds, which in Valverde solidify and turn into damp and drizzle all at once; but the soil of both islands is the same, as is the feeling that they have just gone through a savage yet silent fire which has left its trace in a tongue of lava, the light following a disaster.

As soon as you set foot on it, El Hierro overwhelms you; it is the sense of fear one has before feeling truly afraid, as though you were about to feel an emotion different from those on all the other islands: in this mysterious emotion, El Hierro is also like Lanzarote. As though behind this heavy silence, with its echoes of other silences, there were an even greater mystery, a sleeping monster holding in its jaws the unruly cry of time, that great destroyer. The monster of time is asleep here, I thought. And if time itself has hungry jaws, then they are bound shut here on El Hierro, the island which patiently counts life minute by minute.

I arrived by sea and I could enter. Twenty years before, round about 1950, Ignacio Aldecoa could not do the same. In his book he writes of how he was thrown off the island right at the mouth of the harbour: 'El Hierro, according to many, is the island known as La Pluitina, where there is no other water save that which a particular species of tree distils from the fog with which it is covered every day in the mornings: a wonderful prodigy of nature. El Hierro is dark, flat, sour with lava. El Hierro was rounded but not reached. They say—it is a story they tell—that on El Hierro they still maintain the custom of *zorrocloco*, whereby the man stays in bed while the woman prepares to give birth. They told this *godo* things about El Hierro, not always good things. And the sea in front of El Hierro was rough and we went back through its waters like an old sloop, as scared of El Hierro as we were scared of the water and the sharks.'

He could not reach the island. The fascinating entry-point to El Hierro welcomed us the very first time, and now below me I see the vastness of the sea and its pitiless waves. But this time I skipped the adventure.

AS I SAID, THIS TIME I ARRIVED BY AIR, AND I WENT TO HAVE LUNCH IN El Tamaduste, where the air of the island takes a rest and the water too, in the natural pools created to add to El Hierro's air of patience. El Tamaduste is protected from the most stormy seas, which allows the fisherman to have the patience to capture succulent fish, which are later turned into fish soup. With rice, if possible. But there is no fish soup today, and no rice; a lot of people came through before us and the waiter has had to say 'no' to all the hungry mouths who have come here looking forward to the fish soup that is mentioned whenever one mentions the name of El Hierro. With rice, always. We'll have to wait until we reach La Restinga, where the fish is even more abundant. But here, in this bar which is like an alley, I want to stop for a moment to talk about the patience that greets you when you come to the island.

It is here, in these small places within small places, that the legend of Canary Island slowness takes shape. In a time when people praise slowness as a last resort against the hustle and bustle of contemporary life, the pressure which causes illnesses and other forms of hysteria, the slowness of the Canary Islands should be a medicine or an antidote, or at the very least an example. But people who say that they suffer from excessive lethargy use the word *aplatanado*, which derives from the word *plátano*, or banana, the cultivation and export of which has been the mainstay of the Canary Island economy for centuries. The fact remains that if slowness exists and if it is a remedy, then we Canary Islanders have taken it in more than sufficient doses. But the capital of slowness is to be found in El Hierro. Even the air seems lazy here, like the countryside, held fast for centuries in a complicated landscape which has remained almost completely intact, at least until the insolent drill-bit opened up tunnels through the mountains, tunnels which now seem to be miraculous shortcuts preventing the mountains from standing in the way of the inexorable march of a kind of progress which cuts and breaks in order to free the way for other hindrances.

I once spent seven minutes waiting to avoid death by one of these tunnels, the one that leads up to the main El Hierro hotel: there was a sign which said that this was the amount of time one should wait to ensure that cars coming from the other direction had been able to pass through the tunnel. 'WAIT. BETTER TO WAIT A FEW MINUTES THAN LOSE YOUR LIFE.' This blunt statement is perhaps the most direct thing that one can read or hear on this island of slowness and patience. Wait rather than lose your life. El Hierro might even adopt this as a symbol of the apparent attitude of its inhabitants, the attitude of the island itself.

Slowness has its own vocabulary. Slow Canary Islanders are said to be like Galicians, and it was the Galicians, in the guise of the Portuguese, who were among the first Europeans to inhabit these islands, and above all the island of El Hierro. No one ever really knows what people who live here know or do not know; they tend to hide it until they know what you yourself know. And there are memorable phrases connected with this, milestones in the history of the language of the Canary Islands: 'If I told you I'd be telling a lie'; 'I'm not going to say yes and I'm not going to say no.' Worthy elements of discretion, the Canary Islands' way of keeping quiet even while speaking.

It happened in the restaurant, El Tamaduste. We were standing up, the waiter was walking past, sweaty and in silence, carrying food, plates of chickpeas, cuttlefish, fried squid, as though he were providing us with a gastronomic trailer of the delights to come; a little boy was jumping around, young people were laughing as they drank their Coca-Cola, and a man was taking swigs from a vast glass of beer; we looked around, but the waiter did not look at us: one of the great virtues of the patience of the Islands is that of not looking, so as not to be seen. One might say that it is one of the fundamental conditions of slowness: not to let other people's haste disturb your patience. Finally one of us spoke.

'Don't you see us standing here?'

The man looked me up and down.

'I think I noticed something.'

And there we were, standing at the end of the steep cliff which protects El Tamaduste from the wind; the man had noticed us, but he was doing his job, his time was important and our time could wait. We asked for stew and a local cheese, and for some reason, one that can only derive from the Canary Island spirit of the perverse (the idea being to do something unexpected in an entirely natural fashion), the man also brought a jar of honey.

As these things sometimes happen, as they sometimes put something on your table just so you know that they actually have the local products they pride themselves in so much, I asked the waiter if this was honey from El Hierro.

He looked at me and said something almost sublime, which summarises in a phrase a whole way of being, of existing.

'I imagine it might not be.'

THE CANARY ISLANDS IS A PLACE WHERE CULTURES MEET, AND ALTHOUGH El Hierro is the most isolated island, the furthest west, the most separated, the one which seems the most abandoned of these world's ends on the way to America, it was always the crossing point, a sea lane and a lighthouse. It is not that it says goodbye to the world (the Romans believed that this largish islet was the end of the world, the end of the known world), but that it is the place Columbus thought (people say this and Columbus himself said it) he should use to work out which path to take into the unknown. Perhaps because of this the Romans wanted to take control of it, and the French, and the Portuguese. The fact of being at a crossing point has influenced the character of the

Islanders, and this phrase, 'I imagine it might not be', is an expression of a whole way of being, of existing; one both is and is not present; El Hierro is the closest thing, hidden in the fog, to what we dreamed of when we thought of the mysterious island of San Borondón. One day, in 1990, I was walking through a village in Cuba, Las Villas, and I asked a passer-by which way I should go to get to where I was going, and the man replied:

'If I told you, I'd be telling you wrong.'

'I imagine it might not be' and 'If I told you, I'd be telling you wrong' are different ways of saying the same thing, which is 'I'm not going to commit myself, even though I might know the answer'. The Cuban had surely inherited the phrase from the Canary Islanders who travelled in the nineteenth century to look for treasure in Cuba, and this man from El Hierro who was waiting tables with such a lack of urgency was one of those Islanders who prefers the Galician-Portuguese method of engaging in conversation, and prefers silence to any kind of definite statement.

He knew that the honey was not from El Hierro, and it was easy to prove it: in large letters, under a picture of a bee, it said 'Made in France', but I had asked the gentleman the question merely to make him speak, and making someone speak is a task which sometimes is difficult on the Islands. The Islands as a whole, and especially those which we call the minor islands, have always been turned in on themselves, as if they were still scared of an invasion, or a storm that will take from them this almost paradisiacal peace in which they live, scanning the horizon and navel-gazing at the same time

The waiter did not explode or snap at me, but brought, with a humility which he transformed into silence and efficiency, the local cheese, one of the finest delicacies of El Hierro: the thin, sun-beaten sheep have to fight for every mouthful of the grass that the sun allows them, and this leads them to produce pure milk and a cheese which, once it has been cured, has to be eaten with wine, if possible with a wine called Tanajara. It is one of the very best wines that they make in the Islands, and in Spain as a whole. When I finished my trip to El

Hierro I bought two bottles of Tanajara Baboso and a whole cured cheese; they let you carry the cheese on board the aeroplane, but the wine has to go in the hold. The result is a wonderful combination which it is worth seeking out because it gives to one's palate the hidden tastes of this flat and bitter land of lava, as the great Ignacio Aldecoa once called it.

AND THE WAITER AT EL TAMADUSTE GAVE US FRESH BREAD, A STEW OF meat with vegetables and some excellent fried *papas*: the fried potatoes are not always like they were here; they can be failures, poorly-made, carelessly prepared. He also gave us some chickpeas, the larger variety of the Islands, a product which needs to be named among the marvels which my mother made when there was nothing to eat in the house. The large chickpea, the *garbanza* as opposed to the *garbanzo*, has always been an icon of Canary Island cuisine: the person who knows how to cook them well—with meat, with fish, with vegetables, boiled or stewed, all by themselves with oil and vinegar or *mojo*, in a salad or even fried—has known glory, and I must say that this man at El Tamaduste, who brought us the chickpeas with meat, managed to create an extremely tasty dish which made us forget completely the exaggerated slowness with which he worked, his pride in being from the Canary Islands, from El Hierro, from El Tamaduste.

A woman who saw me talking to him, trying to make him speak, trying to make him bring me some food, trying to make him react to my stimuli, said as she left the table next to ours:

'We are not ready for tourists in El Tamaduste.'

But we ate very well, I said to her, and I said the same thing to the waiter, when I was heading out to the dark shadows of the roads that twist and turn as though they wanted to hide the next scene in the landscape.

Behind us lay one of those inns which combines slowness with calm; these two things together define midday in El Hierro, that kind of summer siesta where people live as though their watches have stopped.

WHILE I FOLLOWED THE SILENT ROADS OF EL HIERRO, DRIVING THROUGH cliffs, next to a wild blackish sea, twisting round blunt rocky outcrops beaten by the sea, I remembered something of what I felt in Lanzarote, whose dry, black earth reminds one so much of various corners and landscapes of this western island. I felt that although we were silent there was some kind of music flying above us, as though there were a kind of local musical legend nearby, lost in the air, falling onto the Islands and having its own identity, a kind of soundtrack to the Islands.

I thought that the psychedelic music of Pink Floyd was the sound of Lanzarote. Strident, intrusive and happy, a colourful music, like the extension of some infinite dream. And what about the music of El Hierro? El Hierro is mysterious; it is made of mystery, as though it were protecting a set of feelings that it was never going to reveal, the mystery of a secret kept by every single one of its inhabitants; a music of silence, and how musical, how beautiful is the music contained in the silence of El Hierro. A music which sounds most clearly on the road between Sabinosa and El Pozo de la Salud down to the black sands that seem to push through the sky like a twisting, lost highway until they reach, after a series of dangerous curves that are almost like nightmares, the viewpoint at Bascos, from which the island bids the rest of the world farewell with a majestic insolence. The viewpoint at Bascos is a discovery; if the road is indeed dangerous because it loses itself as though it were ascending into the sky, and gives the impression that there is no one and nothing on either side of it, and that the road stops in mid-air, then the landscape which marks the end of this risky journey is incredibly beautiful, unforgettable.

BUT A LONG TIME BEFORE REACHING THE VIEWPOINT AT BASCOS, I WAS thinking about the music of El Hierro as I walked down to Puerto de la Estaca after leaving El Tamaduste. There is a feeling, like a jolt of strength and vitality, when one sees old landscapes in which one has felt almost simultaneously the sensations of fear, nightmare and delight, and this was what I felt as I went into Puerto de la Estaca, which I had first visited at the end of the 1960s. Back then El Hierro was a more ramshackle island, much smaller—if I can put it like that—and more virginal, and to touch down, to drop anchor here was a much more dizzying journey than it is now. The music that accompanied me at that time was Albinoni's then omnipresent Adagio, and here, in the year 2009, I was listening to silence, by itself, the silence that one looks for after having been overwhelmed by so many of the sounds of the world.

Forty years ago, there were great old ships that came to the island, limping, defying the inclement waves that lifted their keels so high it was as though they were flying; we went there, scared of sinking, scared of not making it, scared of having to reverse our steps on this laborious journey which we had undergone ever since our departure from the western capital of the Islands, Santa Cruz de Tenerife. Ten years before Aldecoa had not been able to land here; on my first journey to El Hierro we were about to turn back as well, about to go back to where we had come from. The boats were old, and everything smelt of salt; the journey took more than a day, you had to sleep in the boat, you came up on deck in the morning, still sleepy, and found ahead of you a huge peak of reddish rock, which is what the modern-day traveller sees as well. Although today, in the twenty-first century, you reach the island in boats that are much faster and less unwieldy, and the anchoring manoeuvre, which once forced sailors to engage in extremely dangerous hijinks, is now much easier, unless the waves decide to make the boats fly in the face of the reddish and inexpressive peak which looks at you as though you were being observed by prehistory itself. El Hierro resists, just like the waiter, and holds its silence like a black stone. It is solemn when it greets you, as though it were subjecting you to an interrogation. It is a mystery island, a question island, it welcomes you but does not give itself up to you immediately; you have to stroke it, as Tony Gallardo did, the artist from Gran Canaria: stroking the stones to fit them to his hand. Tony showed you the stones as though they had grown from his hand, happily, he was like a big child saving the most overwhelming gifts of the ocean from the water.

AND SO AHEAD OF ME IS THE PUERTO DE LA ESTACA OF MY CHILDHOOD, looking back at me, now that I am sixty years old and heading back to a landscape that used to scare me, and I am filled with a new unease. Now I ask myself if coming back, coming back by boat, would cause me the same fear, or whether time calms all fears. Here I am, facing the old port which is now a port just like any other, filled with pleasure boats; a sailboat cuts through the sea in the distance, like a dove: the loneliness which hit us forty years ago is now a question of nothing more than memory. Time passes and El Hierro remains silent, and the music is a music of the sea, which rings out as though in stereo.

Today the port of El Hierro is like a party where friends are waiting for Gatsby to show up: there are yachts, pleasure boats, a few fishing tenders waiting for fair weather, and the old boats no longer exist, those ramshackle and rusty vessels are present only in the memory of those of us who can feel nostalgia, or melancholy, even for the things which scared us in our childhood as we headed for an island that seemed to be some kind of ultimate secret, in the middle of an unencumbered sea, a sea which I remember as high, set on a slope, looking out into the infinite as though it too wanted to head off, as though the sea itself wanted to run away, the dark blue sea licking at the black rocks, jet black, like the black rocks on the beach of my home town, Puerto de la Cruz in Tenerife.

I described these rocks as though I were describing my childhood, and I walked on the scarce black sand around La Estaca as though I were treading on my past, the past of El Hierro and my own past, the past in which the first people came, those who believed that the sea was the house where the Islands lived.

WHEN I CAME HERE FORTY YEARS AGO IT WAS AN ISLAND FILLED WITH borders: these have now all, or nearly all, been knocked down. There are three or four tunnels where there used to be impenetrable mountains, and one of these tunnels, dug into a rock whose emptiness now seems to be a symbol at the end of which one sees the enlightenment which the Islands were looking for, is that which allows access to the main El Hierro hotel, where I stayed. On my first visit I stayed in the Valverde inn, a cheap hotel which had a sink in the corridor; among all the cold air and fog of Valverde, the hotel was the most civilised inheritance of a world of poverty which had once tithed the island to unusual extremes. The island, a little over a hundred square miles in area, the smallest of the Canary Islands and the youngest in geological terms, was the final point of the known world for Europeans; from it you went to the New World, and thousands of inhabitants of the island went to Cuba, and Argentina, and Venezuela . . . Between the nineteenth century and the middle of the twentieth century, the island had slightly more than three thousand inhabitants; it was old people and children who stayed put; the adults left in order to find a means of sustenance which was always more difficult on El Hierro. Survival was a miracle and their journey was an obligation imposed on them if they wanted to stay alive. If it had not been so painful for them, their hunger would have seemed like something out of a fairy tale.

Dearth was still visible when I arrived on the island in 1969, in the farmyards and the villages. At a house in Salmor, where the enormous lizards live who make the island into a scientific curiosity, I once saw a sign which I cannot find now, many years later: it read 'Thank you, Venezuela'. One of the emigrants who had gone to Venezuela trying to find a different life from the miserable one which he suffered in the beautiful and defenceless villages of the Islands was the only night taxi driver in El Hierro, Antonio, who told me some things about how those times had been. There was nothing in his home in 1956, and his parents asked the police to witness a document allowing them to send their son, still a minor of sixteen, to Venezuela. He got aboard one of the boats that travelled from Tenerife to Caracas, arriving at midday in the Venezuelan capital. Two hours later he was working in a market, 'counting oranges by the hundred'.

Lots of people also left my village, a great number. In my immediate family it was only my father who did not emigrate, perhaps because he was the most adventurous of his brothers, but wanted to live the many adventures he dreamed of back on his native land. What is certain is that back then, round about 1956, when the largest emigration took place, I was a boy who had learned to read and write, and the wives of the emigrants came to me to get love letters (or break-up letters) written to the people who had left, abandoning their wives either provisionally or for ever, without either party knowing if the abandonment was temporary or forever. It was as though the men were reborn on their journey and as though the women died a little because of their partners' voyage. They told me what they wanted me to write, and I took notes as in that Brazilian movie, *Central Station*; I was the amanuensis to the tragedies and hopes that the queue of women brought to me, filing past the little table where my papers and their stories accumulated . . .

The stories were moving, stories of loneliness and abandon; sometimes I felt that I was the repository of a series of heartfelt confessions which made me feel ashamed or compassionate, and never indifference; the women would lean down and whisper into my ear, and would speak to me as though I were a father confessor and not a child, not an adolescent who would be hurt or confused by all the events which took place right next to my home without my hearing any part of this dull murmur of loneliness and tragedy, misery and hope.

Just like the protagonist of that Brazilian movie, I sat there at my desk holding a biro, sitting in front of a page of airmail paper, ready to be put into one of those prepaid red and blue envelopes shaped like an arrow, listening to the most diverse confessions. All of the letters written by the wives or mothers or sisters began in the same way, at their dictation: 'Dear son [or husband, or brother], I hope that when you receive this letter you are well. We are well, thanks to the Lord.' After this hortatory introduction, the invocation of the Lord, who appeared in every single letter I wrote, the women would start to dictate to me their family dramas, illnesses, deaths and other suffering; then they would ask me to read them back the letters I had written for them, from the date at the top all the way to the signature at the bottom, and then they themselves would put the letter in the airmail envelope, lick it shut and carry it to the post office as though they were carrying a will, or else the memory of an embrace. My mother wrote letters as well, in her large and capricious handwriting, to her brothers and sisters, her nieces and nephews.

She told them of her own miseries, and her hopes as well, but she did not need to resort to me; she had her own handwriting, her own form of thankfulness. Those years were so poor that I can remember precisely the afternoon when poverty in its strictest sense left our house. It was when an uncle of mine, who drove a truck for a dairy company in Maracaibo, Venezuela—Leche Carabobo—came home for a visit, bringing a certain amount of silver he had earned ('silver' was what the emigrants who travelled backwards and forwards between the Islands and Venezuela called their money), and decided to buy my mother a gas cooker.

And so the petrol cooker vanished for good, that old cooker which filled the house with black smoke and harmful smells, especially harmful for me, the asthmatic son; some men came and put in the new cooker, and the next day at around four o'clock in the afternoon, that hour which still seems to be a time of absolute silence in my house, my uncle appeared: he looked in from the courtyard, checked that the white new cooker was there, and said nothing. And my mother said nothing either, but that was how people expressed their gratitude back in those days. With silence.

BUT THAT IS A PERSONAL STORY. WE WERE IN EL HIERRO LOOKING through the symbols which connect the island with the essential history of the emigration to America of so many Canary Islanders, a history which is not a fairytale or the plot of a movie, but which is rather a story of risk and poverty. Round about 1970 a little boat, *El Fausto*, left El Hierro and was lost on the journey; the story, which it was up to me as a junior reporter back then to tell, runs that the boat was lost in the fog which always accompanied every dramatic incident on the Islands, headed for somewhere which is still a mystery; some people say that the boat was headed for Gran Canaria, just a stone's throw away, still in the archipelago itself, but others say that the Islanders in the boat went off course or were driven off course by the wind, and carried on towards Venezuela; they say that if you throw a bottle into El Golfo, on El Hierro, then sooner or later it will end up at the port of La Guaira in Venezuela, which is where Antonio ended up; Antonio, the only night-taxi driver on the island. But the passengers and crew of the *Fausto* never arrived, neither at Gran Canaria nor at Venezuela; they live on in the drama of myth, they live in the memory when they are deliberately evoked, as they are here.

The *Fausto* is a metaphor of something that has happened so often: urged on by poverty and hunger, islanders from the whole archipelago have taken on, in equally miserable circumstances, the risk of a journey that may have no end.

However, the emigrants whose wives came to my house so that I could write letters for them did make it across the ocean; they were the people whose earnings propped up poor and even not quite so poor families; some of them came back rich, and built houses which were like the ones they had seen in Caracas or in other parts of Venezuela (Maracaibo, Valencia, Puerto La Cruz . . .), and the ones who did not come back rich tried not to come back at all. The emigration was a lottery, but it was also a race: if you didn't finish it then you would be considered a failure in life. Sometimes a man came round to our house who had made his fortune, and he came by showing off his 'silver' to my father, so that he would know what he had made by his adventures in Venezuela. I still have in my mind a clear image of this man, who came round to the house at dawn to pick up his false departure papers, the ones that would allow him to board the boat, make the journey, and settle into Caracas life without any bureaucratic problems from that country which was so used to receiving Canary Islanders. The money people earned was useful for the Canary Islands, and emigration was helpful for affluent Venezuela, which needed labourers at all levels of the workforce. The first gas cooker to be installed in our house, this gift from my uncle who drove lorries for Leche Carabobo, was more a miracle than a gift, and when cheques came from Caracas, the whole neighbourhood felt as people from poorer districts now do when they win the lottery.

El Hierro made a great deal from this miracle, the miracle of Venezuela. A singular figure, the journalist José Padrón Machín, who wrote almost simultaneously, under a number of pseudonyms, in all the papers of Spain and the Canary Islands, and who showed me El Hierro for the first time in 1969, called it the Seventh Island, because it is the seventh one if you count from Fuerteventura, although it is the first if you are counting from the west . . . The nickname stuck, the Seventh Island, and this is the name given to it in the papers, and even the Islanders themselves refer to their home by this name. But Venezuela was called the Eighth Island. Caracas is one of the places in the world with the largest population of Canary Islanders: three hundred thousand Islanders live there (Las Palmas, the city in the archipelago with the largest population, has four hundred thousand inhabitants); their number is diminishing, because the poverty which beat us down back then now beats down, in some kind of infernal cycle, on the Venezuelans and the Canary Islanders who stayed there, or who were born in Venezuela. Whether emigrants or born there, we are all a part of the same community: to talk about Venezuela in the Canary Islands is to talk about an extension of the Islands, and the same thing has happened and still happens when the reverse takes place. José Martí, the liberator of Cuba, spoke to the Canary Islanders as a part of the population of Cuba; Bolívar did the same in

Venezuela; they were not seen as being Spanish, but rather as Canary Islanders (Bolívar would give speeches in which he spoke of 'Spaniards and Canary Islanders'), and in Latin America, above all in Cuba and in Venezuela, it is still a valid distinction. 'Islanders', they call us, even in Cuba, and Islanders is what we are; what distinguishes us is the fact of being from an island, and I don't know a better metaphor for the idea of an island than that huge rock which rises up from Puerto de la Estaca and which is called El Hierro.

IN ANY CASE, LEAVING NATURE AND ORIGIN TO ONE SIDE, LEAVING ASIDE unlucky and fortunate emigrations, in this journey which is taking me through the Islands, which sometimes takes me in one direction and which sometimes leads me in another, sometimes directly and sometimes by indirection, because for me the Islands are a kind of memory and memory mixes everything together, on this journey I was travelling towards the main hotel on El Hierro, travelling from El Tamaduste, and I was waiting at a traffic light that was taking an age to change, in front of a sign that told people to be patient and wait for the light to change. Don't be in a hurry to die: that seems to be the motto of the island. Patience keeps you alive: look at the sea; it never gets old. The sea's patience is infinite. And infinite is the time that you spend waiting for the stoplights on El Hierro to change. The time can be spent, if one is patient and sets oneself to the task, in thinking about the capacity which mankind has to pierce the earth until he changes the thick rock into a hollow at whose end one can see the light, destroying distances which would otherwise make travelling so smoothly impossible on an island with El Hierro's particular nature.

This tunnel, which is a mirror of the patience of the Islands, is 3,100 feet long, and the stoplight keeps us waiting for seven minutes. The landscape around us is dry, with a few yellowing cork trees, a landscape as dun-coloured as Platero, the donkey in the Nobel Prize winner Juan Ramón Jiménez's novel *Platero y yo*. This landscape, with the donkey included, appears in many of the areas of the island, where the green foliage, the upright and infinite palm trees, even the juniper trees which are usually a separate item among the island's vegetation, give a kind of olive-coloured counterpoint to the landscape, in which there are always flowers, and the impatient passion of water to transform places into little gardens: an island of lava and greenery, a fist that is dour and soft at the same time. El Hierro is an abrupt poem which suddenly transforms into a winding path along which one might lose oneself forever, oneself also transformed into silence.

There, at the end of the passage which releases the island from the burden of one of its most unbearable journeys, the passage which leads travellers to the Parador, the island's main hotel, one can see the ghostly figure of the future, a light which grows larger and clearer, until you come out and face the enormous reddish cliffs which the sun wraps in all manner of different light; one looks on the sea from the Islands as the thing which changes, a surface that is constantly portraying itself, and finding superlative tones as it does so, as in a bolero, but the thing which truly changes is the landscape itself . . . The island is, and then it suddenly is not, or is something else. The myth of San Borondón, the island which only exists in dreams, may perhaps have been born from this fact of nature: that the Islands keep on changing as the hours go by, as the clouds go by, and there is an instant when it appears that they have disappeared. It is an illusion out of which emerge mythologies like that of the island nobody has seen, but which truly exists . . .

Speaking of Fuerteventura, at the other end of the archipelago, where the islands are truly a part of Africa, a Catalan academic who studied the urbanisation of Barcelona in the nineteenth century told me, as he ate some fresh fish in a restaurant right at the south of the island, that what was fascinating for him about this place which moved Miguel de Unamuno so much was the fact that the landscape was the land and that was it. Everything else is added by the hand of man, and sometimes man does not add anything.

WE WILL TALK ABOUT FUERTEVENTURA AGAIN, AND ABOUT THAT FEELING of standing on untouched land, but it is certainly the case that what this Catalan intellectual said is more generally applicable to all the islands, and especially of those Canary Island territories which do not appear to have been too greatly touched by the hand of man. El Hierro is absolute: if man were to disappear, then the landscape would still have its own personality; there are islands which are designed for solitude, and islands which are solitude themselves, islands which are entirely solitary; the landscape of El Hierro is the landscape of loneliness itself. The archipelago has a lot of areas like this: parts of La Gomera, parts of La Palma, the lonelier parts of Fuerteventura, Lobos island, almost the whole of Lanzarote . . . In all these spots the landscape has its own particular aspect, its own depth: the land at Gran Canaria is yellow as dates; on Tenerife the landscape alternates drought with the colour of pine needles and the reddish or green rocks of Las Cañadas del Teide; La Palma is green; La Gomera is an island of water to one side and austere drought to the other; Lanzarote is black, pure black; Fuerteventura is land and shadow, a land that seeks its shadow.

And then there's El Hierro.

El Hierro is a landscape in itself, each square foot of the island is already a landscape which has everything: shadow, land, relaxation, the abyss, an island and its own ghosts.

AN ISLAND IS A GHOST WHICH HAS ALREADY LIVED THERE. I HAD THIS feeling when I was on El Hierro and it was so strong that I still feel it now as though it were the light that I saw at the end of the tunnel that took me to the Parador. Later, after checking in, I looked out of a window and saw a red cliff: then I thought that the rock, insolent and solemn, was looking at me, and I adapted myself to its height as though it were an accusatory finger, or a shadow, falling over me and over my memories of the island, forcing me to look with different eyes at the island where I had just arrived, perhaps for the fourth or fifth time. The memory which the island imposes on you is so powerful that you can remember the exact number of times that you have arrived there, as if your memory were associated with its own smells and tastes, with the vision which the island leaves in the memory of your eyes.

The first time I was there something very similar happened, after being impressed by our landing at Puerto de la Estaca: for the very first time a sea rock caught my gaze, this time at dawn. The boat drew out of the harbour with the grace of an elephant, or a dinosaur; those of us already on solid ground went to Valverde, which was a display of fog with the light of a bar at one end of it, a bar called Los Reyes, which owes its name, as do many things on El Hierro, to the Virgen de los Reyes, the holy patron saint of the island, the virgin before whom even atheists break down in tears. In the Los Reyes bar I saw a man drinking a small glass of cognac and slowly smoking a cigarette, while the owner of the bar cleaned, with the inherent patience of the inhabitants of El Hierro, the zinc counter on which he topped up the little glasses of wine. I kept in my mind the image of this man, tall, thin, perhaps a little too tired for such an early hour of the morning, and knew that he was a doctor. A while later I went back and there was a space at the bar, the doctor wasn't there, he'd left: I asked the journalist Padrón Michín, the man who knows everything, about him. The man, the doctor, had gone on the run because he had killed a policeman in a knife fight that was like something out of the Wild West, which is an attitude and a geography that is often repeated in the Islands, especially in the south, as something inherent to farmers, or else something that seems to be born from the cliffs and fix itself in the timeless gaze of the silent peasants.

What had happened to the doctor? Padrón Machín, who was an encyclopaedic and absolute chronicler of the Islands, who wrote of the moods of El Hierro as though the island had a soul of its own, never wrote this story down, but that day when I asked him he told me, and a long time later he told me again, right there in front of the

Los Reyes bar, in fact: the bar was closed, or being sold, but the mystery of the murder was still there, going round in my head like someone else's bad memory. This policeman, the *guardia civil* in his tricorne hat who both protected the citizenry and threatened them, but who in the Franco period did a lot more threatening than protecting, was an arrogant man who made fun of the citizenry, and he laughed at the doctor, using sarcastic and chauvinist language which eventually annoyed the medic. Until one day, in the middle of his insults, the doctor decided that he had had enough, and took out a pistol and shot the policeman; the policeman fell down dead in the middle of a crowd of people who all, in relief, took the doctor into hiding. The murderer left the island, helped by the complicity aroused by a mutual distrust of the police and general disdain for this particular policeman.

Who was the murderer? Nobody said anything at all, and justice on the island was so slow that the doctor's act of revenge remained unpunished. When I reread what Ignacio Aldecoa had to say about El Hierro ('They told me things about El Hierro, not always good ones'), I remembered this incident, the violence enclosed in it, and the patience with which the hatred carried on building up, until finally, in a spot as calm as a bar on El Hierro, a kind of anger was unleashed that one would normally only imagine existed in bars in the Wild West. But no, this really happened, on El Hierro, in the same place where, two generations later, a young man told me the story as though it were one of the legends of the island.

The anecdote is filled with all the symbols of the time, the excesses committed by authority, the dictatorship's abandonment of responsibility, and what island solidarity is capable of when it shares in the rage of an individual. Padrón Machín was protected by his fellow islanders after the Civil War; he had been a court employee during the Republic, and a triumphant Francoism looked for him everywhere, but, as happened here and in many parts of Spain, the citizenry was brave enough to hide a number of the fugitives. Machín, the chronicler of the Islands, learnt from these experiences how to hide himself, and in the 1960s, when we went to look for him so that he could show us the island, he would appear from the strangest nooks and crannies, as though he were still living clandestinely: he would come out from under his bed, or else from behind a kind of screen that he had used to make himself a secret study where he could use his typewriter lying down.

But we were in the hotel, and I got carried away by the story of a murder, instead of telling you about the impressions I had after leaving the ochre lights of the headland behind me and discovering a line of trees, at the back of the sky, which were a contrast with the sad old vegetation of this part of the island, the southeast of El Hierro, an area bathed by an insistent and orderly sea which ends up on the only sandy beach on the whole island. They call the spot Las Playas, which means The Beaches, and it is well-named, but it could have been named in the singular, The Beach; it is a modest beach, black as jet, seemingly abandoned in front of a sea which is always bidding it farewell, a strong and querulous sea where I saw stones that were like the stones of my childhood in Martiánez, in Puerto de la Cruz.

They are round stones, like little mountains, very unlike one another, always rough to the touch, but seeming very smooth at a distance, like the sculptures of Henry Moore which always come to mind as I walk these desolate, black shores. Sitting in front of them, in front of these stones, I was reading an old book by the old historian of El Hierro, Dacio Victoriano Darias y Padrón, a man whose name is very typical of the Islands, and in particular of El Hierro. Reading this book I refreshed my memory of some of the references spoken of so often among us, the Islanders, which are now a part of the legend that surrounds us. For example, Dacio recalls in his book that Pliny the Elder wrote as early as the first century AD of the origin of the name of the islands: there were so many dogs on them that they became known as the Canary Islands. *Multitudine canum ingentis magnitudines*. But earlier in that same century came Strabo, and he called them Fortunate, *Fortunatae insulae*. Perhaps the name came up, Dacio says, 'because the Islands were close to the place where myth and po-

etic legend situated the Elysian Fields, although other people say that
the name derives from the gentleness of the Islands' climate.'

WE ISLANDERS HAVE SOMETIMES FELT HAPPY AND SOMETIMES EMBAR-
rassed by what Strabo said, his good will having inspired him to say
something which we now see as flattery.

Fortunate? For centuries we have lived through times of great
misfortune which the undeniable beauty of the Islands has done little
to improve; it is a fact that the pleasant nature of our climate has
helped our development and attracted tourism, which for a long time
has been and still is the major source of wealth in our fragmented territory.

But really, fortunate? Perhaps it is better to say that we are situated in a favourable position on the way to America, close to Africa,
but a long way from the hardships of Africa, safe from wars but also
a point of strategic importance for the powers that fight: consider the
Second World War, for example, when Nazi Germany wanted to
transform the Islands (in particular El Hierro and Fuerteventura) into
observation points in case the theatre of war should move in that
direction.

Fortunate to be protected by the climate, but really, truly fortunate? The post-war period, in which all of Spain suffered, was here
extremely harsh, not just for political reasons, but because of the
hunger which the Islands suffered, and which perhaps sank the character of the Canary Islanders even further into that sleepy memory
which we find it so hard to escape.

My teacher Domingo Pérez Minik, who is the author of an important account of the time André Breton and his surrealists spent on
Tenerife, gives us in his published speech, *The Human Condition of
the Island Dweller*, a few indications of how it is to be a Canary Islander, influenced by history to the extent that at times one feels extremely lucky and at times one feels sunk into miserable confusion.

Pérez Minik says, in a passage beginning with Miguel de Una-

muno's feelings when he lived on the wasteland of Fuerteventura:
'And when Miguel de Unamuno lived on Fuerteventura as an exile,
the things that he thought, the anguished poems that he wrote, the
interpretations that he made of the character of the islanders, none of
this has anything at all to do with the Canary Islander himself, this
non-transcendental realist, always possessed of a sense of humour
about the circumstances he lives in, suspicious and bittersweet, a simple sailor without any of the airs of the coloniser, who in his struggle
for life has no other aim than to escape from his isolation, to de-
mythologise his sea and detach himself from his own intimacies. Man
is existence and being, without a doubt. But for the Canary Islander
to stay standing, he has to engage in permanent conflict.'

His nature, the nature of the Canary Islander, is at once melancholy and struggle, and his existence derives from the struggle with
his environment, which is pleasant to look at and to stroll through,
but at the same time very hard to dominate. Steep and solitary lands,
land that you can work but which is also rebellious, land from which
the Islanders have managed to raise a harvest, but at the cost of great
suffering . . . This speech of Pérez Minik's is extremely important because it is not always the case that we Islanders have considered the
isolated character of the Islands with such non-jingoistic lucidity, with
such a degree of passion to find out who we truly are, without thinking about the flatteries of others, men and women who have written
about our lands without thinking that isolation doesn't always turn
these lands into a kind of paradise. Far from it, in fact. Pérez Minik
was a socialist and a republican, who was locked up at the beginning
of the Civil War. He gave this speech when he was older, when Franco
was still in charge in Spain and when it was not particularly common
for people to think of the Islands as anything other than fortunate,
back in the time when they were normally only mentioned in order
to praise their beauty. 'We know,' Pérez Minik says, 'some contradic-
tory properties of the character of the Islander, which flourish like a
living green-black water, bright and dangerous, and which have
granted to him an intimate perception of his freedom: his way of being

both tolerant and dour, polite and suspicious, focussed and expansive, narcissistic and parochial, always with an aggressive sense of humour at his fingertips, but one which contains within it a very touching melancholy; but with all of these elements, we still don't know the invisible axle of freedom around which he turns.'

'I will say it again,' Pérez Minik continues, 'that living in the Islands is both a punishment and a pleasure, both purgatory and paradise. Between these two biblical states, the Canary Islander travels both eagerly and painfully. [. . .] Isolation is favourable for development, in animals and in trees, in larks and laburnums, and in the human soul. It is favourable in many ways, but harmful in others. There is a deep and wide trench between the world of biology and that of human history which we cannot simply jump over. An island is always trying to deal with two irreconcilable forces [. . .] It is very common to see on all islands, from Japan to Crete to the Canaries to the Antilles, common elements which give them a surprising character: the lack of any uniform kind of space, the sense of enclosure caused by the sea, and the feeling that one is living in a place where time has stopped. These elements make it possible for one to create a paradisiacal environment, but at the same time make it difficult for the development of higher culture, which requires an environment full of stimuli, of movements and responses, of fundamental changes to the body and the spirit.'

This is how things are: a truly paradisiacal land could be ours, where time stops in order for men to enjoy themselves, in order for men to enjoy the gifts that nature has apparently set aside just for us. It could be like this. In the world of insular jingoism, which has a long history and which survives right up to the present day, it is usual for someone to observe that we Islanders consider ourselves to be responsible, more than for nature, for the advantages which nature has given us; so we are responsible for the fact that Mount Teide exists, we built the dunes at Maspalomas with our bare hands, we cause the waves of the sea to beat against our shores angrily or calmly, and we can be proud of the shores themselves. We have lived, and we still live, in possession of this character, turned in on itself, vain, a natural tendency of us island dwellers, an Adamic tendency to believe that nature and mankind are designed to be together, as if nature were not something that existed before mankind ever did, and man did not have the tendency to despoil the land which is given to him for free. Although it is true that it is because of their nature that the islands are called Fortunate . . .

But are the Islanders themselves fortunate? Quite the contrary, we are the slaves of an 'oceanic oppressor', and free at the same time, as Pérez Minik says. He puts it as follows: everyone who travels to the Islands and writes about them 'forgets that the Islanders, we ourselves, faced by the dangers of our earthly paradise and the drama of our purgatory which is both concrete and decisive, have had to transform everything, to solve our urgent problems, to live in constant danger of change in order to survive, if we don't want to turn once again into our Guanche ancestors, Neolithic shepherds, Arcadians, separated radically from the constant transmutations of history.'

We were no longer Guanches, we were no longer the descendants of tribes from the north of Africa sent into exile by cruel Romans, dispossessed of our lands and even our language; we were the descendants of the Spanish conquistadores and other voyagers who have transformed the Islands into a mixture of populations which came and settled and took on the human condition that Pérez Minik talks about; we were a consequence of the 'constant transmutations of history', and all that remained to us of fortune was the legend hurled into our faces by Strabo in the early years of the Christian era.

IT WAS A FORTUNATE LAND, THERE IS NO DOUBT ABOUT THAT; WE STILL live in this climate, there is no doubt about that either, the climate has made us fortunate, truly, and the climate conditions the landscape, which makes us, let's make no bones about it, fortunate; our fortune is right in front of our eyes, it is the landscape . . . Halts on the journey and strolls down the paths give some idea of the pleasure that many people have felt here, at different times and in different places: Breton, Humboldt, Bertrand Russell, Agatha Christie, Oscar Wilde's father, Friedrich Dürrenmatt, Miguel de Unamuno . . . And this pleasure is physical, you can sense it at the top of El Time on La Palma, in Garajonay on La Gomera, on the sandy plains of Fuerteventura; you can walk on it in Las Cañadas del Teide, in the waves beating against La Punta del Viento of Puerto de la Cruz; you can feel it while eating fish in San Andrés, next to the Las Teresitas beach, in Santa Cruz de Tenerife, in the marvellous tranquillity of Bajamar, past the mountains of Anaga, in Tenerife, on the Las Canteras beach, in Las Palmas de Gran Canaria . . .

As I write this, as I go over this geography of fortunate pleasure, now no longer on El Hierro but instead in a house in the north of Tenerife, hearing the noises of the birds and the wind in the nearby palms, under the northern sun, watery and milky as the clouds which dominate us and cover it, I feel the climate which my forefathers spoke of; it never gets higher than thirty degrees, and if it does then the winds will come from the sea, the trade winds, to soften the weather and turn it into true springtime, the eternal spring that they always write about in the tourist brochures. And they are telling the truth: sometimes tourism has something to do with reality; it even turns it into a manifesto. The tourists, of whom there are both good and bad, noisy and ill-mannered and silent wanderers along our paths, discoverers and despoilers, teach us how to see the Islands, to discover their secrets . . .

THE DESIRED ISLANDS

S O FORTUNATE WERE THE ISLANDS THAT EUROPEANS DESIRED THEM FROM the fourteenth century onwards, right in the middle of the dark fog of the Middle Ages; the Genovese Lancerotto Mailosel arrived in 1312 on the island which now bears his name, Lanzarote; he was the first conqueror of the Islands, but they had already been populated by people from the north of Africa who, according to legend and iconography, and many recorded testimonies, were tall and handsome, sometimes with blue eyes and blond hair. Little by little they were exterminated, or sold as slaves; the current mania for discovering them in the appearance of the contemporary inhabitants of the Islands breaks down against the evidence that most of the Canary Islanders who have lived here since at least the nineteenth century are in fact the descendants of those who exterminated the people we now call our ancestors, most of them Guanches, although there were not only Guanches on all the islands, and some of the islands had no Guanches living on them at all. But this name, which is the correct term for the first inhabitants of Tenerife, has been extended out of laziness or majority use to cover the primitive inhabitants of each of the seven islands.

What is a fact is that Lancerotto Mailosel came to the island, and he kept it. There is a document of the writer Boccaccio's dating back to 1341, in which the Canary Islands are mentioned, and this is the second mention after Pliny's description of the many dogs on the Atlantic archipelago. The news spread: here is beauty and life, and the conquistadors of the time went to look for it: some of them were pirates, lots of them were adventurers, and some of them were advance guards for their empires, such as Horatio Nelson, the English admiral who wanted to take control of Tenerife in the eighteenth century and who found himself face to face with a population (led by General Gutiérrez from Extremadura) who, in command of a limited arsenal, not only held off the overwhelming English fleet, but also took off Nelson's arm with a shot from the Tiger cannon, an object still highly venerated in Santa Cruz.

This episode, the last of its kind that the Canary Islands have suffered to date, ends with a scene which is still recalled in the Islands as an example of their character: once the British navy had surrendered, the victors took Nelson in and looked after him, they gave him an island cheese as a present, and in return he gave the people who had defeated him a barrel of beer. One of the leafiest streets in Santa Cruz is named after the admiral, whose defeat is also commemorated each year with great patriotic fervour, just as the 1808 revolt on 2 May against the forces of Napoleon is remembered in Madrid. What would have happened if Napoleon had definitively got his hands on Spain? They say the same kind of thing in the Islands: what if Nelson had got hold of Tenerife, and then the other islands? And what if the Canary Islanders had stopped the advance of Franco, who left from here, from Tenerife, to initiate the bloody adventure of the Civil War, or, as the Spanish academic, the Harvard professor Juan Marichal put it, the Uncivil War? What would have happened? Virtual history, of course, but a history which would have made various important aspects of our past very different . . . The Second British Isles: it's not a bad idea.

A long time before Nelson, of course, the islands of Lanzarote and Fuerteventura were visited in 1402 by the French adventurers Jean de Bethéncourt and Gadifer de La Salle. Gadifer came to El Hierro and gave his opinion: 'Harsh and difficult to access from the coast, but verdant and beautiful in the interior, with great forests of evergreen pines and a lot of rainwater.' Bethéncourt didn't waste time with

descriptions: he took Fuerteventura (and made his capital on a beautiful hill, calling it Betancuria, which we have already visited) and
tried to do the same with the island that was then called Canaria, as
round as a pudding; it is with a great deal of patriotic pride that Dacio
notes that in Canaria Bethéncourt 'suffered a complete defeat, which
is why the island is now called Great'. Great it is, and Gran Canaria
is its name.

AND SO HERE WE WERE, READING DACIO IN EL HIERRO AND TRAVELLING
backwards in time, back to where the legend tells us history begins,
or vice versa, and I grew tired of history, and also of the legend, and
started to walk out into the landscape, which here in El Hierro is
sometimes a synthesis of other landscapes which one can see in the
Islands. It is true, what Gadifer de La Salle said: harsh and difficult
to access, leafy and beautiful. That is how the islands are, except for
Fuerteventura, which is an open coast, a huge beach of dark or white
sand, almost never black, almost always blond; but the other islands,
La Gomera and La Palma, Tenerife and Gran Canaria and Lanzarote,
are islands which are called upon to be isolated, to stop any invasion
with the hurricane strength of the winds that strike against their cliffs.
Here I am, for example, in El Golfo, which opens out into Sabinosa,
and the landscape seems to be smooth, you walk across it as though
you were headed towards a huge black beach, but what awaits you
in fact is the abyss; huge abysses of stone, black rocks held tight in a
dun and black earth, both humble and great, arrogant; earth which
seems to exist to destroy you with heat or tiredness. It seems to be
saying: you will grow tired of treading on me, and I will beat you. In
this black desert I had the sensation that the land had a particular
feeling underfoot, like lava and velvet both at once; it was as though
the lava were unchanged, recently thrown out by the volcano, still
reddish, angry, taking control of the seashore at the little beach called
Arenas Blancas, White Sands, although there is no sand here and it is
not white and never was. It is a name, Arenas Blancas, designed to

do no more than make your journey a little easier. Names, passionate place-names that mark the route as though they were describing the past. Why is this place called Antoncojo? Why is this one called Tiscamanita? What happened here for this out-of-the-way place to merit the name of Gran Tarajal? Why is this mountain called Tindaya? Unamuno went through Fuerteventura taking a note of all the names; when you note down the names of places it is as though you carry them with you in your memory . . .

Here, in Arenas Blancas, I took some ghostly photographs, which have now been erased, perhaps because the landscape, like characters in the work of Juan Rulfo or certain tribes, did not want to be photographed, and carefully deleted the image that it had given up. In any case, this is what I wanted to say: a few years ago some farmers from La Palma thought that here, in Arenas Blancas, was a place where they could grow bananas, tomatoes and fruit: the size of the terrain seemed sufficient, it was also a good idea to grow so near to a port; they built and they planted, and prepared the ground to receive their seeds. But they didn't take the wind into account, or the salt, or the sun, and little by little this land which was born to be a desert turned into what it is today, a devastated expanse on which the image of agricultural failure is painted: it looks like a painting by Fontana or Pollock, perfect lines expressing the metaphor of what it cannot in fact be, a great expanse of the kind that Malevich might have painted, white on white all the way to the horizon, all the way to the perfect line that is the horizon drawn by the sea on the magnificent distance, only occasionally broken by a sail.

Once Padrón Machín, the all-seeing chronicler of the island, said that El Hierro was the island of the future, just as Stefan Zweig said of Brazil: 'It is the land of the future, and it always will be.' Perhaps Machín was thinking about this wasteland; here you have it, a landscape which explains why the land and the elements will always be more powerful than mankind; Arenas Blancas is an allegory of the persistence of nature, above and beyond the avaricious will of mankind, clinging on by tooth and claw to the beauty we now observe before we start our journey to the viewpoint at Bascos, another place that, like Arenas Blancas, prevents mankind from ever controlling its gales.

This image of human failure reminds me of the traces I saw in some parts of England where there are cemeteries: everything that grows on this surface, even after centuries have passed, maintains within itself the persistent image of the peace that was there beforehand, the silence which the earth respects forever, like the wrinkles on a forehead or the relics of a religion.

It is an overwhelming kind of landscape: not just for what it shows you, but also for what it hides from you. We wanted to climb up to the Bascos viewpoint and the lighthouse at Orchilla, where the island bids farewell to everything that it knows, to the world as it once was, and we climbed up over this fire-devastated and time-devastated landscape until a curve, which seemed to lead us to nowhere, showed us abysses to either side, and as though we were being held back by a careful rather than diabolical entity, we turned back to the landscape which we had abandoned, as if this landscape which had earlier seemed so inhospitable were in fact capable of welcoming us better than the abyss. Fear is not a good word to describe one's state of mind when confronted by the abyss: perhaps stupor is better, or else paralysis. It was also a fear of beauty: up there, between the void, the wind, and the black landscape, you feel like a white kite hanging from an invisible thread, and we returned. There was another way up to the viewpoint: a man told us when we reached El Pozo de la Salud, the Well of Good-Health at Sabinosa, which had been discovered centuries previously: it was found that the livestock which drank from the well were healthier than those that did not, and the water also proved to be a source of health for the men who drank from it as well; now it is closed, being renovated, but the water is still there, and we were there too, looking for peace after the anxiety which our interrupted ascent into the abyss had caused. And so, here is a piece of advice for travellers: if you travel the winding roads of El Hierro and feel an attraction to the abyss, then be aware that there is a way back, and that fear there is not simply a word, but rather a physical sensation, an absolute proof that nature will still impose its limits, and that you are not brave simply by pushing against them until the inevitable happens . . .

WE FOUND A STONE HOUSE THERE, PROTECTED FROM THE WORLD BY THE Canary palm (*Phoenix Canariensis*) and by verode (*Kleinia neriifolia*), and every kind of aboriginal flora and vegetation, as well as by lizards, and young juniper trees which were now learning to adapt themselves to the wind so as to be able to survive for hundreds of years, producing wood and the succulent smell of wood that only juniper trees can produce. It is a resistant wood which has been used to make the roofs of rustic houses since time immemorial, because it is resistant to a particular type of insect which eats all other kinds of wood. There were juniper trees here, and then we went to El Sabinal, the Juniper Forest, where the juniper tree grows in a spectacular fashion, a metaphor for resistance, a symbol for the island: short, fragile, tortuous, but upright; an island struggling to resemble its natural landscape. The juniper tree is like that: the clearest symbol of El Hierro; the Salmor lizard is a gigantic saurian which appears furtively on roofs and among the cliffs; it is the softness of the earth, the capacity which both man and lizard have of adapting themselves to the landscape; but the juniper tree is more like an extension of the earth, with its baroque style, like a scream, a wooden fist held against the sky, shaken by the wind, the wind in wooden form, if one can put it like that. I said as much to Enrique, my friend who was putting me up in his wooden house, and he, always the philosopher, said:

'Nature runs the show, that is what creates harmony.'

He came here, aiming to cultivate this landscape by looking at it, by blending with the stone, with the lava, with the lizards themselves: he's a painter. With his partner Marta he has built, both of them working with their own hands, a whole universe in which nature indeed runs the show: we sat down to eat cheese and to watch the world. We were recovering from the effect of the abyss, sitting on the ground; they had white wine, very dry; if we fell silent in this paradise we would most likely hear the voice of our ancestors' silence. That's what I felt there, sitting with my friends and the wine, and the cheese.

But let us get back to walking over this young island which is, for me, the figure of all the other islands, a discovery: you should make this discovery as well, but not to touch the island, to leave it as it is, to let it be always the memory-island of what an island has to be . . . Enrique said that if the Canary Islands had been made over the course of a year, then Fuerteventura would have been made on the first day, and El Hierro would have been done in April, in the foggiest months of spring; colonisation and tourism (which at times have been devastating) would not have happened until the last second of the year, but have still had a great effect. El Hierro is a hundred million years old, but some of its sites, such as Frontera, which is where I am now, are only 50,000 years old. Seated on top of these 50,000 years of history we take up a cured cheese with our hands; the bread is still hot, the wine is harsh, as though it had only recently been harvested, and the landscape is like the wine. With these flavours in our mind we carry on walking over this island which is the memory of what an island should be.

I DON'T KNOW WHY, BEFORE WISHING US FAREWELL, ENRIQUE SHOULD have spoken of the volcanoes: the Canary Islands are not a volcano hotspot; there are no eruptions due; the ones which took place are now long past: the eruptions were a drama, but they extended the Islands. They made this island larger; they made La Palma larger, and Lanzarote . . . In Tenerife, the Trevejo volcano devastated the beautiful town of Garachico.

But we had to get to the Bascos viewpoint: it was not just a route to take; it was turning into an obsession. One cannot travel to El Hierro and stop before reaching Bascos and seeing the juniper trees, that prehistoric forest next to the hermitage dedicated to the Virgen de los

Reyes. One cannot leave without seeing this magical place, slowly, as though the wind were a part of the miracle, as if this were one of the places where the air turns round on itself, as in Timanfaya on Lanzarote, or in Maspalomas on Gran Canaria, or on the whole island of Fuerteventura, or in the house in Tías on Lanzarote where the writer José Saramago lived until his death, who once said to me:

'They can take everything from me, but they can never take this air.'

IN ORDER TO GO TO SEE THE JUNIPER TREES, THIS SIGHT WHICH SEEMS TO have been brought to life by the power of a group of witches, they showed us another route, through the forests, far from the abysses of the sea, and that was the route we took, surrounded by green and by all the colours of the Pinar highway. I recalled the road covered with its perennial rain in La Gomera, although on El Hierro there is less water, no water at all. The vines and fig trees give a sense of peace to the landscape, a sense which does not exist in that landscape of dark lava which had stopped our passage that morning, had stopped us out of pure fear in Frontera and Sabinosa. Up there at that height it is as though you were alone on the island, surrounded by fog and by greenery, surrounded by the soft and omnipresent pine needles, a kind of volatile ground laid on top of the sullen and firm ground beneath.

This idyllic surface also has cows walking on it, keeping their monotonous gaze on the dry and difficult grass next to the juniper forest, one of the most fascinating landscapes of the Canary Islands. They are prehistoric trees, the ones in front of me, the ones that look like disembowelled women—their centres open in order to show their baroque and sectioned nature—with their hair all awry, like vegetable paintings which have been alive forever representing a wild despair, and they produced in me once again the impression that has made me come back to see them again, which keeps me here petrified, as if I had never before been in any other spot in the whole world, as if I would discover here in this one landscape all the landscapes of the Islands.

The blue of the sky, the sea sounding in the distance, and these confused plants with their sparse manes exposed to the wind.

When I saw this forest for the first time, life for me was still a breath of youthful air, and back then this place was for me the mirror of age, a place where you have to stop and think about what time might have done to end up creating sights like this, and that it is only nature which is capable of holding out for so long in order to create such miracles.

FASCINATED BY THE JUNIPER TREES, WHICH ARE LIKE A ROW OF WOMEN running away from some terrifying spectacle, I went to the Bascos viewpoint, which I had never before visited; I thought that it was no more than a viewpoint, a place for tourists to take photographs in order to carry them home and stick them into some clichéd photo album. And when I climbed up there, assaulted by the wind which came from all sides, as though it were being blown at me by the juniper trees themselves, I realised that what one saw from this viewpoint was fear itself, the mortal fear of the abyss, that what one saw from here was the abyss itself; below you there is landscape, earth, dryness, the sun, the sea, the whole Atlantic passing by smoothly, but determinedly, towards other coasts, other islands. But when you are up there, there is no such thing as any future or any journey or anything, there is nothing but the abyss, the present, and terror, the calm of absolute mortal fear.

The word is vertigo; if this landscape had been available to Hitchcock then he would have come here to ensure that his masterpiece of suspense was filmed hanging from the Bascos viewpoint, where one feels the unhealthy illusion that there is another world into which you are, helplessly, going to fall.

You can only escape from this vertigo by leaving, and I went to the lighthouse at Orchilla, a blunt mass at which the light says farewell to all of this. There is a monument here with a line on it (a line which was the subject of a film by Andrés Koppel, the Canary

Island filmmaker), which marked for centuries the zero meridian of the ancient world; Greenwich may have taken the distinction from El Hierro, but the line is still here, next to an abandoned volcano and an ocean which bids everything a vast farewell.

I went back by the same path, overwhelmed by my discoveries on this island, which seems unknown, secret, an example of distance itself, still calling to visitors who have seen it once and who retain in our memories an almost photographic representation of the place which is now revived with an enthusiasm which we wish to share. I returned to the northeast, the black sands and the rocks which are like the rocks where I bathed as a child. I returned through the tunnel where the stoplight, the only stoplight on the island, holds you back and warns you: 'Do not risk your fate for a few minutes of waiting.'

I did not risk my fate; I waited. Later I met the taxi-driver, Antonio, who told me about his journey to Venezuela when he was sixteen years old, in 1956. A few years later his life became so happy there, so far from the poverty which assaulted his homeland at that time, that he wanted to symbolise his happiness by sending something home: he was the first person to send pine seeds back to El Hierro, and now the pine is visible all over the island. 'I sent the first seed.'

LET US TRAVEL WITH HIM TO THE SMALLEST HOTEL IN THE WORLD: THREE rooms (it appears in the *Guinness Book of Records*); there is a Swedish man who comes back every year just to see the ocean reach his balcony, where he sits and fishes; he tells me about the dancers who travel with the Virgen de los Reyes as she comes down to the capital from her refuge close to the juniper trees. The dancers are like Turkish dervishes; they go into a trance and kiss the ground. A friend, Rafael, tells me over a plate of parrotfish and comber (two species of fish which are eaten throughout the Islands) that the island used to be poor, but it always had everything, even now that people have all kinds of food in the kitchen gardens in front of their houses. In order to survive people needed to buy only two things, coffee and yoghurt, and any other luxuries they could afford; but everything else, the basics, the food that Juana served us in Garajonay, the food that my mother put on the table, that they had. This self-sufficiency, which Rafael thought of as a symbol of effort, is what makes El Hierro, once again, seem an absolute island.

The juniper trees offer a form of vegetal fascination. In El Lajial, the fascination is volcanic, looking at the lava carrying out its whims. There are forms in the rocks at Las Cañadas del Teide like that as well, capricious, airy, round, spectacular, but the ones on El Hierro seem sculpted in order to be symbolic; in the dry south of the island, there are two oases, the one at Tacorón, a pool of clear water where the sun appears a red stone, and the one in La Restinga, a former fishing village. El Lajial is an extension of the mainland where the lava carried out its diabolic sculptural flourishes. Time is a great sculptor, Marguerite Yourcenar wrote; here the sculptor that is time has left human forms, the shapes of animals, flowers made of stone, and everywhere, in a shadow which the inclement sun has allowed somehow to survive, a patch of greenery, a verode, a little flower growing as though the greenery itself were fighting for its life in the spaces calcified by the same nature that Enrique told me about in Frontera.

It is like Pompeii, but in stone; I recovered from the impression which El Lajial had made on me with its surf of lava in Tacorón, lying down on its black rocks, looking down into the depths of its primitive and still crystalline waters, and then I went to La Restinga, to eat fresh fish, which they have here in abundance, and then I went to look for the Garoé tree, which no longer exists, although there are signposts to it from the highway as you head northeast towards the spectacular viewpoint at La Peña.

The tree is no longer there, but there is a spot at the highest point of El Hierro (which has been prepared for visitors with an impressive installation) with trees that gather water from the air and store it at their roots. The inhabitants of El Hierro describe this as something attractive and of exceptional value.

The tree is no longer there, but it remains in the legends of the

Islands, it was a sacred tree which gathered water and the people loved it; they thought that it wept for unrequited lovers. As I carried on with my journey I came across the viewpoint of La Peña, where the artist César Manrique has created a space where one can eat and look out at the same time; we will talk a great deal about César later on, about his beneficent influence over some of the Islands, and above all about the miracle which he performed on Lanzarote. Here he has created a synthetic viewpoint, which respects its surroundings, as was always Manrique's custom; Enrique said that nature always should take the lead, and without a doubt it led Manrique. One sees nature's control in everything Manrique did, one sees the influence of nature in every bowl, in the contents of every frame, as though he had gifted his two hands to the service of nature.

From this viewpoint one can see all the way to Sabinosa, and one can see, as though it were a distant shadow, the highway that led us to feel the fear of heading upwards through two abysses. But above all what one sees here is peace, which is an island feeling that dominates everything here; peace and the enthusiastic sea, unalterable, majestic, filling the whole world, hiding itself as it fills the world. They told me that it is the crow, that bird which seems so malignant, so perverse, that is responsible for the fertilization of the juniper trees, the most airy beauty of this land, and one wonders at such a perfect beauty coming from such abject stomachs, the sublime appearance of vegetal life coming from the most dilapidated of all elements, the crow giving birth to the still life of the landscape. Disgust creating its landscape . . .

The juniper trees are the children of the crows. The crow eats the seeds of the tree, it regurgitates them, its hardy, efficient and violent stomach acts upon them, and it throws them out into the world at precisely the right temperature for them to germinate. I thought about this, surrounded by birds in this nature reserve, sitting at the viewpoint at La Peña, looking into infinity and asking myself how it could be that I had taken so many years to come back to El Hierro, and, now that I had returned, how it was possible that no one had told me that I should come back to see one of the freest and most intense natural environments of the whole Canary Islands. The fault is mine, to spend so much time without visiting the island which contains the metaphorical memory of all the Islands.

Well, I was here, and my time here was unforgettable, as though I had dreamed it. They asked me what El Hierro was to me. I said: 'An open hand.' That is what it is: the lined palm of a young hand in which a crow leaves a seed that grows into a juniper tree that shouts and blends its cry with the wind in the Bascos viewpoint.

Go there, but do not touch.

OH, THERE WAS SOMETHING I FORGOT FROM MY NOTES. SOMEONE TOLD me, one night while we were drinking beer and eating fish in a neighbourhood bar, near the smallest hotel in the world, that there is a place in El Hierro where they still keep preserved the cave for the communal coffin; for years and years it would be taken out for the funerals of poor people: no one had to pay for the coffin, and when they died, the families of the poor were able to make use of this collective coffin. It is a brutal indication of the level of poverty in the island.

And I also forgot, among many other things, the slim, incredible figure of a beautiful horse, brown, walking in lonely elegance across an empty field, near the La Peña viewpoint, near the sacred tree. The horse stood there, upright, looking to one side and then the other, with the sense of curiosity which horses have, and I wondered for a moment if it might in fact be there forever, keeping guard without any weapons over the beauty of an island which had overwhelmed me once again, as though the island itself were a single lonely horse.

THE BEAUTIFUL DESERT

WHEN YOU ARRIVE AT FUERTEVENTURA, JUST AS WHEN YOU ARRIVE at every island, you should look out of the window of the aeroplane, if you are not coming by boat; in the case of Fuerteventura, this is obligatory in order to see if Miguel de Unamuno was right when, living here in exile in the 1920s, he said that you have to approach this beautiful desert with a clean soul. Unamuno said as much in a famous sonnet from his sequence *From Fuerteventura to Paris* where he wrote that that Fuerteventura is a skeleton of an island. And that is how you see it from above: a skeleton which grows larger and smaller, like a size-shifting lizard that somehow manages to stay alive and vigilant no matter its size; wounded or whatever else, the lizard keeps on breathing whatever its dimensions.

And that was how I saw it from the air; Fuerteventura is the air itself, like the air of the earth; it is an island in search of shade, and it is a skeleton. Unamuno compared it with *gofio* as well, the major source of food for the primitive inhabitants of the Canary Islands, and of all of us who have continued to think of this food as the symbol of all our meals; if you say 'bread', then you are talking about the basis of your diet, and if you say '*papas*', then you are talking about what the Canary Islanders and the Southern Americans eat, and if you say '*gofio*', then you are referring to the Canary Islands, or to Fuerteventura in particular. The same Fuerteventura that Miguel de Unamuno saw.

So, when I read Unamuno and saw him identify the island with *gofio*, I felt that he was my poet, that he knew where the Islands' childhood came from, how we were able to survive when there were only *papas*, fish, *gofio* and cheese, the basic elements in the diet of generations of Canary Islanders. And Fuerteventura, which is an island that has been extremely isolated by its poverty, felt more than any other island, at least as much as El Hierro or the south of Tenerife, the humble solidarity of *gofio* with one's stomach.

But we had reached Fuerteventura, and some verses of Unamuno took me back to everybody's childhood. Now a great deal of time has gone by, and childhood no longer exists save as the memory of a memory, or the distant gleam of an event in the past, and Fuerteventura is a different island from the one which welcomed Miguel de Unamuno (which embraced him, literally, preventing his exile from turning into an imprisonment). Back then Unamuno—who was the rector of Salamanca University in 1936 when Franco started the Civil War, but who in the 1920s was a thunderous professor, a republican member of parliament, and opposed to the soft dictatorship of General Primo de Rivera, who had him sent into exile—scandalised the whole of the conservative society of the capital of Fuerteventura, Puerto Cabras, now known as Puerto del Rosario. He led his discussion groups here; his was a peripatetic discussion group, as he had been forbidden from speaking to many people: he walked through the streets, stopping here and there, in bars and at the windows of people's houses, and added voices to his poetic, political and philosophical chorus. His ideas derived from a militant Catholicism, but also from a struggle to identify the true identity of God, which was his great battle, his great agony, a word which is fundamental for his philosophy and its evocation of the struggle—the literal meaning of the word 'agony' in Greek—which he forced himself to control.

AND SO, FROM ABOVE, FROM THE WINDOW OF THE AEROPLANE, FUERTEVENtura looks like a series of large dun-coloured lizards, a kind of ghostly island which opens up in the middle of an eternal or probable sand-storm, and which looks—how could it not?—like a skeleton made of *gofio*.

The sensation of sandiness which one feels upon looking at Fuerteventura is not surprising; Fuerteventura is sand, is only sand, succulent desert sand, scattered with occasional humble trees which give an ever-greater sensation of loneliness; a sandy fortress stained with the sand of the sea. In the atmosphere there is sand; there is sand on the roads, and they used to be covered by even more sand; in Corralejo, near the capital, Puerto del Rosario, Puerto Cabras as it was in Unamuno's time, the dunes rolled onto the highways and the roads; now the dunes are smaller and they don't cover the highway except in particular parts of one's journey.

Everything is the colour of sand. In some places, such as Corralejo, the sand is whiter; and in the very south, in Cofete, the sand has the colour of millet *gofio*, or else wheat: a light brown shading into dark brown. In Corralejo, which is where I went the first time I visited Fuerteventura, forty years ago, the sand is like an addition to the sun: a clear, sparking sun; crystal-clear, pure waters, and as a result of this combination one feels a sense, physical, pleasurable, of joyous delight, almost like the sense one feels at Famara on Lanzarote, the beach where the artist César Manrique grew up, the best, most mysterious beach of all the Islands. But we will get there later.

Now we are in Fuerteventura, and travelling south, although not to the very south, not to Cofete. We are arriving at the Costa Calma, which is given that name for obvious reasons, and to a particular spot where I want us to travel together, my readers and I. I came here because the poet Pedro Lezcano recommended that I do so, years ago. He went here every summer; until he was more than eighty years old he did scuba-diving and underwater fishing here, and this is a wonderful spot for looking at the bottom of the sea, not simply at the sea itself. Lezcano stayed in a hotel, the Hotel Los Gorriones, which was like an old car with soft leather seats; there was a bar which was like the old bars of the Islands, with a slight English air to it, like the bar in the Hotel Mencey in Santa Cruz de Tenerife, which is also a hotel of leather and wood, a kind of dovecote where it looks as though the clients will spend their entire lives sitting with a whisky in hand, just as in those dangerous parties that Gatsby used to give . . . Perhaps I am idealising things here, but in my memory the bar at the Hotel Los Gorriones is like that, just as I remember, and just as the poet spoke of it to me: a comfortable bar, darkened in the afternoons so as to be able better to see the sunset, which shaded with melancholy the farewell the sea was bidding to the sand . . .

It is likely that this memory, which is perhaps a false one, has been made larger by the actual evidence available to me, because the bar has now disappeared and in its place is a chill-out lounge which I doubt would have been useful or pleasurable for my friend, the poet Pedro Lezcano. But here we are, and we are not walking towards the hotel anymore, but instead strolling along the beach. Fuerteventura from the air is a lizard, but at ground level it is a beach, many beaches, beaches of all kinds: large, long, wide, white, black; this one in particular, the beach where we are, Playa Barca, the Beach of the Rowing Boats, as it is called for obvious reasons, looks like a real beach: narrow at the ends and wider in the middle, and you walk along it as though you were dancing in the middle of an agreeable desert. Like every beach on the island, it is entirely clean, and this is another symbol: it is not that the sea has taken away the rubbish, but that people have not left any. It is the responsibility of the Pájara local government, the largest local authority in the whole of Spain, but it is also the consequence of a tradition in Fuerteventura, which is that the beaches should always look as though they have been recently swept. The wind contributes to this miracle, without any doubt.

In any case, the Beach of the Rowing Boats is lots of things: a distance (four miles), an aesthetic, a pleasure . . . It is a good representation of the metaphor of the beach, the metaphor of Fuerteventura itself; your gaze loses itself in the distance, because the beach is distance itself, and your footprints follow you and are immediately blown away, because the wind shifts the fine sand with great skill, and the marks you leave in the sand are filled as though no one had ever walked there. It is a beach from which to go diving, a beach where you can swim, a beach to observe. It is a metaphor of the island itself. If you take photographs of Caribbean beaches down to the Playa Barca and compare them carefully, then you will see that there is a lot of overlap between the photographs and the beach in front of you. This is not a coincidence; it is a copy: many of the beaches in the Caribbean sell themselves, in Spain at least, by using photos of the Playa Barca; it's easier to use these photographs than to go to the Caribbean and take proper ones yourself.

Although it is a major part of the life of the island, not everything is to do with the beach. No sooner had we left the Playa Barca, heading down towards the very south of the islands, my friend Andrés Duncanson, a journalist and fisherman, spoke to me of a tradition connected with another product of the island: its wool-bearing livestock, its sheep and its goats. He pointed towards the dull and dry hills and told me about the great livestock drives for sheep and goats which took place in these dry areas, all the way as far as Cofete, every year. The goats graze at their leisure and are gathered every year in order to be slaughtered. They belong to their owners; everyone knows who these free-ranging goats belong to; they graze by themselves at their liberty and eat what they want, nature gives them what little it has; wherever there is a shadow, behind every tiny rock, among the cliffs, there is some little piece of greenery, and this patch of green is where you will find the goats. The goats and the sheep do what they want, but their ears are marked, and the mark shows who they belong to. The livestock drives are necessary to check that everything is well with the animals, and to divide them among their owners; the money made from the sale of their meat will be divided between the owners of the various earmarks.

We are in the Jandía National Park, and this is where the goats graze peacefully; all of their customs are peaceful and familial: the

kids, the *baifas*, only suckle from their mothers, and follow them with
the devotion of the needy; the owners of the sheep pay most attention
to the wethers; Andrés tells me that theirs is the most succulent meat,
and the most succulent part of their succulent meat is their forelegs,
which is where the animal makes least effort when walking. These are
country tales, from the shepherding tradition of Fuerteventura, which
has not been eliminated, although it might seem so, by the tourist in-
flux, especially by Germans, which has turned this island into one of
the most desirable sites in the world if what you want is beaches and
places where you can take the sun, go swimming or windsurf.

Andrés tells me that there used to be two available distractions
in Fuerteventura: looking at the goats walking around, and looking
at the dunes moving onto the roads. The dunes are now calmer because the roads are better and more controlled, but they used to create
their own landscape, which was never the same from one day to the
next; the dunes at Cofete, which is where we headed, were universes
with their own dynamic, the poetic and secret dynamic of the dunes,
guided towards the smooth and sinuous mountains by the same wind
which has made these southern coasts the best place in the world to
practise competitive windsurfing.

Goats, dunes, sand, beaches, donkeys (there are many donkeys,
and all of them sad, as all donkeys are, on Fuerteventura) and suddenly, of course, advertisements for McDonald's and Coca-Cola.
Tourism is now another aspect of the landscape. We travel past the
Jandía salt marshes, the Jandía spurge bushes, we see the Jandía lighthouse, elements of the landscape that has always been here, but there
is another landscape here which looks like all other landscapes everywhere, the landscape of tourism, all the same at least until we make
it past Morro Jable, the most densely-populated nucleus of the Jandía
peninsula. And after Morro Jable there is a track of stone and earth,
which is occasionally enlivened by the goats and the donkeys and the
beaches, and which takes you to coves which have their own history.
In particular, this track leads you to the La Señora beach, which owes
its name to a lady who was a lover of King Alfonso XII; she was ex-

iled to Fuerteventura in order not to upset the peace of the king's family, and this was where she is supposed to have gone to swim. The beach now has another meaning connected to it, because it is the first place where the bodies of African immigrants wash up from their dinghies that they have used to escape the misery of their homelands in search of what they believe to be a better life in the Canary Islands or in Spain.

The shadow of the dinghy deaths marked the inhabitants of the coast of this island for decades, until better vigilance, or the final understanding that this better life was also a Utopian dream which cost people's lives, convinced the people who were tempted to emigrate not to do so in such a risky fashion, crossing the ocean from the coast of Africa.

Andrés, the fisherman, tells me that these beaches have good fishing; as though he were making a synthesis of the sea and the land, he fishes for parrotfish, the subtlest and tastiest of all the rockfish of the Islands, using the tip of a goat's horn as a float. 'It's an orgasm, the feeling when a good fisherman gets a bite, the feeling as the line goes tense, the weight on the rod that shows you've caught something leaves your legs trembling.' Different strokes for different folks . . . When we sat down to eat by the Jandía lighthouse, Andrés took some rods out of his bag, ready to accompany the guitars that rang out at the other end of the bar; a second later and there was party in full flow; behind us now was the anxiety we had felt earlier: Andrés believes that nature can be overcome, and took us to a beautiful cove which one has to enter by defying the theory (and practice) of gravity. We flew through the air and landed on the wonderful sand of the secret beach, the welcoming sand. The leap was a sudden one, dangerous; luckily enough, there were no rocks below, but only the miraculous sand that has been there since the prehistory of Fuerteventura. We came out alive, but we needed to eat and drink in order to overcome our fright.

This spot, Puertito de la Cruz, is a kind of lawless Wild West town, where there are caravans that look as if they have been there ever since the hippies decided to live in a commune: but here they have food that can help you recover from any kind of fright. In particular, they sell a kind of soup made with fish, onion and saffron, and on the side *gofio* with salt and raw onion. And a good ice-cold local beer (I recommend Dorada, it's my brand) encourages you to forget about what happened on the secret beach, encourages you to join in the party that's kicking off at the other end of the bar, and encourages you to live, to imagine the clean water, crystal-clear, the metaphor for all the waters of the sea that was waiting there after the risky flight that left us on the welcoming and now unforgettable sand. And while we ate the delicate fish, the women at the counter sang; I feel as though I am in a place where the world says goodbye to everything among the sand and the crystal-clear water, as if after tonight there would be no more ports, no better state of health, no easier or more beautiful happiness.

What happens on these islands is that every time you touch the sky you end up touching the ground. And you think about metaphors, but you end up accepting them wholeheartedly: this fish soup, made of wreckfish—a salty fish that can also be very dry, but which here is as soft as the soup itself, which you eat with *escaldón*, that is, *gofio* mixed with water and stock, and raw onion—becomes a metaphor for the patience of eating, for the baroque way in which we Canary Islanders treat our food.

My mother used to mix everything together, she put all the food on the table, and thought that you could eat the solid parts of the meal and the liquid ones at the same time, as well as the sweet bits and the savoury bits: she invented fusion cuisine ahead of her time. This is something she has done and that millions of other Canary Islanders have done over the course of time, usually compelled by necessity, when there was only saltfish and *gofio* and a bone in the house with which to make a soup. And it is from this need that our humble cuisine developed, passing these satisfactions into culinary history. Here I am seated in front of this vast soup tureen, made of hot zinc: inside it is the fusion, the fish, the *papas*, the sweet potato, other vegetables.

Andrés says that it is not so simple, as he sees me stirring the pot: you don't just stick everything in and later take the fish soup out; it's not so simple. You have to watch the time; time is patience, and cooking is patience as well, and that is why they have taken so long to bring us the food; they have put our patience to the test. You might come from cities where there are noises and traffic lights, and find yourself face to face with roads on which you can travel for whole afternoons at a time, while you adjust your gaze to the sight of immense safe beaches, where there are no mosquitoes or anything else that is not nice to look at.

And this slowness is like a lullaby which is later turned into the form of food, food which comes when it is ready, and when, if I can put it like this, one's patience is at an end, only because it is now no longer necessary. Andrés even says that they have brought it a little bit too soon, that the fish is not quite how it should be. But one never knows, and I eat it with the delectation it deserves. Out there, on the dirt, the children are playing in among the dusty caravans; there are dozens of them, quiet and dirty; there is a warehouse selling a whole load of junk just in front of us, like a set from *Easy Rider*. So far away from everything, Puertito de la Cruz. And there, opposite us, looking out into the particularly blue sea, is the lighthouse, just one more lighthouse; the Canary Islands delimit their world using lighthouses.

The women are still singing; they are singing Maná's version of the song *Probablemente*, a song from Mexico, which fills me with nostalgia and a kind of unsteady happiness while I eat a fish soup which is like something my mother would have made. 'In the same place as always, the same city and the same people,' as the song goes. They are singing, the women are singing. Andrés raises his fishing rod to them, like the fine musician he is, and accompanies them, and while the melancholic music plays I feel in my depths the noise of fishing rod knocking against fishing rod, enlivening the party as if it were going to last all evening and for the rest of all our lives, like the fish, like the stewed *papas*, like the greenery which gives a bit of life to the food, like the Dorada beer that has just fallen like a cold lifeline into my throat.

There are other things that people call happiness, but this small pleasure is happiness itself, here and with these people. We serve ourselves green *mojo* and *mojo picón*; these sauces, the *mojos*, are a part of the humble (or grandiose) theory of cuisine; they are both a luxury and a necessity, there is no flavour in the food of the Islands which does not allow one to add a *mojo*, *mojo* with everything, *mojo* with *gofio*, *mojo* with *papas*, *mojo* with meat, *mojo* with fish.

'The tasty sauce of the Islands is called *mojo picón*,' as Caco Senante, a star of the 1980s, once sang: he is also the originator of a kind of sarcastic slogan used to apply to people who leave the islands and go to live in Madrid: 'What are you doing here, a seagull in Madrid?'. . . Well, here we are, in Puertito de la Cruz, this Wild West village where the remains of what used to be the hippy world live alongside the nostalgia of the farmers sitting dreaming at the bar as though they were lost stills from the films *Baghdad* or *Paris, Texas*.

They are used as though they were a form of condiment, the different types of *mojo*, and cover up all other flavours. The Catalan academic who studied urban development in Barcelona so far away from where we are now dipped his bread in *mojo*, we pour *mojo* on the *gofio* with which we accompany our soup; all around us the Germans and English order their food, dip it in *mojo* and for the first time try this sauce, which is like a sign of identity in some ways.

Mojos, mojos, the Canary Islands are summed up by their *mojos*. *Mojo verde* is the smoothest, made with cilantro, or else parsley; *mojo picón*, sharp *mojo*, is made with red pepper, and is sharp, as the name suggests, it's used to make the taste of whatever you are eating even stronger; if you use too much *mojo* then your food stops having any flavour at all, *mojo picón* can take on all-comers; the green variety is much more simple, a friendly kind of *mojo* which enhances flavours without overwhelming them. For a long time I used to eat both kinds, but now I prefer to eat my *papas* with oil and vinegar, which is also, for me, the best way of dressing a salad. They didn't give us a salad at Puertito de la Cruz, and now I imagine the flavour of the salads they normally serve in the Canary Islands: with millet, palm hearts, avocado, *guayonge* onions (which are bluish, tasty, grown in the area from which they derive their name, in Guayonge, a part of Tacoronte on Tenerife) . . . But there was none of that here; here there was only onion, and it was not blue, and it was what we used to eat the *gofio*, as though it were a spoon. Salads are a ritual that comes directly from the fields; if you want to believe that the Canary Islands are there, right there on the table where you're eating, then apart from the *mojos* and the stews you need to order salads, and you have to insist that they contain onion. And if it is blue, that strange blue onion which they grow up on the cliffs, then so much the better.

As we finished eating, the women were singing *El rey*, by the Mexican José Alfredo Jiménez. *Pero sigo siendo el rey*. But I am still the king. This is the kind of place where the music takes you away to anywhere at all, and we were simultaneously in the Canary Islands and in Mexico, in the Wild West, and in a paradise where the wind moves the sands in order to put them in their proper place. The Catalan academic, the expert in nineteenth-century urban planning in Barcelona, ate a huge fish, fiery and red, and made a few notes. I spoke to him directly. His name is Francesc, and he is on the island 'to disconnect for a bit and to study a little'.

Can you do the two things at the same time, disconnect and study? Yes, he says, you can.

I like to speak to the foreigners who visit the Islands; they all see things which we never see; I have always spent my time watching them and trying to talk to them; one of my first jobs was looking after the children of some foreigners, and as a child I used to run after them and beg for pennies, and speak to them; the first words I ever saw written down were foreign words ('Trulsa ös mormor'); in a general store which had some goods imported from England, I saw the phrase 'Good because Danish', and I noted down the following Portuguese phrase from a jar of Nescafé: 'Mantenha a lata bem fechada' (Keep tightly closed). The Canary Islands have always been, and still are, the site of an immense and constant traffic of foreigners who have transformed our language, connecting our vague borders with the border of the world. It is impossible to live enclosed within the Islands: the Islands are a window which has been open ever since I was a child.

And so I spoke to Francesc as though this Catalan academic were a foreigner and asked him if you could combine study and disconnection. And looking down into the bottom of his plate, covered now in *mojo*, bread and the remains of the fish he had eaten, that parrotfish which he dissected as though he were studying it, he confided in me a discovery which I now copy from him: 'I like the fact that it is not greenery which defines the landscape here, but rather tectonics.'

It is not greenery which defines the landscape here, but rather tectonics. He said this in Fuerteventura, of course, where the greenery is either artificial or distant, set back from the parts that the sea and the sand can reach; in Puertito de la Cruz and in all the surrounding countryside you see wretched little goats, but never any grass; perhaps there is grass or some kind of plant hidden away in the stones themselves, where the animals all gather like thirsty men meeting at an oasis.

There is no greenery here, there is only tectonics. He said this as though he were laying a hand on the earth. It is true. There is little greenery; there are a few little trees which stand by the side of the road, clinging to the ground like limpets, which I have on occasion stopped to photograph, bending down to the ground until my chin is almost touching it; but this is greenery which gives no shade. Andrés has pointed out to me a tiny plant which hides crouching next to an equally small rock. But there is no greenery here; in the distance, sometimes, you see in the deep south occasional strips of palm trees or hedges which give you the impression of facing an oasis, but Jandía was not made for greenery, and so what Francesc said was just what everyone feels, that it is tectonics, the structure of the landscape itself, which is the most important aspect of Fuerteventura, even the air is made of sand, it is as though it will soon solidify. We live in the midst of a sandstorm that sometimes unleashes itself absolutely, but which otherwise hangs in the air like a threat.

BUT THE MAN WHO HAS NOT VISITED COFETE AND WHO HAS NOT CLIMBED up to the viewpoint, a rustic type of construction, deforested by the wind, has not truly seen the extent of the loneliness which transforms this island, as Miguel de Unamuno said, into the skeleton of an island. We are in the Jandía massif, we have left behind us the house which they say that a German engineer, Doctor Winter, used during the Second World War to provide fuel to the German submarines that passed by the Islands; we have seen and thought about this mystery which is one of the legends of the Islands; we have marvelled at the fish soup; we have been about to die leaping into the sand of a secret beach: but even so, none of us is prepared for the impression which strikes us as we round this curve in Cofete, harried by an endless wind. What you see is a virgin extent of nine miles of beach up against a massif which looks like God's own open hand throwing its shadow down on the earth, aided by some greyish clouds which make the ground on which we tread seem even more ghostly and hallucinatory.

At the end of this smooth greyness are enormous lonely beaches, and a ghostly cemetery, like the memory of a mysterious cemetery where the dead are eternally doing penance for the sin of having been buried where there is nobody, not even God.

COFETE STOPPED BEING A TOWN IN 1960 AND THE LAST BURIAL IN THE cemetery was in 1953. It is strange to see here, amid all these succulent beaches, which call out to people to indulge in the pleasure of bathing or losing themselves, the presence of a truly marine cemetery; it is a construction which is now truly a part of the sand, which gives it a particularly symbolic appearance, as though the sand were going to cover it fully one day, and indeed is now covering it fully, in the face of the air's indifference: the air here is like time and patience itself, a constant steady breeze which seems, like the lost souls buried here, to be a part of eternity.

Time is the inheritor of this cemetery, and the air here is the earth which hides the cemetery as it marks time. Here I felt once again the sensation of being inside a film, hearing once again the music of *Paris, Texas*. I saw abandoned palm trees, sometimes standing in little clumps, completely dry; I have seen volcanic landscapes intermingled with fields of palm trees elsewhere on this island, which on clean sunny days give the impression that we are between the desert and paradise. And if this is paradise, then paradise must be a lonely place.

THEN WE RETRACED OUR FOOTSTEPS; IN TEFIA WE SAW THE MONUMENT to Miguel de Unamuno. Upright, alone, the philosopher who stood up to Franco, to Millán Astray and to the fascist battle-cry of '*Viva la muerte!*' during the first years of the Civil War, was here, resistant as a palm tree. Unamuno has transformed himself into a kind of lay patron saint of Fuerteventura; his verses are recited as though they had been written by a native of the island, a *majorero*, and we ate gooseneck barnacles here, the food which he helped to discover as though he were its creator, inventing food in order to make people's life on the coast happier, at least on the coast of Gran Tarajal, which was where I ate them for the first time in my life, almost half a century ago.

The other symbol of the island is more purely of the island: it is a mountain, Mount Tindaya. I went to see it once again; years before I had been to it to describe it for a newspaper article; now I approach it as though I were carrying out some kind of religious pilgrimage, in order to see what I can hear, if I can hear something at the foot of the mountain.

Tindaya is a perfect relic, a construct which nature has transformed into a kind of caress of the land, undulating, a wave of land balanced above the wasteland. The primitive inhabitants of the Islands transformed it into an object of veneration, and although people later made use of its stones (trachyte, valuable as a building material) and damaged it, the people who lived there realised just how valuable the mountain was only when a Basque artist, Eduardo Chillida, wanted to transform it into a temple of light, the house of the sun.

It is strange to think of it now, that three Basques should be so connected to the mythology of the Islands: Chillida, the sculptor; Unamuno, the philosopher; Aldecoa, the writer. One of them from San Sebastián, one from Bilbao, and the last from Vitoria. The Islands are a magnet, but the magnet only works when there is a poetic gift that can recognise its qualities.

Well, there is that.

As the result of a coincidence which I have mentioned elsewhere, I had something to do with the dream of this Basque sculptor.

Chillida, who died in 2000, after suffering from depression and Alzheimer's disease, said in around 1990 that he had a dream, and spoke about it to the press. In his dream he had found a mountain that he could hollow out, in order to make it into a receptacle of light, the light of the sun, the light of the moon, a receptacle for light in general; in his dream the mountain turned into a kind of temple in which the light of two particular heavenly moments would be gathered: the light of the full moon and the light of the sun at its peak. An architect from Gran Canaria, José Miguel Fernández-Aceytuno, and his partner, the writer Yovanka Vaccari, knew that I was in semi-regular contact with Chillida, for professional reasons, and asked me to share with him an idea which they thought fitted perfectly with his dream: to consider the mountain at Tindaya. They had made a sketch of their dream and its consequences, the top of the mountain transformed into a site such as Chillida had spoken of, and they handed it to me on a vast roll of paper. They had made their drawing following a commission from the government of the Canary Islands, which wanted to protect the mythical mountain. 'Culture and art against mining', was what Yovanka said to me. The dream was passed into the hands of Chillida, who wanted to hollow out a mountain.

CHILLIDA WAS A SCULPTOR AND A POET. HE HAD PLAYED SOCCER, BEEN A goalkeeper, and that, he said, gave him an exact idea of spaces: the ball fits into your hand, and the space that one's open fingers can contain is the perfect space. He told me this as we strolled on the beautiful paths near La Concha, below his studio in San Sebastián, surrounded by playing children, perhaps just as he had done at the same age, leaping around among the adults on this peaceful path. Some of Chillida's best drawings are studies of hands, open hands, fists, closed hands, expectant hands, hands asking for help, hands offering it, hands held up to prevent another's approach, hands which fly, empty hands.

Chillida was a dreamer and an ingenuous man, and strong until Alzheimer's took hold of him. But back then he was in great shape, and received the stimulus of Tindaya with great excitement. Yes, the mountain on Fuerteventura, which was both a closed hand and a myth, a kind of recreation of the dark myth of the cave, was the perfect spot; this was where he should hollow the world out to make his secular temple to light.

And here my work as a messenger ended: I left the plans for the Tindaya mountain with him and went away, my mission accomplished. Then the technicians were called in; Chillida worked with an engineer, whom he called the 'engineer of shadows', José Antonio Fernández Ordóñez, who worked out the ways in which the mountain could be hollowed out without affecting its shape, the ways in which Chillida's dream could be carried out without breaking the mountain.

But the ecologists of the island did not think the same way, and little by little, between their opposition and the slow political management of Chillida's idea, the project started to fade away in a haze of ecological accusations and indications of political scheming to get hold of the valuable trachyte in the mountain. Chillida was obsessed with light: it was not at all odd that he should have found a mountain like this, on an island where the highest value is placed on light. It was a symbol of all he aimed for as an artist: capturing light.

When I took him Aceytuno and Vaccari's proposal, it was round about 1995; I heard Chillida talking to Fernández Ordóñez, the engineer, about his obsession, his obsession with light. The engineer reminded the sculptor how he always managed to interpolate lightness into weight; the Spanish poet Jorge Guillén, whose poetry added so much to Chillida's concepts of space and light, said that lightness is what weighs the most. And then both of them, the engineer and the sculptor, started to talk about concrete as though it were a material from a dream. And Chillida put his hands together as though he were crumbling concrete into crumbs. Or as if he were turning it into an accordion which he used to accompany the powerful silence of his hands . . .

This was the same way he put his hands together when he found out that Tindaya existed and that it was on offer for him to fulfil his dream. In this session with the engineer, he said: 'We see nothing without the light. I am working on the Tindaya mountain in order to be closer to the light.' Light is what it is, Chillida said: 'It is everywhere; in alabaster, in marble. It is here, in this paper.' He went to the mountain. He visited it to see what it was like. He returned absolutely fascinated with the island and the mountain. He worked obsessively on the project; it was his last great work; for him it was alive in the moment. But Chillida died a few years later; when his project started to be picked apart he began to feel a huge sense of melancholy, as though the light had been covered, as though his dream had been killed. He wanted Tindaya to be a part of the mythology of the future, and also to respect the mythology of the past, without harming the legend of the mountain, and preserve it forever by stopping people from speculating with the value of the material which made up the mountain; he wanted to create a space 'in a mountain set aside for people of all races and colours, a great sculpture for tolerance'.

TINDAYA IS THERE NOW, I SEE IT THIS AFTERNOON IN THE MIDST OF A grey cloud; it is dull brown, like the skin of a donkey, and its base seems lightly chewed. Nearby there are adverts for petanque competitions and rock concerts; there is an old, silent house, an adobe and stone construction next to this silent mountain which Chillida wanted to turn into the house of the light, and I look at it all, trying to remember the expression on the sculptor's face when he got this strange commission to fulfil his dream.

I carried on walking, surrounded by these bare mountains, by cultivated terraces, by lonely palm trees which live by spreading their shade over time itself, and I felt that Fuerteventura was some kind of musical rhythm, was architectonic, that there was an odd harmony to the island. On that occasion when I heard Chillida speaking with Fernández Ordóñez about air and light, he said the following: 'When I walked into the cathedral in Sofia, Bulgaria, I felt I was walking into the lungs of Johann Sebastian Bach.' Well, when you arrive on Fuerteventura, whether by air or by sea, it is as though you are entering a score written by Albinoni or Vivaldi, with all the force of their melancholy, or even a work by Vangelis or Theodorakis, and here is the proof that all forms of art and music can coexist. And you always feel as though you are hearing the chords on the soundtrack of *Paris, Texas*, the melancholy of the desert following the route of an island that seems to have sunk into sand.

But if you walk through the mountains, at some point, inevitably, you will see a sign advertising a McDonald's.

There are places where meeting these perverse signs of the future (trash food, trash traffic, trash tourism) is impossible: I recommend travelling by a route that avoids them. If you go from Morro Jable, which is where all the 'Mc's have their headquarters, across to Puerto del Rosario, or Corralejo, or Pájara, then take the road that is marked 'To La Pared', because it will take you to a little village called La Pared. Lanzarote stands out from the other islands by having whitewashed its villages—an initiative of the incomparable César Manrique—and a number of the villages on Fuerteventura have followed its lead, and here is where you will see a number of them, La Pared among them. But the important thing here is to look at the perfect symphony of mountains succeeding one another, brown and red, always smooth, sometimes appearing to have almost human, feminine shapes; in order to see them properly, you need to link two of your senses, touch and sight, and the combination of the two is the true pleasure to be found in looking at Fuerteventura.

FUERTEVENTURA IS NOT A FLAT ISLAND, ALTHOUGH IT HAS A GREAT DEAL of flatness to it, and a single man up in its mountains can dream, both accompanied and awed by the calm there, a calm that carries you to Betancuria, which is like Tindaya but with its own history.

Before reaching Betancuria I climbed up to a spectacular viewpoint that allows the visitor to look out onto a boundless loneliness, a solitude that is complete, generous or pitiless depending on your state of mind. The palm trees that I saw from there reminded me of palm tree in the Gran Rey valley on La Gomera, which filled me with a kind of melancholy, because landscapes covered with palm trees have the air of being unattainable and tiring and always fill you with other memories of other places.

There are thistles here, tomatoes, cactus pears; a cross made from thistles remembers someone who died in a car accident . . . It is common in these areas, especially in the rural parts of the world, for families to make these memorial crosses out of the widest variety of materials, and this gives the sides of the road a ghostly atmosphere of memory and sadness. And the Islands in themselves are melancholy; the series of crosses turns them into a physical geography in which the sorrow of bereavement becomes a persistent shadow, impossible to forget.

This is how the landscape is, halfway between deserted and subtle, until you reach Vega de Rio Palmas, where the vegetation has all gathered as though expecting a visit.

And here is Betancuria, with its history and air and mountains, and the sound of a goat bleating that is just the same as the sound I once heard on La Gomera.

BETANCURIA WAS THE ADMINISTRATIVE AND RELIGIOUS CENTRE OF Fuerteventura until the seventeenth century. But now it is nothing more than the shadow of its former glory. Its population hovers around five hundred people, and it depends entirely on tourism, on people who come through looking for a souvenir of the island's past. It is the only tourist site on the Canary Islands which has saved itself from the cement that has buried the sea-views all along the coast on almost all the islands.

Betancuria is the majesty of silence. This is silence that has been present for centuries, and which still falls over Betancuria with the moral force of a mystery. But today we are greeted by a flock of crows who are waiting tirelessly for the baby goats to die, those little animals who are grazing here with the playful passion which distinguishes these sun-loving animals. A man told us that Betancuria is like 'a village that has been beneath the sea. But without drowning.' And the same man also told me about how time passes here: 'It is as though time had stopped and we were clinging on to the hands of the clock.' Betancuria is a stopped clock.

It is in the very centre of the island, hanging up there, looking down; it was the religious and administrative capital of the island. In the fifteenth century it fell into the hands of the French coloniser Jean de Béthencourt, which is why it is called as it is; successive dominations have not managed to delete this first impression, of which all that remains is the skeleton of a convent.

But now Betancuria is no more than the shadow of its former self, of which it retains this convent and some other ecclesiastical relics, and the silence which will surely never leave it. The population, as we have said, is around five hundred people, and the silent, dry streets are filled with absences, except when tourists to Fuerteventura come in search of a souvenir of the earliest history of the island. And there are not so many souvenirs to take away.

From above, this closed valley is clearly visible as the strategic site which Béthencourt chose to protect his conquest, and you walk across the plain as though treading on history. You hear your footsteps on the stones, and you feel, when someone asks you a question, that the intimate, almost wild, sometimes savagely timid, character of the Canary Islanders turns these questions into what amounts to an examination of intimacy, a knife into the silence. It is better not to ask questions, to walk by without asking questions, not to scratch the silence with our impertinence, to walk by without anyone seeing you.

Canary Islanders don't like people asking them questions; the Canary Islander is definitely someone who wants to be intimate, but whose shyness is the defence of a form of separation, the Islander feels better alone, in his corner, looking at the floor, speaking with an inner mirror that will never let him down or abandon him; the Canary Islander is like one of Juan Rulfo's Mexican characters, like Juan Rulfo himself, in silence, hidden under the shade of his hat. This is something I saw in Betancuria above all.

Pérez Minik says, in his speech on the human condition of the Islanders, something sensible about our willingness to speak to foreigners and strangers and also about our willingness to remain in obstinate silence, the consequence of our refusal to make a free gift of our intimacy. He says, as he writes a kind of history of the (difficult) construction of our national character: 'The geographical conditions of our Islands made this kind of stagnation possible, made our calm possible, made the Garden of the Hesperides possible, the inheritance of our idyllic Guanche ancestors. If the Spanish had not arrived, then this state of affairs could have been prolonged infinitely and placidly.' This could not have been the case (luckily, I add now), because 'in order to protect themselves from these immense dangers to their physical and mental health, the Islanders had no other option than to exile themselves deliberately from their homeland and then return with the treasures they had gathered from their long journeys all over the world, or else to stay permanently in their paradise, calling upon the foreigner to come to visit them, and the more foreign the visitor the better, either to live together in friendship or else to keep a fertile debate in play, formed of hints and suspicions.'

Pérez Minik was a cosmopolitan, and the inheritor of a cosmopolitan tradition; his spiritual nourishment, in these islands sunk in their post-war isolation, was foreign radio (from Paris and London), foreign newspapers (*Le Monde*, above all), and his daily walks, which he made until he was an old man, out onto the pier at Santa Cruz de

Tenerife, whose large and small boats he knew by heart. From his attitude there arose his belief that the Islander, in general, relies on the arrival and departure of foreigners to the Islands, and from this fact arises his conviction, his cosmopolitan affirmation which fits alongside the spirit of the Canary Islanders, especially the inhabitants of the larger islands, the ones where the large capital cities are to be found, Santa Cruz de Tenerife and Las Palmas de Gran Canaria.

But the Islands are now calm; they are not sought after; as Pérez Minik says, the descendants of the former pirates now come here only as tourists. 'We must state,' Pérez Minik says, and I cannot be sure that he speaks without nostalgia, 'that in these days it is now difficult for other populations to come to the islands with a view to conquest, given the current economic climate, and we have no other recourse than to wait for the arrival of foreigners.'

The foreigners for whom we are waiting represent 'for our time, to the child of the archipelago who is trapped here definitively, the same as the Chinese did in later Japanese civilisation, or the Saxons in the development of Great Britain, or the Spanish in the conversion of the Islands themselves.'

BETANCURIA REPRESENTS DISTANCE ITSELF, A POINT THAT ONE REACHES only in order to travel through it; its situation as a space lusted after by the greed of the conquistadors is long behind it. Foreigners come and go, but they never stay; there is a provisional degree of noise and hubbub stirred up by them, just as there is for example in Taganana on Tenerife, but then silence once again fills the air . . .

The town of Betancuria, where we pause to eat a bit of cheese and drink something, lives off the visits of tourists; this, along with a little livestock farming, with whatever agriculture remains, is what provides the locals with any hope of survival. The survival of Betancuria depends on whether or not the tourists come to walk its streets, to see its monuments, to try to find among its stones something that even they cannot identify. But if the tourists don't come, then nothing at all will happen:

there is no custom of asking for help on the Islands. If there's cheese, and *gofio*, and *papas*, which taste so good here, then we can all struggle on, as the old men said to me as they waited at the house where the post was delivered: a few letters that are then shared out among the houses . . .

A GIRL, VANESA, TOLD ME THAT BETANCURIA WOULD ONE DAY BECOME a ghost town. 'Because not even old people will be here.' I'd heard this before. I heard it as soon as I arrived, when I came into Betancuria accompanied by the chattering of birds. It was a young man who works as a lifeguard in Pájara who said as much, José Hernández, the son of the local magistrate: 'And what if I get married, what then? I don't know, but it would be difficult to live in Betancuria.'

It would be difficult, but for the time being it is a pleasure. The houses are as old as the world, and one day they will collapse and there will be not a single trace that remains of Betancuria. A young student said so, pointing to one house in particular: 'Now it's nothing, but it will be a ruin soon as well.' There is something akin to an air of collapse in the midst of a music which the palm trees turn into the healthy monotony of a village asleep in their murmur.

At the top of Betancuria, where the crows were, the local magistrate José was coming to look at his flock. He said, with a laugh, that 'animals are better than people'; some you care for, some you judge. He has five hundred goats and their kids, and a few sad donkeys, grey and melancholy, as well as a camel which twists around nervously or flirtatiously, and it was as if we were in the midst of a fog that separated Betancuria from the rest of the world. Across from where we were looking at his collection of fauna, José pointed out the clarity of the air: 'there's not a single cloud in the sky,' he said, and it was true, and this clarity made the presence of the waiting birds even more ominous.

The magistrate's farm smells of cheese; we came into his yard and the noise of our feet on the gravel was for a time the only sound that had been heard in Betancuria for centuries. The donkeys looked at us with their inexpressive yet mysterious eyes, and we stroked the head of a kid as though we were greeting the whole of the traditional livestock of the Islands.

THE CAMELS—THOSE MYSTERIOUS ANIMALS WHICH AT SOME POINT WERE the standard means of transport for the whole of Fuerteventura—walk in a way that makes one unsure whether they are uncomfortable or flirtatious; one thing that is for sure is that they do not look out at us with the same nobility as the donkeys do, or even the horses, and I walk alongside them as though in their troubled gaze there were some kind of threat that is intensified by their large yellow teeth, the cruel zip of their mouth. José showed me a machine which allows goats to be milked automatically, while they listen to music; they relax and their milk is better, and there is more of it. So music can calm goats as well.

There was a sensation which I felt in Betancuria that one can feel in a number of villages that are high up in the hills, next to the clouds or next to silence: it is as though time has stopped; it is a feeling I have experienced in Arona on Tenerife; I have felt it in Teguise on Lanzarote, in Arucas on Gran Canaria; I have felt it in Valverde on El Hierro, and more than anything else I have felt it on La Gomera, in places like Chipude or Agulo, and one feels it strongly here as well, in Betancuria, as though Béthencourt the French adventurer were a contemporary of Franco. A young student of history told me that here this sense seems to be concentrated on the past, as though the goons and chieftains of the Franco period were still in charge, and that this is probably an illusion (or delusion), but the truth is that sometimes in Betancuria one has the impression that time has stopped and that you are travelling backwards, to meet with a universe that no longer exists in any other place, or even in reality. But the historian, who is from here, loves to return: it is, he says 'my place, my life, a paradise'.

José Luis took me to look at the monuments that were still around, the relics of this history which we still appeared to be living through. Some of the houses were ruined, some of them were closed and ransacked. But they still have—according to Doña Milagros, who has always lived here—the devil's tail! She says that according to the legend the hermitage at San Diego was built with stones carried by the devil as a penance, and when the task was done, he left behind the rope which they used to tie him up and his tail as well.

There is a sensation in Betancuria that time has stopped still. And there, lying on the white sofa at the entrance to his house, is one of Vicentito's crutches; Vicentito, whom everyone refers to as the ancient eyes of the village. He is more than eighty years old, friendly and uninhibited in his speech; one of his nephews, Paco, tells us that we're going to need several of the notebooks we have with us to record everything he's going to say. Vicentito is out at the moment, making his regular round of the neighbouring villages with the postman, whose name is Bernardo; when they get back they sit down to have breakfast together like comrades who share confidences at the same time as food. Their meeting has something about it of the atmosphere which Gabriel García Márquez found in the smaller villages of Colombia, and above all it contains elements of the attitude towards his correspondence of the colonel that nobody writes to. 'And what are we going to eat tomorrow?' 'Tomorrow, we eat shit.' The postman tells us that every day he delivers about one hundred and ninety letters, adverts, bank statements . . . There are only five or six families that still exchange letters, with Cuba, with Venezuela . . . The world does move, but it is as though it moved backwards in Betancuria.

VICENTE, WHICH IS A NAME IT FEELS ODD TO USE, RATHER THAN WHAT everyone else in the village calls him, Vicentito, says with a laugh that he is the head of the village. To him Betancuria has always looked as it does now, and he imagines it will carry on looking the same for ever. There is an air here, an air of resignation and of the past, as though time might crack if you tried to force it in either direction. Talking to the postman, Vicentito says that one of the signs that the village has not changed is that you still do not need to lock your door when you leave the house. This happens in some villages, but does not happen everywhere, and given that they lack other sources of pride, this is one of the sources of pride for the inhabitants of Betancuria. 'There will only be old people here one day,' Vicentito says with a laugh, 'and why would you want to rob old people? Old people don't have anything.' The young people left, and he left too, to go to the war with Franco's army; here he is, in a photograph: there they are, with the mayoress, who was his wife, standing next to the Generalissimo. He was a builder, but the best building here is the village itself, he says. 'People think that Betancuria has always been here, that it's old, the oldest village on Fuerteventura, but I remember the days back before there was electric light.'

Marta, a Colombian, walks over the stone pavements of Betancuria; she passes this way every day to get to the restaurant where she works, walking past the impressive church, the cathedral which looms over the village with a majesty that contains within it centuries of silence. Betancuria reminds her of the villages near Tolima in Colombia: the sense of peace, the little houses . . .

And it is as though we had moved into another world. 'It is as if time had stopped,' José Luis says, and as though we were hanging onto the hands of the clock. Something traps you and you want to come back. Here everything is different: time, personal relations, life. This is what I have to explain to my brother when he comes to visit. He comes from New York, from the world of new technologies, and probably doesn't really remember how things are here. It's as though we were a village at the bottom of the sea, but without drowning. It's the opposite of Tibet, which is so high up and where it's impossible to come down . . . We're at the bottom, and how do we go up?

A stationary paradise.

THE DANGEROUS CURVE

Unamuno said, José Luis reminds us, that Betancuria was like a whitewashed tomb. In the silence which reigns over it one can hear the strange sound of quiet places. The people who think that Betancuria is a paradise would miss there being a sound that connected it to the world. Some people believe that this would have been the work of César Manrique, the artist who saved Lanzarote.

But time caught up with César Manrique, a contemporary myth, in September of 1992, when a car took his life just as he was driving round a curve in his own car, next to the space where he collected all his invention and all his art, in Tahiche, Lanzarote.

And here we leave Betancuria, alone, in the majesty of its silence. A village that is an island hanging from the roof of the world, in a time that is defiant and placid as the donkeys who live there, as calm as the palm trees and the goats.

Let us leave Betancuria and think about César, a spectacular man, an artist who took an island and remodelled it until it was no longer an island but also the image of its recreator. César was an island.

Allow me to introduce him.

He was a visionary. Imagine him at dawn one day: almost seventy years old, in 1992, living in a landscape which he seemed to have invented. At this uncertain hour of the day, when the cool of the night has not yet passed to the warm air of salt and lava of Lanzarote, this man, with his clenched mouth and large eyes, the most active animal on the island, was already stretching on the cool stones in front of his house. This house, the one where he is at the moment, is his house in Haría, in the cloudy north of the island; he has gone there, after searching over the whole island, because this house gives him the melancholy and the loneliness which he now cannot find in Tahiche, where he built his first melancholy house among the volcanoes, the one that appears in every catalogue drawn up of wild and strange dwelling-places. Tahiche was a village, and still is; he discovered the open mouths of an extinct volcano, and thought that this was his territory, a space that had been invented for him. Under the earth, in the suffocating heat of a ground that was fire itself. And here he built his house, the joy of generations of artists whom he invited to come to visit him, as though he had managed to enclose the dream of an island underground. One day, when he was almost seventy, he abandoned this luminous and buried house and went to live in a larger place, much darker, where he could hunt for the comfort of his last years; this retirement from the world reminds me of Picasso's in his old age. There was something about this journey to the north, towards Haría, which was like César's farewell. But he did not close Tahiche, of course not, this volcanic site was like the root of his life.

And there, in Tahiche, his foundation has been set up; we can say that he is not truly dead; we can follow his itinerary and say that this is his foundation, and that he comes here every day, early, as though the sun rose with him.

IT IS EARLY, THEN, WHEN CÉSAR GETS UP AND WANDERS THE ISLAND, AS though he himself were waking it up. He wants to establish, at this time when the light is still uncertain, a relationship of gratitude between the earth and the day; it is his way of praying: getting up early. And his relationship with life is one of gratitude. Everything is ordered in his house, and he leaves the house as though he had fulfilled a pact that he had agreed with sleep: to sleep in order to live. He would prefer to be always awake, his huge eye fixed on life as night fell, and he prepared to hang himself from sleep just as birds hang themselves from threads of light. To play a little, he opens the lid of the piano and sounds out a few arpeggios; to play a little, because the piano is not for him, a friend has come, or will come, who needs the piano to express himself or to brighten up the slow afternoons in Haría; but César just likes putting his hands on the piano, making music, picking out a few notes so that Corcho, his dog, a beautiful Labrador, thinks that his master is talking to ghosts.

And so César gets out of bed and leaves the house's large bedrooms, says a joyous hello to Corcho, his friendly and well-mannered dog, who sees him at a distance with the grandiose indifference which is the property of all melancholic dogs, and Corcho gets up slowly to come and meet his master, walking over the gravel that separates the house from his kennel. César gives him a kiss and laughs, that's my dog, that's my Corcho, and Corcho is grateful for the hug with which César celebrates all the life that surrounds him; the dog licks his cheeks, runs around him, returns the caresses that his master gives; in the midst of this recent dawn silence, the man and the dog look as though they are trying out dance steps, happy but also lazy . . . César is a happy man who does his morning exercises.

He has found *nopales*, cacti, in the luminous kitchen, as well as milk and cold water; he peeled the *nopales* the evening before; they are always there, like a greeting that he himself has prepared for himself, a breakfast with life to it; he is vitality and lightness itself, he is ready for the joys that the day will bring, and he eats and drinks as though this were the first time in his life he had eaten or drunk, because life begins anew every day, he says, and one needs to celebrate the fact that everything is always starting again. And so he starts his life, then returns to the piano—if only I knew how to play, he says— then touches the book he is reading, as though objects had a life of their own that they will live while he's out of the house, when he's in Tahiche, the house which is like a root to him. I found this book there, a book of poems, after César's death; the book was open at a particular page, I picked it up and then put it back down again, as

though César were going to come back to touch the silent keys of
that piano.

BUT LET US GO BACK TO THAT DAY, WHEN THE ARTIST IS GETTING READY
to live through all the hopes and dreams of this particular day in September, a day, as his Peruvian namesake César Vallejo said, that one
remembers before it starts . . . The car is outside, he looks out at the
spectacular hillsides of Haría and listens to the cocks crowing, but
above all, from the hollow where his house is set, he appreciates the
persistent breeze which makes the few remaining hairs on his shiny
head wave a little; his head is a noble sphere which he strokes as
though he wanted to stroke his entire personality as well, the site of
his thoughts and dreams, the violent conjunction of harmony and revolution which gives life to his solitude and his nights, his parties and
his melancholia. His heart is everywhere, and at the moment he feels
his heart in his head.

When he starts the car and feels the strength of the engine under
his feet, the Jaguar in which he is about to cross the island as he does
every day, the image of the Universal Expo in Seville comes suddenly
into his mind, a spot where they have an exhibition of his work—we
are now in 1992—but why should he travel to see it, I imagine him
thinking, for the first time affected by the melancholy that accompanies travelling or any kind of effort: why travel so much, why do so
much, why not stay here, in this little spot filled with silence and calm,
why not just be Corcho for a while, or even for ever; the dog looks at
him. He has made his Haría house for this purpose, so that the war-
rior of the island can rest, like Picasso looking for an escape from his
melancholy in Vauvenargues.

There are other images that pass through his mind, among them
one in particular, the image of his house in Tahiche, where he started
to calm the volatility of his genius, where he became a real artist.
Tahiche, thousands of square metres laid out under the lava, a fig tree
in the middle of it all, reds and blacks, a swimming pool among all

the lava, a skylight to make the light that picks out the bedrooms more natural, his huge dark bedroom, black sheets, the pleasure of touching life itself; he needed the darkness of love, a degree of melancholy, bodies walking naked through the white rooms, figs in the kitchen, a hint of music coming from the dark rooms. But one has to carry on, and one has to travel between Haría and Tahiche, to look through papers to find old memories which give some sort of meaning to what he is planning . . .

He cannot go and leave this island without his voice speaking up against those who would destroy the work which he has spent so much time patiently building up, to turn the whole island of Lanzarote into a marvel of red, white and black; he has to stay here; he is a witness and his words are whips that warn people about what could happen to this landscape if it were left alone, if there were no one to defend it. He is the shield of the island. He invented it, if one can put it like that; he invented Lanzarote, because it used to be nothing more than a piece of land and now it is the right eye of the archipelago, a place which attracts speculators from all over the world, people who come to speculate with this beauty that is rigorous, and clear and extraordinary, in which the air twists and turns, perhaps ecstatic at its own eternal perfection. He looks up at the sky, it is always cooler in Haría, and there are clouds now, the clouds of autumn, dawn has broken already . . .

Every time he recalls the previous poverty of the island, poor at a time when everyone was poor and all the islands were humble, César imagines himself sitting down with Pepín Ramírez who at that time, back in the 1970s, was the President of the Lanzarote local government, both of them sitting on the edge of a cave which back then was nothing, a hole in the ground, just another hole in the volcanic soil of Lanzarote, a passageway left there by the fire. César was a young abstract artist who had just come back from his adventures in New York, and also from a personal tragedy, because his wife had just died. Pepín and César were friends and each of them listened to the fantasies of the other, and César had just come back from a long journey and must have had at least something to say.

César was having one of his most exuberant days that day, for him the world seemed to be filled with marvels, and Lanzarote was one of them. What, this poor island? This poor island is one of the wonders of the world, César said. Now as he starts up his heavy car in order to drive through the Cactus Garden, a kind of living symbol of the dryness of the island, César remembers the foundational moment for what one might call César's Lanzarote.

He was not an architect; he wasn't even a landscape artist; he was an artist plain and simple, a vitalist who had experienced in New York the vision which sometimes dominates the dreams of every immigrant: to return to his native land in order to make it into a work of art, in order to turn it into the greatest place in the world. And this was what César said to Pepín.

'Pepín, we're not going to be wretched our whole lives.'

'. . .'

'We are going to start making Lanzarote the most beautiful island in the world. Will you help me?'

PEPÍN WOULD DO WHATEVER CÉSAR SAID HE SHOULD DO, AND WHAT César offered him was a fantasia on the Lanzarote which he could now see from the car which drove him slowly, heavily, down the road; the car in which he travelled with a certain degree of internal joy, as though he were travelling across a work of art which had no frame and which was not a sculpture, and didn't even fit in the memory of any single man: the island of Lanzarote. The mountain over there is luminous; Lanzarote is always like that, like a shadow that had been born from the earth in order to head up to the sun or to the infinite, although the old clouds of night grow complex over the shadows of the palm trees in the headstrong presence of the glowing embers of the salt water. The artist who made the island looks down at all the efforts the local inhabitants made in order to help him to create the genial harmony which is what now makes this island, this island which used to be, when he and Pepín agreed to refound it, nothing more than a wasteland which evoked the word 'misery' as though it were a wretched glove laid over the real island.

First of all came this cave, the Jameos del Agua, and then the Cueva de los Verdes, a kind of spectacular natural prospecting of the lava underneath the earth, and then came the mysterious, overwhelming path of Timanfaya, the black and red park caused by the eruptions in the middle of the island, which created a new landscape, a future which seemed like the future of poverty and which is now a landscape of an almost airy, musical beauty. And then there come back to the memory of the artist as he retraces the origins of his version of the island other facts which turned Lanzarote into his pride and his greatest memory, and just at the moment when his tired eyes look at the island's nascent sea, his memory returns to the Mirador del Río, across the strait from the island of La Graciosa, where he imagined the Basque writer Ignacio Aldecoa in his fight for life, the life of this novelist who reinvented the lonely island, a kind of fist made of sand in which César also saw a reproduction of the perfect islands, and in the Mirador del Río César offered an explanation of the reasons why he carried on covering the island with new attractions; we need people to come to visit, because the Islands are not trying to become virgin territory, but we don't want there to be too many people coming; this is a delicate island, it can't get filled with cars, with people and hamburger joints; what we have to do is create the need here for people to come and travel through the landscape.

But now, as he travels through the landscape, it is 1992, and the island is overflowing, with cars, with people, with smoke, with freeways. This makes him feel both angry and exhausted; he wants to fight against it, and so he has created the Fundación César Manrique, which is where he is headed today, where he goes every day, even though today is Friday and why not stay at home in Haría painting in this house which he has set up for his last years. But he has never been able to stay still, never, not since he was a child, when his parents took him to the vast and stimulating beach at Famara, facing La Graciosa, underneath the Mirador del Río. This was his sea, these were his rocks, a beach filled with wind and with salt, there, in the restaurant which looks out onto a boat that sank so many years ago that it now resembles a sculpture made by time and rust . . . this was the beach were César ran 'like a mad goat': he was Lanzarote, but Lanzarote, more than anything, was this young beach where he had run as a child.

And this is the Fundación César Manrique, in Tahiche; this is his day-house, if one can put it like that; it was here that the light was born which César wanted to gift to himself; like Chillida before Chillida invented the mountain of light, César made the light of Lanzarote out of lava, out of the heart of lava. This is the result of his quest, his pride: his former house, the house of a madman who felt the enlightenment of colours, the summary of his work of love and friendship; Lanzarote is his space, and the house was his refuge, and now he seeks refuge in Haría, with Corcho and the piano, and the fig trees. Here in Tahiche are his paintings, his projects which he has created in almost all the islands, the collections of other people's work which he has put together and which are now the kernel of an extraordinary collection of abstract art, made at the movement's moment of greatest euphoria in the 1960s and 1970s.

Here it is, and here he comes, to see what it contains, to walk from one side of the old house to the other, the old house which is no longer his house but rather his memory; he travels its labyrinths again, he looks at the poem which his old friend Rafael Alberti dedicated to him, and he sits in the shadow of the fig tree which was the symbol of this house and the symbol of the whole of Lanzarote itself. The ancient sound of the lava is over his head, and in this solitude, so far from the noise that one would tend to associate with such an active man, the soul of his best memories and his chief melancholy flies overhead: his melancholy is that life should not be eternal, that he is not able to be alive forever, to gift life forever. This morning he designs new places—in Puerto de la Cruz, in Tenerife, in El Hierro, in La Gomera; in El Puerto he has successfully created a new coast, as though he were capable of defying the sea, which beats on the coast here like the hand of God—he receives commissions to transform them into more beautiful corners of the world, just as he transformed Lanzarote. But it is late now; by the end of the morning of 25 September 1992 he had given everything he could give that day, and it was time for him to return home, to the piano and Corcho's willing and puzzled back. Before he goes, he speaks to Pepe Juan's son, his godson, the grandson of Pepín:

'I'll bring you the picture of the camel this afternoon.'

And so here is César, this vital man, filled with enthusiasm, stepping once again into his car, where music and solitude are like an air of the earth, pressing the ignition button, driving to the no-man's-land where the freeways end and which he knows well as though he had seen them in a nightmare, but he cannot see, he cannot see as well as he used to, and his tired eyes don't warn him about the world coming to throw itself upon him, this end that is approaching, and when he is finally finished, finished forever, then a blanket of grief and confusion falls over the island, César is dead, the accident was terrible, no one can believe it, there, just next to the Fundación, where he always told people to drive carefully, another car killed him, he didn't realise it was coming, his eyes, his eyes aren't as good as they once were . . . He died on that day, on 25 September 1992, a day I always remember . . .

In Lanzarote, César, the visionary, was everything. Just now, while I was in Fuerteventura, a rapid memory of salt and earth brought that day in September 1992 back to my mind, as though it were only yesterday. He was everything for Lanzarote. César was everything, a lighthouse, a beacon for the Islands.

LANZAROTE IS A PERFECT METAPHOR FOR A STRANDED ISLAND, SURrounded by the cleanest of possible atmospheres, looked at by a calm sky like blue lead. It holds in its bosom a perfect combination of every single natural element, which sometimes coexist in a single space, just like the water which the lava ploughs through in Los Jameos, or the power of the earth, harmonious and surprising, in the Montaña del Fuego, or Timanfaya. I remember one day there, with Günter Grass, the German Nobel Prizewinner: in the face of these sand-built rocks, the writer (and painter) asked us to stop the bus, got out, took out his pencils and started to draw the plastic result of the lava's actions like someone doing a court-side sketch of the beginning of the world. And here his friend, José Saramago, would walk as if flying, and the air was sketched out by the ancestral whistling of mysterious birds; the air is like the most transparent place on earth, and here it is in all its fullness. Here is the air that Saramago thought they would never be able to take away from him, not even after his death. And this is the air they have in Femés, a village up in the mountains, where the writer Rafael Arozarena found the materials he needed for the earthly inspiration of his poetic novel *Mararía*, which was born from a dream, perhaps from the survival instinct of Lanzarote itself. Carlos Fuentes came here to see if it was true, what Breton said of Tenerife: Lanzarote is also a surrealist island. And when Susan Sontag's *The Volcano Lover* was published in Spanish, she came to see Saramago so that he could show her the mysterious sound of the Timanfaya volcano.

Lanzarote is the remains of a volcano. Between 1730 and 1736 it underwent the largest eruption in its history; the lava flowed down and buried several villages in what is now the Timanfaya National Park. Thirty-five craters exploded and their rain of fire and lava buried a third of the island's surface: the most fertile third. In one of the holes which had sunk into the lava, César Manrique would one day build his house. And here, in the middle of this wasteland which the lava had left behind, I have seen Susan Sontag fascinated because the heat of the earth is enough for one to fry an egg in a hole dug in the volcanic sand; a huge cauldron of boiling water was later to frighten her, as the author of *The Volcano Lover* saw the spectacles which the passage of this devastating sheet of fire that helped create the island again left behind it. Aldecoa left a description of it in writing: 'Tao, dragon, Timanfaya, fire mountain. Tinecheyde, hell mountain. The massive mythology of volcanoes is something that spills over into the place names of the island. The tremble that might signify awakening sometimes runs over the island, the shiver of morning fright at the idea of the first day, the signs that the earth is about to wake up. Huge cracks open in the ground and the fire is born from them. You only need to dig down about a foot to find that the earth is burning. Pits of water boil and bubble: Satan, who has been put in charge of finding proofs for the ignorant and the faithless, keeps a close and malicious eye on them.' The presence of the volcanoes lighting up the peaceful earth while a song, perhaps something by The Doors, plays in the background, is a majestic presence to the contemporary mind. In contrast, Aldecoa's mind received the following message: 'Fire mountain is beaten by the winds. Neither the winds nor the years have managed to cool the mountain down. When it rains, the mountain is veiled in water vapour.' It is a question of temperament, Aldecoa says. The mountain's temperament, the temperament of Timanfaya, the temperament of Lanzarote itself.

Lanzarote is an island that walks by itself; it is as though it is laughing at time itself. Conquered land, there is a monument in Teguise like a colonial Castilian castle right next to the continent of Africa. The Janubio saltworks is a ghostly site, like the remains of some sea lying on the ground, a surrealist sight which fascinated one of the greatest Canary Island writers of the twentieth century, Agustín Espinosa, the author of *Lancelot*. And, in the mythology of the Lanzarote landscape one also comes across La Geria, a large county completely covered in volcanic ash, planted largely with vines and figs and other fruit trees. As a place for growing food, La Geria is an outlier. As a space, as a monument or a place with a focus, it is something special. It was an archbishop's fault: after the eruption of Timanfaya, which buried a great deal of the arable land of Lanzarote, he ordered that holes be made in the ash and lava in order to recover or uncover the land and get back to planting in it. As they did this, the farmers discovered that the volcanic rock retained the morning dew and this allowed them to develop an entirely original method of cultivating their land: which consists in carrying the quarried rock (or *rofe*, as they call it on Lanzarote, just as they call it *zahorra* on Tenerife) to the areas that have not been covered by lava, and laying it down there before planting. Semicircular structures of rock, which also protect the vines and fig trees from the wind, give a great deal of beauty to this landscape. This is where the malmsey is made which Nelson tried after his Tenerife defeat, and which Falstaff drank in Shakespeare's play: the cosmopolitan connections of an extraordinary island.

I WAS TRAVELLING FROM BETANCURIA TO CORRALEJO, TO ILLUMINATE myself with the blinding light of the beaches that look out to Lobos, the loneliest island, and Lanzarote. From here one can see two islands successively, one is a lizard that looks a little like a smaller version of Fuerteventura, and the other one holds itself upright, black and majestic, like a sleeping volcano. I am on the beach; this is where the dunes have made themselves urban, but they still maintain their own light. When you climb up them and see the sea close up, it's as though you have made a journey towards a pure beauty, the pure beauty of Fuerteventura's metaphors.

As I left, on a plane once again, to travel to Tenerife, I made some notes. Fuerteventura is the image of vastness, of the sky, of the earth, of the sea. Of the air.

And this is a sensation which you perceive everywhere, especially from the Cofete viewpoint, which is where the air turns round.

Fuerteventura. Let us turn back for a moment. There are sensations in the air which I do not want to lose. A desert like the desert at the end of the world, the sensation that you are living in a novel by Unamuno or Cormac McCarthy . . . The index finger of the archipelago, pointing towards Africa and moving away from Gran Canaria in order to come closer to Lanzarote and the wind. Beaten by the air which seems to be made out of sand, and which is sometimes violent, like an eternal whirlpool, it is a clean island, as though a hand were stripping it clean every night in order to make it even more deserted, more uninhabited. Forced into the interior by its history, it is in

Betancuria where the island's silence lives, and its greenery is preserved in La Oliva. Professor Brian Morris from the University of Cal-
ifornia, who studied the surrealist movement in the Islands, told me
that when he reached Betancuria he felt as though he were at that moment the only inhabitant of the island; that his voice was the only
echo up there. In La Oliva he felt, as I felt too, that he had reached an
oasis, but that the desert was its destiny. On the coast, from Gran
Tarajal to Jandía, the beaches are the permanent quintessence of this
island which bids you farewell and then returns, and is never the same
because the wind continually moves it.

It is as flat as Lanzarote, and its undulating movements seem to
be bodies sculpted by Henry Moore. Although its agriculture has been
elusive, beaten down by the sandy wind, the Islanders have sharpened
their imagination and found ways to survive off their livestock and
its products: cheese, meat; they also eat the fish of the sea. The cheese
of Fuerteventura, just like that of La Palma, or El Hierro, or the Flor
de Guía cheese from Gran Canaria . . . One cannot leave the Islands
without a piece of this cheese and a glass of wine.

And here, I have said already, Miguel de Unamuno lived out his
exile; it was from here that he set off for Paris, from the dryness of
the island to the damp of the Encyclopédie; to Paris from Puerto
Cabras, which was what they called Puerto del Rosario until 1957. A
land of contrasts, Fuerteventura holds its whole way of looking at the
world in Puerto de Rosario: here is its beaten topology, dampened by
the vibrant sea, young and almost insolent. The island itself is an
index finger held up to the wind.

AN ISLAND UNDER CLOUDS

NOW, AS I AM GOING TO WRITE ABOUT TENERIFE, WHERE I WAS BORN, there comes to my mind like an unpublished image, insistent and marvellous, something never before photographed, and never before seen. It was late afternoon in August 2009, and I was returning to the island from Madrid via the northern airport, Los Rodeos. You couldn't see the island; you could only see the clouds: they were red, still, immense, infinite, mysterious; I saw them from the aeroplane as though it were for the first time in my life, or at least the first time I had wanted to see them. Like many people, I am scared of flying, and I have always tried to avoid sitting in a window seat as I fly. On the window side of the aeroplane your proximity to the abyss can make you behave rashly, and I had grown accustomed to taking a central or aisle seat, but I was less crowded in my part of the aeroplane this day and I plucked up the courage to take a look out into the abyss, and I saw Tenerife . . . Drowned, submerged, an island beneath the clouds.

It was a fascinating vision.

It was a summer evening, around nine o'clock, twenty-one minutes before the plane was to land in the middle of a particularly clouded, perhaps the most clouded, part of the island, near La Laguna, the first university city of the island, the place where I had studied, next to the Monte de las Mercedes, near Mount Esperanza, on the foothills of Mount Teide, without any doubt at all the highest mountain on the whole archipelago. A guardian of the Islands, a dormant volcano which one ascends in an almost ritual fashion, in order to confirm that the mountain is strong, powerful and tall, filled with veins and colours, beaten by a wind that is at times frigid and at times hot but which never manages to dominate the mountain.

BUT NONE OF THIS WAS THERE TO BE SEEN. ALL YOU COULD SEE WAS THE red cloud, the sea of clouds which completely covered this part of the island. Little by little, as though a figure of authority were forcing its way through a crowd, Mount Teide emerged from the red and white landscape, monotonous but fascinating, and now what could be seen of the island was this black and red peak, a kind of fist held up to the sky, as André Breton called it when he came here to see it in 1935.

It was, I will admit, an extraordinary moment, a rediscovery. I was alone in the aeroplane, was reading something, any old thing, a newspaper; I had books lying by me, poems, and I was well provided for by my own memory; I was remembering, as happens when one lands in a plane, other landscapes of the island, the things I was going to see, a good meal, the laughter of my friends, the familiar sensations evoked by a return to the place where one was born, but this way of returning to the island was for me entirely new. Everything conspired together to make it exceptional, first of all the weather: it had been hot the last few days, and the island was burning in the sun, perhaps because the whole world, or at least Madrid, which was where I was travelling from, was burning too, as we were right in the middle of summer; but this particular part of Tenerife had clouds squatting over it, and the sun, which had heated the earth throughout the day, seemed to have departed, leaving behind a spark of fire to which the clouds were testimony, refreshing the space into which the aeroplane was going to fire itself like a shell.

What happened were several minutes of ecstatic contemplation, and the evocation of this and of other landscapes: then I wondered if I would ever be able to see the island again from this perspective, with these red clouds; a lot of coincidences would need to fit together, among others the idea that I would return from a journey at this hour of night and that I would look once again through the window next to me, and that my eyes would be able to capture in all its variety the spectacle that I have just tried to note down for you here on paper.

This will never happen again, because no island is the same as any other, and because the island (not this island, and not any island) is never the same as itself, just as man is never identical to himself, man being an island in and of himself, and never the same as he was the instant previously; a dune is always a different dune, constantly different; the sea is always changing, every second; the mountains hold one colour and then another; and it is clear that people change from one moment to the next, and I am not the same man who saw the red clouds hanging over my island.

This joy in change is one of the most notable expressions of the nature of the landscape; greenery is not a landscape, as Francesc said, that Catalan student of urban development, the man who was eating fish soup in Puertito de la Cruz; landscape is tectonics. This is what César believed and what Unamuno believed too, and I would be willing to bet that Aldecoa believed the same. Landscape is hidden inside clouds, inside what changes, what makes imperceptible changes: landscape is not greenery. I am writing this now in El Médano, in the south of Tenerife, and the wind is blowing, and all around me there is sea and sand, and this spectacular confluence of ungraspable elements is what makes up the landscape.

Landscape is not greenery.

Well. That is why I spent so long looking down from above, as though I were going to stay hanging there in space forever, seeing how the island is while it is not there. Lewis Carroll has a magnificent phrase: 'She tried to fancy what the flame of a candle is like after the candle is blown out.' That day I had the chance, along with all the passengers who were looking out of their windows on the same plane, to check what the truth of this phrase is, using Tenerife as its protagonist: what the island is like when it is not there, or when it is buried by the strange magnificence of clouds.

Is the island there, are the clouds there? The land is very often the same thing as the clouds, something cloudy which hides behind the cotton-like mystery of the sky; one describes what one remembers of the land and very often this includes the clouds; I feel, talking about this and about other islands, as though I were myself hanging among clouds, describing a reality that at times is tangible but which many times is also simply a sentimental reality, within which one has never stopped living, even though one might have left the island a thousand times and come back a thousand times, even though one might have landed in the middle of this dreamlike landscape only once, this landscape which can be remembered only in fragments of memory, which is never described, only remembered. Samuel Beckett, talking of his homeland of Ireland from abroad, said: 'I thought I had left the island; poor fellow; the island can never be left, it always travels with you.'

And so the most tangible thing I found among the clouds was perhaps this, that the island travels with me, like the island that always accompanied the author of *Waiting for Godot*.

IT IS ODD THAT SAMUEL BECKETT SHOULD HAVE COME UP WITH THIS quote on the memory of the island; many years ago, on one of my annual ascents of Mount Teide, lying in my bed in its calm, handsome, fortunate hotel, I read a book by this sceptical, angry Irish writer, and I came across this phrase which every islander, myself of course, could apply to his own relationship with the isolated terrain on which he was born. And then I sat up in bed and looked out of the window, as though reading Beckett had been some kind of spring that impelled me to confirm my physical relationship with the landscape, with the physical island itself, not just with the mental island that us islanders have forever embedded in our mind and in our souls. I looked out of the window at the rocks, the lava, the stolid Teide, a mountain that is young but still ancient, majestic, looking down arrogantly from its peak that has been scarred by the ancient eruptions that took place in its now silent crater.

I looked out over the cavernous rock formations, down to the geological constructions that tourists have, with good reason, photographed a million times or more, and I focussed my imagination and my eyes on Llano de Ucanca, where all the shades of all the colours alternate, where Raquel Welch filmed the movie *One Million Years BC*, where UFO hunters and other oddballs claim that aliens and flying saucers come down to land, or at the very least spirits which come down to the earth via the Teide valley. I looked out there as though I could touch the place, as though I were touching an essence, the essence of the island.

THE TRUTH IS THAT UP HERE, MORE THAN NINE THOUSAND FEET ABOVE sea level, the silence is overwhelming; just as the stars are overwhelming at night, just as the sun is overwhelming when on hot days it lays itself over your head like a mantle of hot lava. Albert Camus spoke about the exceptional silence of the beach where *L'Étranger* took place. Up there, where I had just read this phrase of Beckett's, the island is an exceptional silence, like the earth, a reflexive silence, where the earth is still and it is your footsteps which break the extraordinary harmony which surrounds you; here you can abandon yourself, think that the world has decided to make a pause in its journey and has left you to the mercies of whatever the landscape wishes to do to you. You can see here the poetic peculiarity of Mount Teide: there are millions of mountains in the world, and there must be many that are more beautiful; there may be many that are better preserved because back in the 1970s this mountain had a wound inflicted on it which has never yet healed: a cable car that takes people all the way up to the base of the crater . . . There is the cable car, like a small embarrassment to which the mountain has become accustomed; I went up in it once. What is clear is that speed diminishes the mountain, takes its solemnity away, puts it on the same vulgar level of the men who go up and down and say that the mountain's not up to much, that anyone can climb it. No, not anyone can climb it, because this is a mountain that has to be climbed on foot: that is the tradition, and that is also what this incredible landscape requires of you, to dominate it on foot, as you would have done in the past . . .

There are more beautiful mountains and better conserved ones, but this is our mountain. My mother never climbed Mount Teide. She looked up at it from the La Orotava valley, that spot where, as legend has it, Alexander von Humboldt fell down in submission; but she looked at the mountain with the eyes of the island's first inhabitants, like a mythical mountain which passed on secret signals to the inhabitants: for her the snow, which always stood on it during the winter, signified love and Christian behaviour, but its mere presence meant protection and respect. For the first inhabitants of the Islands the volcano also meant refuge, and fear: fear of the eruptions, of the fire, but the fire was also what was attractive about the mountain; it was like mother earth, and now it is the mother mountain. I do not know if it is true that Humboldt fell to the ground when he saw the valley and wept at the virginal beauty of the sight; I do know, because he wrote it down, just as he did not write down that he fell to his knees on seeing the valley, that Mount Teide made a huge impression on him, that he deliberately disembarked from the boat that was taking him to America in order to evaluate the qualities and characteristics of the volcano. But in any case, whether Humboldt bowed his head or not in the face of such majesty, Mount Teide marks the authority of the island, is its fundamental symbol, its light and its darkness, and so it is not at all strange that the ghostly vision which I had as I returned to the island by plane should have contained within it this generous but abrupt element, the peak of the mountain, in the concrete vision which I had of Tenerife. And it is not strange either that it should have been on Mount Teide that I read Beckett's definition of the island as an eternal fellow traveller, which always, right up to the hour of our death, stops us seeing clearly the inner landscape from which our souls and minds and even bodies derive.

AND SO WE HAVE NOW LANDED, ALTHOUGH WE MANAGED TO SET FOOT on Mount Teide from the air. I was born in the north, in Puerto de la Cruz, the city which Oscar Wilde's father found charming, which was approved of by Agatha Christie, Bertrand Russell, Winston Churchill and André Breton, amongst others, but now I live semi-permanently in the south, which until the 1970s was like an inhabited desert, a place segregated from the rest of the island by abrupt hills which could only be crossed by sinuous roads which helped maintain the mystery of the place but which increased all distances. A freeway—the Southern Freeway, like the title of Julio Cortázar's famous story—broke this curse, if one can call it that, and joined the cloudy north of the island with the dry south, on a route that goes from Santa Cruz, the capital of the island, to Guía de Isora, in the deepest south; the southern beaches—in particular, El Médano in Grenadilla de Abono, and Las Américas, in Arona and Adeje—had attracted local holiday-makers for decades; the freeway and the subsequent hotel development revealed these southern beaches to foreigners as well, and suddenly, in little more than thirty years, the northern primacy was broken and the south started to consolidate itself, economically, as the most powerful part of the island. If one climbed up to a high vantage point, the top of Mount Teide, for example, and were able to see the whole island, the north and the south, and were able to draw a line which divided the landscape in two, then we would have a perfect indication of what it is that divides the north from the south here and in the world in general; the north is leafy, fertile (plants grow here, flowers and banana trees and tomatoes and all kinds of fruit), while the south is a wasteland which can still give the more difficult kind of crop, palm trees and tomatoes, but which is largely a dry area, the place where sun and sand go to hide . . .

Tenerife is a space that is cut in two, and it was even more divided years ago, before the freeway which both divides it and brings it together. To one side it is green, to the other side it is dry. I have already said what I thought of that urban landscape where I ate soup; and I think that here my feelings are similar: the south is a landscape and the north is a landscape, in one of them the only important thing is the tectonics, and in the north the geology is covered with greenery . . . The green north, the dry south. Tradition meant that things were the same for centuries and centuries: wealth on one side and drought-derived poverty on the other, almost a biblical curse on the south of the island.

Now that the curse is broken, if we can put it like that, the unequal division between the trees and the desert has been broken. The south is still the south, with all its characteristics, all its shrub-land beaten down by the sun and the wind, as in El Médano, where I am writing this passage, and the north is still the green expanse it was when Humboldt expressed his ecstasy in the face of the botan-ical beauties of the valley, which was the nucleus of his experience of the island. But the south has taken its revenge, and that part which once seemed lost, a desert facing an ocean, is now cultivated land, cultivated largely by tourism; there were always banana trees and other plants which were sown in defiance of the climate and its consequences, but the true wealth of the south has come from its arid landscape which, while arid, is still calm and sunny; tourists in search of sun have made this part of the world a refuge, a place for the sea and for silence; the north was, and still is, a landscape which Mount Teide beautified from above, and which the greenery beautified with a particularly concrete kind of softness, the softness which Humboldt saw, but the north is no longer the only destina-tion for tourists, who have found in the abrupt crenellations of the desert a special kind of attraction, one to which I myself succumbed as well when I first discovered El Médano, about forty years ago, when I was still a young man and came to this fishing town with my parents, this town which has become a symbol of what the south gives its visitors: the beach, sand and practically nothing else apart from air, a dry wind which at night turns into a violent cold caress.

BUT LET US START IN THE NORTH, WHICH IS OBLIGATORY; IT IS WHERE I come from, it is for me, perhaps, the island, or the part of the island that Samuel Beckett spoke of: the part that you never escape from. I want to speak about the soul of this place before travelling through, as best I can, the memory of this island which I saw from above as a sea of red clouds.

The north, which for centuries was a reference point for travellers, is green and silent and naval and exuberant; it has lived for a long time calmly confined underneath a sea of clouds which filter the Atlantic sun until it blinds you with the quality of its light. The place where I saw the island for the first time, in my childhood, was an uneven symphony of banana trees and cheap houses, round a cliff where children and adolescents would go to look for scrap metal. The adults, men and women, got up early in the morning to water their plants, water their bananas or tomatoes, and many of them worked all day to pack their fruit into enormous warehouses where their produce would arrive entirely *au natural*, without having been cleaned at all; there, in the warehouses, it was all prepared. This work was a kind of prelude to the only source of income that there was in the Islands, which were divided between the poverty of the many and the wealth of the few, the *caciques* who had always been rich, and the nobles who had only recently become so. Tourism did away with a great deal of the poverty, and the wealthy were now not only those who owned the arable land, but also those who owned the plots by the beaches, first of all in the north and later in the south.

My family lived right in the heart of what Humboldt had seen; back then, from above, from what would later become Humboldt's viewpoint, in the shade of the La Orotava mountains, all that could be seen was green, the green of the banana trees, and some paths; at the end of the 1940s, when I was born, the land still looked like the steep and exotic greenscape which the German scientist had studied. But then the foreigners started to come. At the beginning of the twentieth century there was one hotel that people could go to in the north,

the Hotel Taoro in Puerto de la Cruz, which was in the middle of the
national park which bore its name, the Taoro Park. Here there also
started to appear private houses which reflected the economic situation of their owners, who were the masters of lands and plantations.
This was how tourism entered into Tenerife, and one can perhaps say
that this was the entry point for tourism into the whole of this Atlantic
archipelago.

Even today the Taoro park maintains the stately decorum of previous years. The existence in its heart of an Anglican church, which
was also there back in the days when Spain was much more cohesively
Catholic, back in the Francoist dictatorship, gives some idea of how
tourism influenced the development of the island and how it became
ingrained in the customs of the Islands. This air of polite cohabitation
which the church shows, this metaphor, is complemented by the
stately air of the buildings, which is connected in La Orotava and in
certain streets of Puerto de la Cruz, and in other places such as
Tacoronte, Garachico or Icod de los Vinos, with the signs of a period
of great wealth that occurred because of successful agricultural trade.

Taoro Park has always seemed to me, out of all these buildings
and all these places, the one that best embodies the idea of perfect
peace. Still today there is a hotel there, the hotel Taigaga, which keeps
to some degree the distinction of older hotels in the Islands and in the
world as a whole; regular clients are received as though they were a
part of the history of the establishment itself. The Taigaga was
founded by a German family, the Taigs; it has just celebrated its fiftieth
birthday. When I started writing the book I was sitting out on the
hotel terrace, looking out at the invariable beauty of Mount Teide. I
suppose that over the past fifty years thousands and thousands of
travellers have felt this same excitement, under the sun or under the
clouds, under the stars or under the moon, which I felt that morning,
looking at the way in which my land exerts the same fascination as
always, even though men have put concrete in the exact place where
Humboldt only saw greenery.

BUT IT IS NOT JUST THIS PLACE THAT IS THE NORTH OF MY CHILDHOOD. It was the north of the lizards, of the uncultivated lands, of the mountains that had been eviscerated in order to dig for *zahorra* or sand for building works, it was the north of trees and birds' nests, of goats and cows, of the silence that went alongside you as you walked to the little school lost among the banana trees.

It was the north of *gofio* and cheese, of salt fish; it was the north of the sea beating incessantly against the rocks on the Martiánez beach, one of the most beautiful and sudden beaches of all the islands, where the speed of the sea and the narrowness of the stretch of sand turns a simple bathe into a struggle against the violence of the waves, against the speed of its flowing and its riptides; bathing here meant being bathed by a powerful hand, in the south it was the hand of the wind, and in the north it was the hand of the sea.

Now that I have gone back to live there, up in the cliffs above a beach which looks like this one from my childhood, El Socorro beach in Los Realejos, I have heard the sound of this sea, insistent and powerful; for years, so that people would feel safer, they hung a rope out into the sea so that the bathers had something to hold on to, and this part of the beach at Martiánez was known as the Charco de la Soga, the Rope Pool. The requirements of safety, and probably a desire to make more money from this abrupt and beautiful beach, steep and difficult, surrounded by caves that evoke the caves of the ancient Guanches, led the authorities to ask César Manrique to design a plan to make the space less dangerous, and Manrique built them a new coast. Lots of what Manrique did was good, and his enthusiasm to make sure that the Islands would be happier and more prosperous is something that his admirers, among whom I count myself, praise at the tops of our voices, but not a few of us would have preferred the beach at Puerto de la Cruz to have been left forever as a little range of miniature archipelagos, black and savage rocks, with the sea beating against them, the same sea which I can now hear, free, beating against the foundations of my house, just next to La Romántica, near

the Rambla de Castro, one of the most beautiful parts of the touristic
north, to which I have returned as though I wanted to recover the ancient aromas of what is now nearly nothing more than melancholy
inhabiting the landscape in which I grew up.

And I have recovered them, I have recovered these aromas. I
have been in the Plaza del Charco, in Puerto de la Cruz. Surrounded
by the ancient taro plants, as green as the greenest thing you could
possibly imagine, the Dinámico bar is still there, as are the swings
which were the gift in the 1950s of an eccentric Catalan called Tomás;
tourists and locals still walk by just as in the old times, enjoying the
climate which gained this place a reputation for being the land of eternal spring. And I was at the stream where the old fishmongers used
to wash the mackerel which I bought early in the morning to take
home to my mother. And opposite this stream, in the centre of this
little pier from which the fishermen leave, I have seen the splendid
house of the Yeowards, British merchants who set themselves up here
so as to be at both ends of the trade route in their exportation of bananas. Now the Yeoward house is the site of a permanent exhibition
of surrealist and abstract art collected by Eduardo Westerdahl, a critic
and painter of Swedish extraction, who was the man who brought
André Breton here from Paris in 1935, in order to mount the first international surrealist exhibition; here it was that Breton said that
Tenerife was a surrealist island. He would later say the same thing
about Mexico, and other places; the discovery that his praise was
nothing more than a cliché turned Breton, for me, into a charlatan of
landscape. But yes, it is a surrealist island, how could it not be, this
crag which it is better, as Aldecoa said, to describe with silence rather
than with words.

And so I have come back into the atmosphere where I used to live,
and I have taken once again the path down to Martiánez, through
these streets that were once walked by Bertrand Russell, or Agatha
Christie. And I have smelt the sea as I walked, smelt it as one can

smell it in no other place in the world, from La Punta del Viento, that point where the air turns round and which has already been mentioned in these pages for its powerful smell of salt and seaweed. Here, in La Punta del Viento, beyond El Penitente, I used to stop for many years to smell the salt and the seaweed, and now, as I smell this odour once again, it is as though I had grown fifty years younger at least. Below me, beating against the large and the small rocks, are the San Telmo pools, near the old natural swimming pools which Manrique incorporated into his project of remodelling the coast. Above us all, looking down on this spectacle which it now has to reconstruct from memory, is the old hermitage of San Telmo, which is a part of what remains of these memories that accompany me as I walk through what life here used to be like.

I have asked people where I should go to eat some good fish, from Puerto de la Cruz. And everyone says that if I want it to be fresh and recently caught, like the fish that we used to wash in the little stream down by the docks, then I should go to a place about twelve miles away, in El Guincho, on the way to Garachico, a suburb of Garachico, in fact. It is an old house with lots of nooks and corners, like the old houses of the north; they show you the fish in zinc buckets, without any salt, natural, just as it was taken out of the sea. As I drove along the freeway I saw in passing lots of old houses which have been recovered and which are now houses where people live, set among banana trees which survive as a source of income, competing with the true source of income which is tourism. I have travelled through tunnels which have been drilled in order to bring villages closer together, and as I have driven I have seen alongside the banana trees bright terraces which no one now plants, all of them dry and filled with yellow bushes, the sign of the end of an era, or the end of a dream, or simply the end.

And now here, in El Guincho, I wait as the food is slowly prepared; it is as though the Islanders have decided to pay homage to people's perceptions of them and have decided to honour me once again with a display of their patience, as happened in the restaurant in El Tamaduste, by the sea in El Hierro; they prepare parrotfish, and groupers, and zebra seabream; they put green pepper on them, stew *papas*; in order to make the wait bearable they bring cheese with *gofio*, which is a combination that sprang up in other times of need, back when there was nothing in people's houses apart from cheese and *gofio*; but necessity always creates the most flavourful combinations. And so I wait out my meal with this cheese, but they also bring an octopus which still smells of the sea, as if it had been cooked, and it surely was, in sea water.

Everything here tastes of sea and of the countryside at the same time, as though the two kinds of flavour were being put together, and the robust and resigned north were seizing hold of the two styles of life on the island: the land which protects and the sea which caresses. There is silence all around me as though the diners were fulfilling a religious ritual, and the fish were blessed by the same silence which now falls like a hand on all of us in the room, drinking our robust wine that to me tastes like the first wine I ever drank, which must have been in a place like this, with the fish in their zinc buckets.

The people here eat with their heads hanging down; in the room, which is covered with old photographs of the island, photographs of bright goats and old women wearing black hats, there is an atmosphere which is one of celebration and mourning at the same time, an atmosphere which reminds me a great deal of the celebrations of my youth, when I always had the sensation that we were mourning as we celebrated. I don't know if I have brought the old spirit of the Canary Islands to the table with me, or if it is the wine which has put me in this mood, but here I am, in the midst of the history made between us: made, above all, of daily life.

FROM HERE I GO TO A CITY WHICH I LIKE A GREAT DEAL, ICOD DE LOS Vinos, which for many years was the involuntary port of the south of the island, or at any rate the spot through which one had to pass in order to keep on travelling to the unexplored and still savage side of the island.

The other alternatives were crossing the peak, by La Esperanza, in La Laguna, or else using Las Cañadas from La Orotava, or else the paths that led to the south from Candelaria and Güímar, which were, until they built the freeway down to the south in 1972, abrupt and winding roads which took you slowly through every one of the villages and hamlets on the way, a long way from the sea, through what were ever drier mountains on the way down south; now we are travelling in the other direction, to the deep north, Icod de los Vinos, which is now next to Garachico.

Icod is distinguished by El Drago, a tree which we have always said is more than a thousand years old. Humboldt was confused by the presence of this tree, which grows so well in this part of the island, from the valley of La Orotava all the way up to here, up to Icod. And lots of travellers have come to see El Drago, and now very many tourists come as well. We say it is a thousand years old, and for some time we were happy to say that it was far more than that. Nowadays even the people trying to drum up the tourist trade say that it is 'probably' a thousand years old: it could be a thousand years old, it could well be, but it is not likely that it's much older; specialists have concluded that it might even be a bit younger than that. And even Pérez Minik was suggesting things along those lines, that it might not be quite as ancient as we claimed, but when he wrote his book, in the middle of the 1960s, it was very difficult to say anything on the Islands other than that which was canonically accepted by the bigots who governed us.

Whether it is a thousand years old or not, El Drago is a marvel of nature; also, one does not ask trees their age. There are two squares practically joined onto one another by El Drago, or if not joined onto one another then probably parallel, which increase the calm of the place and prepare us for the abrupt access of emotion which the sight of this ancient, or in any case very old, arboreal remnant will inspire in us. I have seen it many times; it used to be possible to see it from the road, you could stop for a moment and touch it, if you were feeling particularly daring, then you could take a strip of its fascinatingly twisted bark away with you. But the bark started to be taken away in ever-greater amounts, to the great detriment of its vegetal health, and scientists decided that they needed to carry out some radical surgery: first of all, they isolated it from all kinds of traffic and limited access to its trunk, and then they inserted cement into the tree to hold it up. And so this tree, which, like Mount Teide, has become a powerful symbol of the island, and has inspired surrealists like Óscar Domínguez, and which inspired the creative soul of André Breton when he first came to the island, or that of Rafael Alberti, who dedicated a poem to the tree—this tree now looks like an old man whose health depends entirely on the aid of his servants.

But it is a spectacle, a true spectacle. If I had never seen it, or if I had never seen it in those circumstances, open to the public, right next to the road, majestic but nevertheless exposed like any common tree, then I would not have recognised it now. El Drago was a symbol of health, a kind of blow struck on behalf of the earth, a tectonic affirmation of everything vegetal, a capricious offshoot of nature, put there by the will of some ancient god who might even have been a metaphor, a point of reference, a mythological plant, right here in this spot on the island, as though set in place to prove that a legend was true. This is how the poets saw it, and how it was easy to see it, because its nature did not only blend with the surroundings, but also with the threats posed by progress. They thought it was indestructible, but it was gradually destroying itself.

And so they isolated it; they put it, as my mother said, in a flask, a kind of glass bell, and surrounded it with rocks; they poured cement into its soul, so that now you see it as though it were in a crypt, in a kind of narrow circle; you are no longer able to touch it; it is sick but it is beautiful, you can see that, it is not necessary to touch it to see that its different illnesses haven't destroyed any of its prestige. I was taking photographs of its belly from a distance; the belly of a colossus, in spite of its weaknesses, is still in its own right colossal. One side is healthier than the other, and that might perhaps be the side which is less impressive. From a distance, the tree's trunk seems to be young.

It is green; ever since the days of antiquity it has kept that colour by which nature identifies its healthy trees. I noted that it seemed to be a young woman, shaded by a palm tree with a great deal of leaves which grows alongside it like a shield, or like its own improbable shadow, 'odd shadow', as I wrote in my notebook.

They have, in order to preserve El Drago, built up around it a park in which they have planted some of the indigenous vegetable species of the Islands as a whole, and so I was able to walk through the past and the present of our trees as though this walk were to calm me of all the violence I should feel at seeing the beauties of this great bleeding tree. I was surprised to see here, mixed in with all these plants, a butterfly house, for I did not remember that here in this part of the island, around El Drago, there had ever been a flourishing of butterflies, such as there are, for example, in *One Hundred Years of Solitude*. But the butterflies are here, perhaps looking for a combination of the kind the surrealists liked when they made El Drago, and its blood, a symbol to feed their metaphors.

I LEFT THE PLACE OVERWHELMED BY MY CONTEMPLATION OF THAT SICK yet still powerful tree. I was walking between the two squares in Icod, and I was entertaining myself by looking at the balconies around the squares, houses that once were the expression of the neoclassical style which came to the island via this town (the house of Lorenzo Cáceres is here, the general in the engineers who introduced this style into the islands in the nineteenth century), and, above all, I was looking at a palm tree which seemed to me to be extremely out of the ordinary: a palm tree shaped like a menorah, with its seven arms skeletal yet powerful, showing the same blend of exuberance and strangeness that in other parts of the island had made the most famous naturalist ever to visit Tenerife, the German scientist Alexander Humboldt, cry out with emotion.

Icod is a place where the darkness of the earth leads all the way down to the sea, down to the beach at San Marcos, where the sand is like all the sand of the beaches along this coast: Bollullos, Martiánez, El Soccorro, La Fajana, San Marcos . . . Black sand, high waves, a lively sea, a succulent smell of seaweed, the loneliness of the sea marking with its sound the lonely northern nights.

I carried on down the road to Garachico. I had been told of so many places there that I needed to see that I decided only to go and look at the sea. I could have gone to the hermitages, the strange houses, the banana plantations which evoke a wealth that is now no more than a legend, the convents, the well-preserved streets (as there are also in La Orotava, Puerto de la Cruz and Icod), the old cobbles . . . But I wanted to see the sea, which had come all the way up into the town until the violent Garachico explosion at the beginning of the eighteenth century cut off the promising future of what had been the wealthiest town on the island. And so I set off to look at the ocean, as if an old friend was calling to me. There is an old davit there, rusted, which now looks more like a sculpture; it is next to a packaging plant for bananas and other fruit. Garachico is festooned with hills of the produce of its extremely fertile land, the banana plantations are still, obviously, an external sign of wealth, and so here, in this davit, I find a symptom of what was once a rich port and which now is assaulted by the violence of the sea. They are building another harbour in another part of the town, but it was here until the volcanic eruption put it out of use.

Aldecoa, in his *Tourist's Notebook*, explains his impression, which was impressed upon him when he visited this formerly depressed village in the north: 'Garachico, on the edge of the sea, was buried by the lava of an eruption. A rock surged up in the bay, a hump which now houses strange plants, lizards with two tails and black birds known as ospreys. The sea here is deep, and sometimes the sharks climb onto the troubled land. The slope at Garachico is the precise opposite of that at La Orotava. What is green there is here ash, and black rock from the heart of a volcano. A skeleton with no earth to clothe its bones, a petrified storm under a deep blue sky.'

The poet felt like this, but I think he must have been inventing the sharks; I never knew that there had been sharks in Garachico, rather than those black birds; this winged rock lifting itself up into the blue sky of this town battered by the volcanic lava in the past . . .

WHEN YOU ARRIVE AT GARACHICO YOU KNOW THAT YOU ARE COMING to a special place: you know this by the smell of the sea, by the rock (the Roque de Garachico) which is like a dry fist surging out of the sea; you will already have seen the omnipresent banana plantations; to those of us who know that, just as sugar cane and piglets went elsewhere, the cultivation and export of bananas is not a major part of the island's future, this persistence of the bananas seems to return us to a memory of a landscape, the landscape of our childhood, when banana monoculture was practically the only way Canary Island families had to survive, both for the rich people who employed the poor and for the poor who were employed by the rich.

And so, when you look at this landscape, which has remained unchanged for more than a century, you see that it represents what the island is, and you do not know for how much longer. This ancient landscape still can surprise the visitor, but it also now surprises the emigrant who returns, when the green of the banana trees approaches and almost touches the blue of the sea. And you can still smell the sea with the same intensity that is proper to the seas of the north, constantly beating the shore, filled with seaweed.

They have built natural swimming pools across the whole of the north of the island, from Punta del Hidalgo and Bajamar in La Laguna, all the way to Garachico, Los Silos and Buenavista, where we will travel later, but the sea keeps on breaking over the artificial barriers put in its way, and keeps encroaching with its scent and its waves, with its irrepressible violence, all the way into the avenues and squares of the town.

And it came all this way as well, all the way to where I am, in Puerta de Tierra. This was the spot where merchandise came into and departed from Garachico; this was the customs post, where the

papers were deposited which bore witness to an exchange which was
a cosmopolitan activity, coming from Europe, from America, from
Africa. This port, in the sixteenth and seventeenth centuries, was a
reflection of the naval splendour of the bay, the principal port of
Tenerife. Agricultural produce came and left, as did wine, sugar,
cured skins, pitch, cloth . . . English cloth came in, French cloth came
in, Dutch art . . . The Italian geographer Torriani described the port
in the sixteenth century as a vital element of commerce in the Canary
Islands, as the axis on which the existence of the island turned. This
was the case until the volcanic eruption of 1706 caused what is
known on the island as 'the catastrophe'. The legend says that the
wealth of the town was such that all the streets were paved in marble;
now they are no more than cobbles: most of them are paved in shining cobbles which give the town a medieval air, the same as certain
Castilian towns possess. But the streets are not paved in marble, and
never were. In Puerta del Tierra—where there is still a bust of Rafael
Alberti, who came here too after his vegetal ecstasy at the sight of El
Drago—one can feel when standing in the Plaza de la Pila or the
Plaza de Abajo that the symbols of the town's ancient splendour are
still there to a degree. But it is in the convent of the Franciscans that
the devastation wrought by the volcano can be observed in terms of
dates and consequences.

Humboldt, in his description of his time on Tenerife, says that it
is 'slightly sad to see a crater in the very centre of a land that is otherwise fertile and well cultivated'. And the German naturalist continues, in a sudden access of pessimism: 'The history of the Globe tells
us that volcanoes destroy what they have created over a long stretch
of centuries. Islands which the action of undersea volcanoes has
pushed above the waves are little by little covered by a rich and cheer-
ful canopy of greenery, but often these new lands are destroyed by the
very same forces that have lifted them from the bottom of the ocean.
Perhaps there are islands which are now no more than mountains of
trash and volcanic ash that used to be as fertile as the hills of Tacoronte and El Sauzal on Tenerife.' And Humboldt, in a heated and some-

what scared peroration, concludes as follows: 'Lucky the lands where man does not have to fear the land upon which he lives!'

HERE, IN GARACHICO, ONE STILL FEELS THE GLOW OF THAT VOLCANIC ERUPTION, which ruined the future of the whole place. Here, in this convent, one of the four or five remaining monuments which the town retains as a part of its worship of the past and of silence, the whole volcanic biography of Tenerife can be seen. Here are the maps, like palimpsests of fear: Chinyero, the last eruption in 1909; Garachico in 1706; Boca Cangrejo in 1492, the year in which Christopher Columbus discovered America, and Fasnia, which began a year before the disaster that fell upon Garachico. This started on 5 May 1706 and continued until 13 May: this was the first phase of the eruption; after a pause it gathered its strength and continued to erupt until 13 June.

The eruption of Garachico destroyed the port, but there were no victims. The population of the town were surprised, but they managed to hide. And Garachico could no longer be the same; the town was 'dominated by seven arms of fire which filled the deepest and most protected part of the port'. Viera y Clavijo, the historian who was born in Los Realiejos and who did so much to bring the *encyclopédiste* spirit to the Islands, wrote as follows: 'One arm broke the port, pushing the sea away and leaving only a small cove which was difficult for even small boats to access. [. . .] The vineyards disappeared, as did the water, the birds, the port, all commerce and the entire neighbourhood.'

Devastation. The more recent volcanic eruptions, of San Juan and Teneguía on La Palma in 1949 and 1971 respectively, caused far less damage. I was a witness to the eruption of Teneguía, as a journalist: it was an enormous crater of fire, black and red, which breathed out terrible explosions that people watched as though they were watching the end of the world. But people did not seem to be scared. The exhibition I saw in Garachico included a report filmed at the time by a colleague of mine, Cristina García Ramos. She spoke to some inhabitants who were looking at the effects of the fire in the distance and listening to the terrible explosions, and one of them said, 'No, I wasn't scared; it's a beautiful sight.' I wasn't scared; it's a beautiful sight. When the tragedy has gone by what remains is a landscape; tectonics, something that will eventually be buried in greenery, something which will at some point in the future once again be soil, a green spot even though now empty, a wasteland. No, I wasn't scared; it's a beautiful sight. Canary Island language in its purest form.

THEY MUST HAVE READ WHAT I FOUND ON ONE OF THE PANELS IN THE exhibition which spoke of these eruptions: 'The Canary Islands have appeared as the result of different underwater eruptions over the last twenty million years. Volcanic islands are still being formed under the water, which will appear in a not very distant future. The history of the Canary Islands is the history of the cohabitation between man and volcano, a coexistence that at times has been very difficult, but which has been in general more beneficial than harmful for the inhabitants of the islands.'

Now that I look at these images, these landscapes which have been devastated or expanded by the fire of the volcanoes, I think about a particular image: the figure of a man who saw Teneguía vomiting fire; he had very little hair, and that hair he did have was white; his name was Telesforo Bravo, and he is one of the great Spanish geologists of the twentieth century; he studied Mount Teide, the volcanoes of the islands; he travelled round the world and went to savage islands, he looked for water in Persia, and here, in this image, he looks like someone who is drinking in an action carried out by the land he knows so well. Now I have read Humboldt once again, I imagine Bravo speaking with the German naturalist about his fears. ('Lucky the lands where man does not have to fear the land upon which he lives!') He would surely have tried to calm Humboldt down, or at least one sees him here, watching as the soil of La Palma burns and smoking his pipe, smiling with the calm expression of a wise man.

Nature is doing its job, and although it may cause devastation, it knows all too well what it is doing.

I left the place and walked through what is now Garachico; I stood in front of a convent where there are still cloistered nuns, and there must be very few of them; it is a single block with white walls, large windows through which passers-by are unable to look. A friend sent me a message to make sure that I didn't miss a thing. 'You can walk through the centre of the town. As far as sites of architectural interest are concerned, there is the convent of San Francisco, the convent of Santo Domingo, the convent of the cloistered Franciscan nuns, the church of Santa Ana, the Casa de los Condes de La Gomera, the Quinta Roja Hotel, the Puerta de Tierra in the Plaza de Abajo, the Camino Real between the crosses . . .' And he listed other places as well which were equally important to understand the patience with which Garachico has protected the past. But more than anything else, I stopped for a while in front of this monument to silence, and imagined the nuns sewing and darning, keeping their silence like an offering or a sacrifice, and I went to listen to the sea, which was a relief after the powerful silence of Garachico.

Above me the climate of the northern half of the island, the haze, the opaque sky; I drank a coffee in one of the hotels which my friend had recommended to me, and any sound, even the sound of the teaspoons, seemed some kind of interruption or an alarm. There, under the white and insistent clouds, I thought about this climate which leads people so much into introspection and melancholy, as though the absence of sun were a door that opened into dreams and delirium, into a lack of physical activity and a need for mental activity, for dreaming, nightmares or poetry. And I made a note: 'A climate that makes it easy to be introspective or delirious; the cloud thrown over the island so fully that it even covers the line of the horizon and gives the sea an almost violent somnolence such as there is in many of J.M.W. Turner's later paintings.'

THE CLIMATE IS A RETURN, TO CHILDHOOD, OR IN ANY EVENT TO ONE'S origins, and here, in the midst of this haze whose calmness is broken by the smell of the sea and the sound of the sea against the rock and against the salty coast of Garachico, I was taken back to the years when I began to discover the island, to live it. By association of ideas, there came back to my memory a scene from Camus's novel *L'Étranger*, when Mersault commits his murder and attributes his stupor to the effective and powerful blanket of warm cloud, to the sweltering heat that lies over his forehead and his soul. And he kills, he has no other way to act than to kill, to shoot several times; I can still hear in my adolescent ears the expression used to describe the impression which the murderer has upon completing his horrid task: 'I understood then that I had broken the harmony of the day, the exceptional silence of a beach on which I was happy.' I did not commit a murder on this beach, and nothing took place to disturb the harmony of the day, but I feel a similar heat hanging over my head, it is the climate which is sending me back to my childhood, to my adolescence, to my reading of that book and to the climate of that time.

I went to a restaurant to eat fish (and ended up eating meat): Casa Gaspar, a restaurant in front of the rusted davit; as had happened to me before in El Tamaduste on El Hierro, waiting for a plate of chickpeas, and in El Guincho on Tenerife, waiting for a plate of cod, the man whose job it was to bring my meal thought that two hours was a decent time for him to bring my order. Our friend Humboldt complained in his book about his journey to Tenerife of the time it took the islanders who were accompanying him up Mount Teide to fulfil their particular tasks: 'Our Islander guides were desperately slow; they had tried to persuade us the evening before to travel no further than Las Rocas on the next day; they sat down to rest for ten minutes or so every ten minutes; they stealthily threw away the samples of obsidian and pumice stone which we had carefully gathered, and we discovered that none of them had yet been to the summit of the volcano in their whole lives.'

Of course, what happens in restaurants is nowhere near as serious as what happened to Humboldt, but it does make one feel a little desperate. I thought, perhaps wrongly, that what seemed to me to be a natural part of El Tamaduste or the moral haze of El Hierro was only a part of the idiosyncrasy of those particular islands, because it is not an attitude, but rather something more, as though it were a part of the climate: the sensation of loneliness, of exhaustion, the fear that walking too fast will lead us straight into the abyss.

Anyway . . .

Before leaving Garachico I went into a church; it was lonely, there were about four people there, all of them praying while moving their lips; the atmosphere was one of absolute seclusion, like that which one finds in the churches in certain villages in the south of Italy; an ashen light came in through the open doors, and the candles that were lit here and there made the church appear ghostly, a place where one might go for a secret meeting or to lie in wait for someone. When I left Garachico, thinking about my childhood, I was tempted to carry out an odd journey, an excursion in search of my father, something that would be logical in a psychodrama but not in this particular exercise, whose aim was to discover, or rediscover, the landscapes which form my life. But my father was a man who created landscapes. He was a driver, an adventurer, he worked as a builder and, in the final phase of his life, he built paths and roads, and as a result of that he also destroyed paths and roads and houses. Once, without him wanting to do so, a truck of his demolished an old house, and then a highway was put through the space, and one could always see the void that he had created. It was on the road from Puerto de la Cruz to La Orotava, via Las Arenas, the place I always go through when I go back to the home where I was born, under the hollowed mountain where they built, with suicidal perseverance, an unnecessary hotel.

BUT ON THIS OCCASION I WANTED TO GO TO LA GUANCHA, NEAR Garachico, on one of the roads near which my father had once left an immense stone which nobody could remove. He insisted that it was a meteorite, a stone that had accompanied an extraordinary phenomenon which had occurred without any warning, and he wanted people to know that it had happened. When I managed to arrange for someone, my friend Salvador García Llanos, to write a report on him and the phenomenon, my father gave a sigh of relief, as he had managed to make someone take notice of what he had discovered as he was digging up the ground. He died a while later, and I always thought that he, insistent and obstinate as he was, a man of absolute convictions, would not have died before the interview had been carried out and the report had been published in the newspaper.

Because of this, because of the memory which he left stuck onto the surface of the island, I spent a whole afternoon looking for the stone, whose whereabouts had become somewhat blurry in my memory. Then, after a great deal of poking around, I found it. There it was; a young man who lived in the area said that it was a 'volcano bomb'. When they were making the highway, the kid told me, 'they found this shape, perfect, round, powerful', and tried to break it into pieces. The rock broke two jackhammers and also couldn't be lifted by a crane. And so the man who was in charge of the development, the kid said to me, just left it here, just left it some space.'

The boy didn't know who the man had been. I spoke to him standing in the middle of a farm which he had inherited, among chickens which never stopped cackling and laying eggs, a farm where my father would surely have been happy, and I felt like the sentimental heir of a stone which is now surrounded by palm trees, like a tumulus dedicated to a unique man who thought that he touched the sky whenever he touched the ground, and who was happy whenever he saw the ground, as if the earth were speaking to him, as if the stones were talking to him.

The boy told me that when they found the stone, drivers at night thought that there were pieces of mica embedded in its surface, 'and that there were, and now there aren't anymore'. They were there: I imagine my father convincing everyone that the stone reflected what people wanted to see in it, a solid testament from some kind of extra-terrestrial. The boy told me he was called Gustavo and that he was twenty-three years old; as I left I told him that the man who found the stone was my father. And then I left as though I were also a part of the landscape.

TRAVELLING DOWN THROUGH THIS LANDSCAPE WHICH I AM FOLLOWING one reaches the south, which is where I am now writing, sitting facing the beaches of El Médano, where I have lived for almost twenty years now, driven here by my desire for health, for sand, for wind, for joy. To get here from the north, I have travelled via the same bus stop that I used to use when my father took me to building sites where he was working in isolated spots in the south which I will reach in a while, from Buenavista.

There were women in mourning clothes who travelled with me in these dusty buses, and workers, and peasants and a great many chickens; I don't know why there were so many chickens in my memories of these journeys, but it certainly is the case that back then a good layer was a form of economic security. The eggs could be sold, could help make a little money, and they were also, of course, useful as food; my mother raised chickens and cows and pigs, but it was only the chickens that got to travel by bus.

Now, however, in this twenty-first century journey (twentieth-century journeys on the Islands were made using nineteenth-century means) I travel in a car which is much more modern than that limping beast in which my father used to drive me back from the building sites where he was working. He took me to Tijoco, near Guía de Isora; he built houses for the agricultural landowners there, along with his team of builders; the lizards scampered over the roof of the shed where he slept like all the other workers, and I saw them; at the bottom of the dry plains, dry as some landscape out of a novel by Juan Rulfo, you would sometimes hear a Mexican *corrido*, which back then was the kind of music they listened to in the countryside, the combination of violence and melancholy that was the sound of the tiny villages out there. Many years later, Jesús Polanco, president of the *El País* newspaper, a noble man who fell in love with the Islands, and especially with the view from the south of Tenerife towards La Gomera, took me out to the abandoned farmland where he would build a hotel, the Abama Hotel; the houses that my father had built were just opposite. It is difficult to say what your memory is trying to tell you when such coincidences take place on the tiny space that is an island and in the vastness or minuteness of a life . . .

And so, in this modern car, I am travelling once again, many years later, to a place which brings a great number of memories to mind, the Tierra del Trigo, high up in Buenavista. A sensual and silent place where I was once decades ago; I remember being there, alone, one absolutely normal evening, shouting out a single word in the midst of all that fog, and I remember the echo bringing it back to me. I don't remember the word; it might very well have been 'silence'.

Now as I pass through the Tierra del Trigo I realise that the reason it has remained so evocative is perhaps something to do with the discovery which I made back then of the echo in the solitude of the landscape. From down here I can see the mountains and observe how the banana plantations head all the way down to the sea, from here to Punta de Teno, on one of the most spectacular freeways on the island. As I travel down this road I have stopped by some geological protuberance which looks like the now vanished Dedo de Dios, the Finger of God, which was so called because it did indeed look like a finger made out of stone; it was knocked over by a storm on Gran Canaria. Here near Punta de Teno there is another Dedo de Dios which has no name and which points up lonely into the sky like a lighthouse or a milepost, facing a clean sea that beats against it with extraordinary violence.

Here is where the island breaks in two. The pure north comes to an end and we enter, buffeted by a wind which emphasises the sense of solitude, into the northeast, or the southeast. This is Macizo de Teno, before which every traveller needs to feel a sense of respect which he should later keep in his memory. We have passed through a wonderful place to eat, El Palmar, where they roast the best chickens on the island, and which is a sensible place for a traveller to pause, if he later wishes to plough through these roads which the people here call highways—technically they are correct, because the roads are paved, but they still give you the sense of fear that driving on an un-paved road over the abyss might provide—with something pleasant in his stomach.

I have never been here before, or at least I don't remember it if I have. From a certain height, once I have recovered from my fear and from the wind that was blowing next to the Tenerife version of the Dedo de Dios, these imposing rocks seem to have been deliberately shaped by the hand of man, and they give a sense of emptiness and danger at the same time, or else they arouse both sensations simply because it is a clear day and it is as though every object you see from so high up, whether it be a house or a goat or a tree, is in fact a minia-ture figure in some diabolical or benevolent world.

It is the end of the north, the beginning of the south; anyone who has been to La Gomera and knows the abruptness of its cliffs will find an even more majestic symphony here, and will want to listen to a calmer music in order to help their spirit become accustomed to these gorges, to these nooks where there seems to dwell a wind that will fly with you among all the crags.

YOU TRAVEL ALONE HERE; SOMETIMES A FEW CARS COME IN THE OTHER direction, and then you need to move to one side, climbing onto the narrow pavements, but you have the reward of imagining that you are travelling across a secret island on which you have the feeling, at any given moment, that you are alone, that it is only you who are crossing the island, that you are hanging from the heights, and not hanging from a stone, but hanging from an emotion or a mystery. Will you arrive? It doesn't matter. And moreover, where? It doesn't matter either. Suddenly Tenerife seems like the essence of an island, a geological event which the hand of man has worked on in order to make sure that the earth is not alone. An island is a rocky surface, is pure rock; men come to do it violence, its destiny is loneliness and we walk over it in silence, as though we were praying to it.

Ay, the paths we have to take.

AND WE ARRIVE AT THE SUMMIT, WITH MASCA BELOW US. I CAME ALONG these paths two or three years ago, through a forest trail that allowed us to escape from the fire. It had burnt the Buenavista forests that lead to Masca; I saw, below in this little village, groups of men crying because they had lost everything, their houses, their belongings, their wooden chairs, their clothes: they didn't have anything, and they were crying. As I left the spot I saw a piece of wood still burning, a little tree perhaps, and thought that this little piece of fire represented the fire itself, was its testimony. Now I have returned and can see them rebuilding the house. And the burnt mountains are regaining their pine trees, although the parts that were burnt by the fire still have black bald peaks. I can see certain similarities with La Gomera in this landscape which takes me to Masca, in particular with the landscapes that you can see, majestic and aerial, as you go down from Playa de Santiago to the Gran Rey valley: huge palm trees which resist the heat and the wind, and here they are, offering leafy paths into which the traveller leans as though facing an oasis after such a curving road.

But then you have to go up again; unlike the mountains of Fuerteventura, which are extraordinarily sensuous, modelled out of an infinite number of silken curves, these mountains are cliffs, like pillars or knives, and as you climb them you can feel them taking their revenge. You get to the top out of breath, and you have your reward there before you have to turn round and head down again. To either side of you, you see the two opposed universes, the north and the south, the left and the right of the cosmos: the north is abrupt and intricate, and the south is vague and flat. The vagueness begins below, in Santiago del Teide, the village from which hangs the immense geological construction which is the cliff of Los Gigantes, which reminds one once again of the natural constructions the sea makes in La Gomera and in certain areas of Anaga in Tenerife.

This path leads me to Guía de Isora; here you can see the dusty villages through which my father drove me as we went to the building sites. One day, more than forty years ago, he left me in his shack and while I dozed and listened to the distant Mexican songs, I became aware of a moving point on the roof of this modest shelter.

It was a gecko, a large and potbellied lizard which seemed to be showing me the essence of the south, the kinds of loneliness which the heat generated. I was in the south and the lizard was its symbol; it was walking its own way and I came out of the shack in a fright, looking for my father's protection against this pest.

I will not see lizards on this trip, but they are there, they are the testament of the sun, and it is a stern sun which falls on me as I walk between the sea and the banana plantations, from the Los Gigantes cliff to Adeje, which is a soft village, something like the capital of the south, up in the hills, looking down what in my childhood were nothing more than tracts of land and which now are groups of houses that look down on the sea, all the way down to the Las Américas beach, the greatest tourist emporium of the island, one of the largest in Spain, where the climate attracted the first colony of expatriates, the Swedish, many years ago.

They were Swedes who were disabled or in pain, people to whom their doctors had recommended a dry climate such as this one, and here the Swedes built a clinic which was also a convalescent home, Vintersol, which means 'winter sun'. When I was a boy and the summer came round, I would see the Swedes trying to recover from terrible illnesses; we lived between Arona and Adeje, in Los Cristianos, at the start of the Las Américas beach, in a village which was like the entrance to the sea. Back then, halfway through the 1960s, there were no iceboxes in people's homes, and you had to bring in ice on your shoulders, carry it in to keep the food fresh, and the streets were made of sand or earth, and there was no light in the houses at night, and no light in the streets, so the adults and the children entertained themselves by looking up at the sky, at the moon and the stars, whose movements we all knew by heart.

Now everything has changed too much. There are still dusty banana plantations on the south of Tenerife, and there are still beaches like there used to be, but this part of the island, which once was the mirror of a desert of sand, is the most cosmopolitan, most inhabited part of the island now; the village on whose beach I live, San Isidro, has one of the highest levels of commerce in Spain, is one of the places with most notaries; the southern airport is nearby, built to give some kind of outlet for the economic and touristic strength of Tenerife, and to compensate for the ancient primacy of the Los Rodeos airport, which brought in life and wealth to the north for decades.

The south now has its revenge.

I live in El Médano, which is a place that I was first taken to in the 1980s by Doctor José Toledo, who was born here, studied in the United States and in England, was one of the great surgeons of Europe, and died when he thought he was going to be able to enjoy this, the landscape of his childhood, for many more years to come. He stood in front of the Montaña Roja as though he were worshipping it, and this vision was enough to make him sure that he was living a happy life. He was a poet, but he did not need to write down his works: he was a poet in his looking at things, and this landscape filled his heart with poetry.

Allow me to speak a little about this village before I head back to the north, this time travelling from the south.

Perhaps it is a symbol of the south in its purest form, this distance which marks the difference from the north, from the green and tectonic parts of the island; here we have nothing more than the purely tectonic, and the man who touches this soil touches a fundamental, dried-out solitude. Back in the 1950s, 1960s and 1970s, houses were rare here, and squat; they had an interior patio into which every room led, so that they could all be protected from the wind which, along with the dunes whose shape imitated that of the hills behind the village, was the morphological metaphor for this place.

The great beach, which now is called Leonardo Machado beach, was the main attraction for those holidaymakers who chose El Médano as a place where they could rest, or simply disappear.

Back in those decades, when tourism was starting to unroll industrially in the Canary Islands, people travelled here as though they were travelling to a foreign country. Things have changed since then, as the southern highway has been built, and the southern airport has started to run flights. Now this little village of local holidaymakers and fishermen is a motley formation which combines package holidays with the tourists who come from the Islands or from Spain and the foreigners who come more sensitively. Foreigners have always given this place a surprisingly cosmopolitan air; lots of Italians have decided to make their homes here, lots of Chinese and Latin Americans, and all of them have set up businesses which make this ancient sandy and half-deserted place into a typical example of the flood which the southern coasts have suffered, both here and in most of the rest of the Islands as well.

This is, let us say, the history of El Médano, which I recommend strongly that you visit because it represents the combination of the sea, mountain and wind which has always characterised it. It is impossible for anyone to see now what El Médano used to be, and to take refuge in that little village which exists only in the memory of the oldest inhabitants of the island is useless. There are other places, like Porís de Abona, a few miles away from El Médano—where the Swiss architect Jacques Herzog decided to build himself a house, an act which caused a new wave of interest in this landscape—which still have the same qualities as they did back in the past, but there are very few places to compare with the beaches near the place where I live. The wind, and the lively sea, which breaks smoothly and decisively on the dark and light sand, has made the place an international centre for windsurfers, who dominate the shore with their passionate struggle to beat the wind and bend it to their will.

Sometimes I stand in front of my window and look at the windsurfers, and the sinuous movement of the kites, and I have the impression that I am on a different beach from the one where I actually live; it is different from the place where my ancestors lived, who would look at the sea as it is now (lively, white, broken, violently stroked by the wind) and see it as a surface that was useless for fishermen. It was a closed sea: the sea was here and the land was there. Now the windsurfers defy this border and fit into the waves as though slipping into a glove.

The great metaphor of El Médano, its emblem, is the Montaña Roja, nearly six hundred feet tall, made of reddish stone, a kind of guardian of the sea. On one side it looks back at the steep cliffs at the end of the beach, and on the other side, like some poorly-trained animal, it faces what is the apparently quieter shore of a surprising and isolated beach, La Tejita, where the sea is high and treacherous, and the currents are peaceful but implacable: a beach for people who are experts in beaches, one of those beaches that needs to be treated with the same delicacy with which one might treat a beautiful crocodile, some soft and sinuous, but equally implacable creature.

Montaña Roja is surrounded by the low hill, dark and green and sometimes hidden by the sandstorms, of its oasis; its height and standing remind one of other sacred mountains, such as the one that the sculptor Eduardo Chillida wanted to hollow out. One can imagine the Montaña Roja, back in the times when El Médano was a practically undefined space, without any tall buildings and with hardly any houses, sending out the message of loneliness that it still transmits today. I like to look at it; I like to think that when I look at it I am using the eyes of my soul just as people like Doctor Toledo did, all those people who admired and who still admire its serene existence, tormented by millions of years of the sun beating down on it, and the wind and the cold, protecting the coastline like an enormous magic dog.

This is my place, I cohabit with this place, I am writing here today, listening to the insolent knocking of the wind against the window, the wind which at the present moment is enlivening the atmosphere of El Médano, next to Cabezo beach; a windsurfer ties his foot to the board on which he wants to reach Montaña Pelada, another beach, a nudist beach at the other end of La Tejita. I have been there several times, it is very sheltered; La Tejita is open to the ocean, but Pelada has a rock which protects it. These are the two vectors of the village; in between them is a population which has a special energy to it, a tiny part of which I have been borrowing for years now.

I CAME HERE FOR THE FIRST TIME WHEN I WAS AN ADOLESCENT; THE EX-cessive heat made me faint and I was revived with cold water and a little plate of Russian salad; later on, round about 1970, I came here with a group of friends to get over an annoying love affair and to get drunk on the empty beach, where I woke up in the middle of an expanse of wild sand, windy at the dawn, facing a clean horizon, the same one I look at today, although from a much more populated coast than that desert which in those days scarcely appeared an any maps. And, twenty years ago, thanks to a playing card which I found in a building site, and which I thought would bring me luck, I bought this house where I have written most of my books and most of this book about the sentimental memories which I retain of my homeland, the Canary Islands.

El Médano, as distinct from that little village of fishermen who lived on earthen roads with their doors open to the street, into whose houses the sand came like just another guest, is now a multinational place where, thanks to the windsurfers who come from all over the world, but especially from the cold north of Europe, breathes regularly an air (a wind, perhaps) that is absolutely cosmopolitan.

Now El Médano, which is part of the Granadilla de Abono district, a place through which one has to travel in order to reach Teide

via Vilaflor, is also next to the airport which, along with the southern highway, guaranteed a tourist boom for this part of the island,
a boom which has changed the face of this entire area and also the
psychology of its inhabitants, among whom there are practically no
fishermen anymore.

FIRST VISIT TO LA LAGUNA

A LONG WITH PUERTO DE LA CRUZ, WHICH WE HAVE ALREADY VISited, this, La Laguna, is my place; I said as much to the painter Pedro González as we drank wine in La Carrera, the street next to the convent of Las Clarisas; here the air which animates my spirit comes into play and this place where I now pick up again my island journey is the landscape which my feet already know; I know that it is a desert, or almost, a place where there are almost no palm trees, almost no plants, but the air, which is its principal inhabitant, wails as though it would destroy the whole world, and memory itself; and one walks into the purest of seas which seems always to be in a state of storm, roaring like an adolescent, wrinkled as though it had just suffered a terrible gale, like the one that scared everyone, even the outlaw (played by Edward G. Robinson, unforgettable) in *Key Largo*.

This is my place, La Laguna. Let me offer up a personal homage, the reiteration of a visit which I always owe it, a journey which I recommend as one would recommend drinking the best water from the best spring in the best house of best memory.

La Laguna is the place where I went to university; for many years it was the only university in the whole of the Canary Islands, and now it shares this honour with the University of Las Palmas. When it was the only university of the Islands, it was the common spot where students from every island came to study, which gave the

City of the Sheriffs (a nickname that dates back to the time of the conquistadors, because it was here that they first drew up the plans for
the exercise of their power) a cosmopolitan air, of course still very insular, but the cosmopolitan air that all students give to a place. They
came from everywhere, and they gave the city a strange bohemian aspect, something which I am afraid it lacks today, because students
tend to live in their houses rather than in shared accommodation or
in the fraternities which were the scenes of an almost legendary wild-
ness in the past.

La Laguna. It is here, in front of me. I can touch it, I touch the
city; it is a tactile memory, I miss it; but now I touch it; it is a city
which exists in order to be touched, it is not just a city, it is music as
well, an inner voyage; it has never stopped having a sound of its own;
the sound of rain, the sound of footsteps over the cobblestones, the
clear sound of the night, the sound of the wind at a street corner, the
sound of winter, the dry sound of summer.

One day in La Laguna, very early, when I was a student, I came
here at dawn. Air is loneliness, the air of La Laguna is solitude, cold
air, open air, as though it were the memory of a child, and I touch the
air, it stands against my face, I walk down the Avenida de la Trinidad,
the statue of Padre Anchieta behind me—this is the spot from which
the man who brought the gospel to Brazil departed, from this land of
air and water. I walk to the cemetery; the morning takes me to the old
cemetery, where a cypress stands up unashamed and calls to the sun
to give shade to the dead. Its blue shadow stretches out and I take
cover in it; the shadow seems like another monument to the city which
sheltered its ancestors.

You come in here, via Anchieta, and as you open your path into
the city it is as though you are headed to a new life: La Laguna is
this, a place where you will learn, you are an adolescent and you are
entering the cradle of the Islands, you are still not aware of this, you
don't know that you are treading on the edges, and finally the body
of history itself, but at this moment, when you arrive, you are entering the past because you are entering possibility once again. In past

centuries it was through this place that literature entered the Islands, that debate came, the *Encyclopédie* . . . It was here that the conquistadors debated, but also historians like Viera y Clavijo, and poets like Viana.

When I enter the city there is no one here, it is early in the morning, but a cyclist passes with a lunch box on the back of his bike, and he nods to me. Everything is new in the city and I am a little kid again, coming to see in the air of the city what life has promised me: the adventure of seeing. I touch it. I touch La Laguna. A German doctor, who is travelling early in the morning too, has picked me up on the road, and we have understood one another thanks to my Greek dictionary. I am headed to the Institute, to do my pre-university course, and this is my first lesson, my baptism in La Laguna.

I touch La Laguna, but today I am in the cemetery, as though a hand were leading me to pay homage to the past. And then I head back to the Avenida de la Trinidad, and other early risers laugh as they cross the road at the same time as a flock of goats. The cobbles are still wet with rain or dew; the young men are all carrying folders and new books. Almost every part of what I am now seeing will remain forever burnt on my retina. My hands are frozen in my cotton trouser pockets, it is autumn and the sun gives no heat; a few men are shouting, coming out of the bars where they have been drinking liquors to fight the cold or else draw a night of partying to an end. There is a drinking culture in La Laguna, and the bars never run out of customers.

The city then opens up into its urban history, and here I am, I have come in via Consitorio all the way up to the Plaza de los Adelantados, and there is one of those cloisters in front of me which adds to the mystery of La Laguna, the nuns inside making sweets, darning socks, praying; the goats have followed me here, and there they go, climbing La Carrera, a street I have heard about in popular songs ('A night in La Laguna | filled with cold and rain | La Carrera was not a street | it was a river . . .); the street ends in an extraordinary architectural statement, the Church of the Conception, which the painter Pedro González transformed in some of his paintings into the cosmopolitan and terrestrial referent of the whole city, surrounded by modern cars and set in the powerful foothills of Mount Teide . . . This is the path which travels past the Cathedral, which is much more conventional than the Spartan Church of the Conception, seeming almost a lay building by comparison: more than a street, La Carrera is a passage that leads to the other exit from La Laguna.

The Ateneo stands in front of the Cathedral: even in the Franco period it was a place for republican or apolitical anti-Franco meetings, a place where famous *bons viveurs* would gather, legendary musicians . . . This is where the long career of Los Sabandeños would begin, the most important musical group in the history of the Canary Islands, the people who renewed the island folklore, the creators of a way of singing old and modern songs which possess the earth, where the earth which they touch is the chief protagonist. And the path I walk along leads to the Instituto de Canarias, where I am going to study, this is my aim in my first day in La Laguna, to start a new life, this is my city, here I am going to create myself, it is now day, but this will also be the inauguration of my nights. I listen to the fountain and hear the wind moving the trees, and imagine Miguel de Unamuno or Benito Pérez Galdos, the philosopher and the novelist, both of who came here, walking through these inner hallways; the kids with their cardboard folders and new books are here already, the ones who crossed the Avenida de la Trinidad at the same time as the goats. And I see them running down these corridors, as though they had lived there last year as well; but I have just arrived, I don't know anyone, even though the city is mine now, I feel that I am a part of it, as if I was born here, I even recognised the light in the cemetery, the city is mine, I have it, I touch its memory.

Then I walk along Camino Largo, the line in the earth, the moss on the walls, the Camino de las Peras, El Pozo Cabildo, the fountains, the cobbles. I am walking on the past. Many years later I touched the same walls, walked the same roads; my hair is white and I am nearly fifty years older, as is La Laguna. But I feel as though I am arriving and touching it once again, and it feels the same as it did on that first morning.

A HALT ON THE ROAD

L ET US MAKE A HALT ON THE ROAD, LET US POUR OUT A FEW WORDS, LET us stop for a while and consider a few common points about this territory to which we are inviting all those who do not yet know it and calling on those who have already been here to return. And let us put a few names on the table.

Telde, El Tamaduste, Tazacorte, Tiscamanita, Tuineje, Tías, Betancuria, Tacoronte, Tejina, Adeje, Tejeda, Yaiza, Haría, Tahiche, Chipude, Alajeró, Vegueta, Arucas, Arure, Aridane, Taburiente, El Médano, Arona.

Names come first.

Miguel de Unamuno noticed these names and used them to write a poem which he considered to be the essence of the Canary Islands: the poetic capacity inherent in its own names. A land that tries to be a continent, an archipelago full of legends, the Canary Islands are above all the result of a kind of harmony; you see this in Vegueta on Gran Canaria, in La Laguna on Tenerife, in the cliffs of La Gomera, in the deserts of Fuerteventura, in the sky above La Palma, in Timanfaya, in the volcanoes of Lanzarote . . . and this harmony is also to be found in the islands' names.

Seven greater and seven lesser islands, as well as their soul and their geography, what the Canary Islands have in common is paradoxically the fact that they are a compact archipelago, a series of islands both great and small which complement one another, because of the landscape, because of the volcanoes, because of their folklore, which they all share with certain subtle or significant differences, because of their gastronomy . . . The seven islands are well set-up. They need one another, but they could still live separately. They look for one another, because there is an inner sense of brotherhood between them which began at the bottom of the sea and in the depths of history, but they also are tempted to exist without looking at one another. This is no longer possible: they are not joined except by air or by sea, by aeroplanes or boats, but they are condemned to be together. They are a single unit. United by the same sea, as one of the anthems of the Islands has it.

They compare themselves, of course, just as all territories which are close to one another or opposed to one another compare themselves, whether they be islands or not; and here, in these comparisons, is the origin of their disagreements, but each island could set itself forward as an example of how an island should be, an island in and of itself in any exhibition of perfect islands that they put on in the world. It is a lie to say that once you have seen one you have seen them all: in order to truly know the Canary Islands you need to visit them all, and maybe also consider in their mythological history the inverted reflection of the Atlantic and the shifting mirrors of the island of San Borondón, that non-existent space which has always been used for the islanders to get used to the concept of limbo.

Unamuno said of the Canary Islanders what he said of his compatriots, the people of Bilbao: they speak of their land as though they had invented it, or built it with their own hands. They did not lay out the beaches of Fuerteventura, nor mould the dunes at Maspalomas in Gran Canaria; they did not hollow out the Taburiente cave on La Palma, and they didn't design the sunsets at Fuencaliente; of course, they didn't heat the lava of Mount Teide. But they could name these things. Most of these names, these names whose poetic softness so impressed Unamuno and even José Saramago, who made his house in Tías the centre of his poetic reflection on the world, come from the Guanche past of the Islands, and others were born to show different aspects of the uneven fight between the aboriginal inhabitants of the

Islands and the Spaniards. La Matanza de Acentejo and La Victoria de Acentejo, the Acentejo Massacre and the Acentejo Victory, both on Tenerife, evoke an episode from the history of the Conquest, a central episode in the life of the archipelago. The Conquest was slow and laborious. The aboriginal inhabitants of the Islands were brutally massacred, or else sent to other regions or countries, or the races were deliberately mixed in order to give rise to the current-day Canary Islanders. In Tlatelolco, Mexico, they say that the Conquest of Mexico created what is the Mexico of today, and that, according to a plaque displayed in the famous Plaza de las Tres Culturas, there were 'neither conquerors nor conquered'. As Los Sabandeños sing, using a poem by Ramón Gil Roldán in their 'The Song of the Wild *Mencey*', the aboriginal races of the Islands 'finished in history in order to live on in legend'.

There is a great deal of history in this legend, and also a great deal of interpretation laid down on top; *el canario* (the Spanish spoken by the Canary Islanders) no doubt derives from so-called 'travelling Spanish'. This, as Álex Grijelmo explains in his book *The Genius of Language*, is the Spanish that was spoken on the Islands in the eighteenth and nineteenth centuries and which was contaminated, or enriched, by the language that travelled from America.

With certain variations, this is the sound of the Islander, the speaker of Atlantic Spanish, and this sound is one of the unifying elements of his presence, his attitude and his spirit. Another thing that unifies the Islanders is a certain melancholic spirit which is represented in their poetry, in their way of being and in their way of singing. Among other songs that they sing, one which represents this particularly Canary Island way of existing, turned in on oneself, is the *folía*. According to some scholars, it is based on a melody which came from Portugal and came accompanied by an extremely vigorous dance used to counteract the effects of a tarantula bite; according to others, it is a rhythm which came through Andalusia in the sixteenth century and from there leapt onto the Islands. In any case, it is clear that the Islanders naturalised it until they had transformed it into a radically individual manifestation of their way of being and existing in the world. It is a slow and sad song (which has nothing at all to do with a tarantula) which speaks of melancholy partings, of distance, of abandonment, but which at the same time is something joyous yet sad to sing. '*Folías*, yes | that's what you want; | you want me to sing | the *folías* of my homeland | which are joyful and very sad to sing', as Los Sabandeños put it, in this version of the *folía* as arranged by my friend Elfidio Alonso, who had the singular skill of reinventing the *folía* and putting it in the service of the folklore of the Islands and of its connections with the poetic and musical language of America as well.

The intense paradox of the spirit of the Islands, one in which sadness and joy are combined in a manner which leads to a certain kind of sweet despair, is, perhaps, the unifying factor of what it is to be an Islander. A kind of Portuguese *saudade*, which the Islanders call *magua*—a word that in the language of the Islands means grief or sorrow—and which has for centuries been the backbone of a way of being that distinguishes the Islanders from the rest of the world. Here it is almost as common as *gofio*.

THE ISLAND IN THE SKY

T HIS IS LA PALMA, AN ISLAND IN THE SKY. THE WORLD'S ASTROPHYSI-
cists discovered it as though they were finding a hidden treasure:
from here one can see better than anywhere in the world all the mysteries of the sky, as though the island had a natural observatory that
enabled one to observe the future via the sky's DNA.

They are on the Roque de los Muchachos, those observatories
which are now the emblem of an island which until recently preferred
to look down to the ground, to its national symbol, the Caldera de
Taburiente, than up to the sky. It is a triangular island, very beautiful,
born to be green and beautiful, a contrast between the lava which
forms it and the trees which have made it the greenest island of the
archipelago.

La Isla Verde. La Isla Bonita. This is what the people who have
come here have called it, and this is what the inhabitants of Las Palmas
call it themselves. Both groups have a contagious devotion for the island,
so that when one comes to the island one is already in the presence of
its adjectives. Verde. Bonita.

Green and beautiful. Here one finds an exception to what the
Catalan urban planner said, eating his parrotfish in Puertito de la
Cruz: here the greenery is tectonic and green at the same time: everything is green, but everything is rock as well; the island is green, and
the Caldera is green, intensely green, and the lava extensions to the
island, thrown out by successive explosions, are green as well.

When he came here, Aldecoa wrote, more than fifty years ago, that 'the island is in the shape of a heart. The island has a heart as well; a heart of fire, a volcano heart. There is a crucible under the surface of La Palma, and Saint Michael, the angel who defeated the creatures of fire, protects La Palma from its own flaming heart.'

Island of legends and distances: its roads are winding, the curves transform a short journey into a long one, and the way in which the landscape is structured has given the island huge patience. It is a symbol cut out of the rock with a pick, an intricate path on which the valleys are the final surprise of a tortuous journey through curves and impossible cultivated land; the island is patient, but its landscape has led its patience to be almost infinite. The beauty of its landscape has to be walked over, or cultivated with extremely patient labour, because it is full of cliffs and slopes; La Caldera, which is so easy to descend, becomes a sheer trench when time comes to climb it, just as the ancient inhabitants of the island crossed the cliffs from side to side: with strong sticks or staffs.

It is the green island, and it is also the island where one can smell the sea the best. It is the island of the Caldera de Taburiente, but it is also the island of the Aridane valley, the island of the abrupt and the mysterious, the island that is closest to the sky, but also the island that stretches out the most before the sea. La Palma is so close to the sky that one has the impression that it would take just a little shove to force it into the sky; but the sea is so close and so powerful that one might also imagine that the island is afloat: looking at the sky but subject to the sea.

There is an important collection of Flemish art on the island, which began with the immigrants who came here from Flanders in the sixteenth and seventeenth centuries in order to help build the ingenious sugar plants of La Palma. They brought sculptures with them, and paintings, and panels which were representative of Flemish art, of the end of the Gothic period and of the Renaissance, coming from the workshops in Brussels, Antwerp, Bruges and Ghent. This influence transformed La Palma into an island with a great deal of cultural ambition and the best artistic patrimony in the whole archipelago.

The first trip I made to La Palma, in 1968, was to meet and interview an old cigar-maker, Don Pedro Capote. Back in those days, La Palma had a significant tobacco industry. Silk was another industry in which it took pride. Both of these activities have faded significantly, and now all that La Palma has are relics of the splendour which, fifty years ago, held it almost at a level, in the case of its tobacco industry, with the island of Cuba, which it resembles so much in so many other ways.

This time I went to La Palma in search of its sounds, its tastes and its hidden routes. I planned the journey the night I met a man, Mauro Fernández, who invited us to a legendary house, right in the centre of the island; the table was laid with the products of island, which his wife Malula had put out with great care, and certain people had gathered there to celebrate some kind of May festival: there are festivals almost every day in the Islands, but especially during May.

Mauro arrived late; when he got home he told us that he had been walking for five hours, in his high boots and his hat and his satchel, along paths which he had not walked until that point, although he knew almost all the paths on the island.

And so it was there that I thought he would be a good companion for my journey, and I suggested it to him a few months later, when I had already visited the part of the island that everyone visits: the Roque de los Muchachos observatories which have placed La Palma at the forefront of our investigations of the sky. Mauro is a man of the earth, and he came to us that night from the earth, and when he met me at the La Palma airport some little while later, he brought me back to the earth.

There is something metaphorical about one's arrival in La Palma, if you come by air, because the airport displays a kind of summary of the island's variety: greenhouses, palm trees, the sea. This is the first vision of La Palma, the one that fills you with the island; you have the sea in front of you, high and clear, carrying boatfuls of passengers to and from the island. Malula and Mauro like showing

people the islands, they told us as we drove through Garafía; there is
an old man with a hat (his 'puppy', as they call it) and his cigar, smoking
it with such enjoyment that one might think he was about to disappear in a cloud of smoke. Mauro has retired now, but he used to work
for Unelco, the Islands' electric company, which allowed him to get
to know the paths all across this island. La Palma, the island of light,
was the first of the Canaries to have electricity, which came to the
island in 1893. After Barcelona and Madrid, Santa Cruz de La Palma
was the third Spanish city to get electric light. And La Palma was also
a cultural centre, open to the influence of the Encyclopédie, and was
also the place where the Islands' first newspaper, the *Diario de Avisos*,
came into being. It is still published to this day.

SANTA CRUZ DE LA PALMA IS A MAGNIFICENT ARTISTIC ACHIEVEMENT IN
and of itself, a historic place. It is a calm city, surprising both in its
beauty and in its cleanliness, as though the city wanted to reveal its
soul or its history in the calm and ancient spectacle of its narrow cob-
bled streets; a city which is like a reflection of the past which still
dwells within it.

The city was born in order to house the Christianity which the
Catholic monarchs exported to the island during the period of law-
lessness under Alonso Fernández de Lugo, in 1492, when he also got
his hands on the island of Tenerife. Fernández de Lugo came to the
island via Tazacorte; alliances and struggles preceded the conquest,
and the island's resistance ended in 1493 when it fell into the hands
of the Catholics. This was when Santa Cruz de La Palma was
founded, and it has always been and continues to be in the vanguard
of the cosmopolitan life of the Islands.

The city of Santa Cruz de la Palma faces the east, as was habitual
back then in the case of cities that faced the sea, and it was built,
slowly, in a linear fashion after the model favoured by the Portuguese,
who had a great influence on the urban and human development of
the territory. In the Avenida Marítima, which is perhaps the most

heavily exposed to the ocean of all the avenues in the Islands, there are still some houses which recall the abundant presence of the Portuguese. Old houses painted in an extremely evocative fashion, with balconies that are only to be seen in this particular spot, covered with shutters to protect them when the sea is too rough. These shutters used to protect the toilets of the houses as well; they were cleaned by the action of the sea when it was rough. Now the friends who accompany me on my island journey have pointed the shutters out to me as a spectacle in and of themselves, like a symbolic remnant of what man does in order to display his inventiveness.

The architectural record of the city is exceptional, one of the most important in the whole of the Islands. I have it noted down in my book that the city has been threatened on numerous occasions, and that it somehow survived the earthquake on 3 May 1632; it was also unaffected by the regular fires, especially that of 1770. It has avoided being ruined by speculation, and this is another miracle of nature, to some extent.

The history of Santa Cruz de la Palma can be divided into two eras. The first begins at the moment of the Catholic conquest and lasts until 1553, when the pirates of François Le Clerc, known as Pegleg, invaded the island. Then the island developed towards the south, and became an obligatory stopping point on the path to the Indies which Columbus had discovered, and here they set up the first Indies court, which was a key to the control and regulation of the traffic which paused in this formerly much-transited port.

The cultivation of sugar cane, especially in the works at Argual, Tazacorte and Los Sauces, brought in commerce with the Low Countries and increased the degree of cosmopolitanism which helps distinguish La Palma, and its capital above all, in the history of the Islands. This was the spot whence the malmsey wine was exported to Europe, the same malmsey wine that Shakespeare refers to so often in his works and which was so popular in the countries of northern Europe. The traffic was also cultural, in that extremely cultured people from Antwerp and other cities in the Netherlands came and settled on La Palma.

The ships that carried the sugar and the wine returned from Flanders with religious trappings, carpets, weapons, bells, paintings, panels, altarpieces and sculptures, which are now treasures that are kept in the capital and on the island. In the eighteenth century, the city which now sleeps in the sun of its history was the third most important port of the Spanish Empire, along with Seville and Antwerp. And that made the island extremely attractive to all kinds of pirate.

But the nineteenth century redeemed the island to some degree, and its capital above all, as one of the most advanced Spanish sites of learning. Here modernism and liberalism set down some roots; here the first printing press in the island was set up; the first newspaper was printed in 1863; electricity was installed. Some of the youth of the city went to study in Paris. Paris was from which came the news that electric light existed. One of the students who went to France, attracted by the idea of culture, came back from his journey telling anyone who would listen that if you pushed a button in the wall then the whole room would light up. This news was the initial impetus for La Palma to get electricity installed in advance of the other islands of the archipelago, and on 31 January 1893 Santa Cruz de la Palma was the first capital to install electric street lighting.

A little earlier, in 1881, the Cosmological Society was founded, with the intention of being the focus for cultural and scientific discussion on the island, and it was the seed of a great library. This quiet outburst was the result of this island, which already had a high regard for culture and science, making a wager on their behalf, a wager that has encouraged the appearance of great people, poets, actors, musicians and even shoemakers, like Manolo Blahnik, a great contemporary figure, well known all over the world. But it is the Calle Real, and its traditional spectacle of dwarves making jokes against Napoleon, its vast artistic heritage, the Descent of the Virgin . . . it is these cultural remnants which are some of the elements that make this island into much more than a landscape and a history. They called it La Isla Bonita, but it would be equally just to call it La Isla Misterio, the Mystery-Island, and to uncover this mystery it is best to come and see it. And to come and see it with, for example, Malula and Mauro, my friends.

MAURO AND MALULA TELL ME THE STORIES OF LA PALMA AS WE WALK through villages which still look the same and are as peaceful as they were when electricity first came to the island: Los Sauces, El Paso, Breña Alta, Garafía, all of them places connected to agriculture and tobacco. Mauro and Malula, and the jeep in which we travel, know all of these sheer curves, all these curves which reveal at every turn a new banana plantation. Up here, at almost 8,000 feet, they point out the Roque de los Muchachos, with its spectacular installations in which a number of European countries have set up their observatories. 'This is the best sky in the world,' they say to me, but the worldly authorities which control the sky have chosen Chile to install what will be the best telescope in the world, and this has been seen on the island as the result of a failure of political will or an offence that the legendary patience of the Islands will have to deal with.

But we are at ground level; here it is the insects which annoy us, or the plants that damage the vine stock (there's a plant called 'cat's tail' which affects the vines); they tell us about them, pointing out the vines that festoon the path like hanging gardens. Presiding over the landscape are houses in the Portuguese style (three windows, three doors), which can be explained by the continued influence of the Portuguese on this and the other western islands of the archipelago. The first books that were brought to the island came from Portugal, they came in the sixteenth century and were written in Old Portuguese. There was a Portuguese man at that time, Gaspar Frutuoso, who discovered the island. He travelled over it step by step, ate the fruit of the prickly pear that they cultivated in Puntagorda; he hired a man to accompany him who said, when they reached Garafía: 'I will not accompany you from Garafía to Barlovento because I do not know the roads.' And this stretch of the journey, which Gaspar Frutuoso would travel in ten minutes nowadays, took him about a day.

Mauro pointed out the cliffs and the little rivers with enthusiasm, he pointed to the ravines and the woods, we were passing though
the Cubo de la Galga, which is a beautiful forest in Barranco de la
Galga. It is such an agricultural island that one would almost say that
it has been fully planted. Fully; there is not a single nook or cranny
on La Palma which does not contain the shadow of a tree, or a bush.
The problem is that fifty per cent of what has been planted on the island is now abandoned. In the 1950s tobacco was grown everywhere,
the island was similar to Cuba, a huge tobacco factory, but the blue
mould came, a plague, and the tobacco was seriously attacked; now
it is only at Las Breñas where they grow any tobacco.

I WAS IN LA PALMA ANOTHER TIME, ROUND ABOUT 1974, AND THEY TOOK
me to San Andrés y Sauces, which is two worlds in one; what I remember of this trip is the huge rocky cliff, next to a double plaza, by
an old yet still preserved church. I was back here once again quite recently listening to South American singing, intoning Chavela Vargas's
broken *rancheras*, and eating *ropa vieja*. Mauro and Malula have
taken us back to this same spot; they serve *gofio*, they give us wine
and cheese; we are on La Palma: outside they are celebrating weddings
or baptisms, it is September, but it could be any of the festival days in
the whole year; there would be the same festive atmosphere, you
would hear the same songs, we would be enjoying the same weather.
The island is blue, it is not at all surprising that the sky here should
be so sought-after.

This place has something about it of a fifteenth-century Italian
town, like much of the rest of the island; the same ability to understand that it is by reading that one achieves progress, the same sense
that the island is public property that has to be left in good condition
for those who will come after. The jingoistic love which the inhabitants of La Palma have means that they are proud of their achieve-
ments (this was where the first shipyards were built; this was where
the first newspapers were established . . .) and also proud of having

one of the best-preserved landscapes of all the islands, including the larger ones. Construction here has been permitted only to a very small degree; you could take a photograph today on La Palma, just as you could on El Hierro or La Gomera, and the image would look very similar to what it would have looked like seventy years ago to Ignacio Aldecoa's travelling companions.

AND SO WE EAT, CHEESE, GOFIO, PARROTFISH, SOLE . . . MAURO REMEMbers a few lines of poetry and recites them: 'In El Cubo de la Galga | under a flowering almond tree | my mother gave my father | love's first kiss . . .' They serve us *escaldón*, *gofio* in stock, like that we had in Puertito de la Cruz. They add the raw onion I want to this dish, the *guayonge* onion, the blue onion which seems both an onion and a colour out of the earth. We go over our plans: on this island you have to go to La Caldera, and you have to go to see the volcanoes, they say. We are in the centre of the island now. The volcano path will take us to the tip of the island, to Fuencaliente. They do not know this, but at the moment that they say the name, Fuencaliente, I am seeing in my mind a spectacular sunset, similar to the sunset I saw from the window of the aeroplane as I came in to Tenerife. They are telling me that it is there, thanks to the volcanoes, that the island has grown over the last two million years; at some point during this period the Benahoarites, the first settlers, came to the island, and 'then we came', Mauro says, with the irony that is so typical of La Palma. La Caldera was over 11,000 feet tall, taller than Mount Teide, but 'two million years ago it collapsed and fell into what is now the Aridane valley'.

Mauro is still holding back a few surprises, in order to show to the traveller some of the places that only he visits. The place where he is taking us is called Rio Muerto, it is a cove that is almost secret, approached by sheer cliffs, and it is on the part of the coast called the Mazo, under the Colada del Volcán Martín, which poured out its lava in 1660; here there are old houses, beehives, ovens; it is clear that man has stepped onto this land, but it is also clear that man comes very rarely to this place where the volcano provides shelter, where we are now in its shadow . . . Mauro and his hill-walking friends travel through these godforsaken places, from La Breña to La Cumbre, five hours walking, five men, under the laurisilva, crossing on paths which are sown with plum trees and through gardens which feed houses that have been here for four hundred years. The church of San Andrés, which they point out to me, has been here since 1515.

The places where we travel are serious spots, they are like Italian landscapes of the fifteenth century, as though the hand of history which makes such landscapes had stopped here; the colours are restrained, almost old; I note in my book that 'from time to time there are dull bursts of a Mexican yellow'.

We are walking along the spine of the island, we are travelling to San Andrés and to Las Breñas, 'this is a fierce tongue of land bathed in a clean sea', my notes say . . . We pass through Hoyo de Mazo, a little winery, a few vines, the Molino de Mazo, the Mazo mill, 'which is like a little sigh of a mill'. In the distance one can see La Gomera, we are standing right next to a solitary palm and some fig trees, on an earthen path, near Manchas Blancas. From here you can see the crater of a volcano, Martín, next to the part of the coast that they call Tigalate Hondo. The goats are ranging free, and so are the little black pigs. 'I have been walking round here for forty years,' Mauro says. We are down now, in Río Muerto, where there are slabs of stones like pillows, sea stones that must have been here for millions of years. This was where Martín erupted in 1646 and the island grew larger thanks to an immense flow of lava which now coexists with the other parts of nature here in this so aptly named Río Muerto, Dead River.

I speak to Mauro:

'It is impossible to know the whole island.'

'You'll never know it all. It is different in winter and in summer, as well.'

The Islands are like that, never the same, never identical; their horizon, as the painter Pedro González put it, marks them out, but the horizon is never the same, it is a turning point, the centre of a wheel. Here, in Río Muerto, I can sense the prehistoric sound which all lonely places retain. I listen to the sea as it forms pools, as though it were an ocean in waiting, dead, or pretending to be dead. In the distance one can see the tip of the island, the lighthouse at Fuencaliente. It was there that I saw the sunset which is still the most beautiful sunset I have seen in the Islands, along with the one that I saw in the aeroplane over the sea, coming into Tenerife.

On the way to Fuencaliente, Mauro points out El Pino del Alivio, which is where in the twentieth century the animals, the mules and donkeys and mares who pulled carriages, would take a pause and rest. A decade later, Mauro tells me in his most serious voice, they buried the victims of the Civil War.

Mauro likes telling us the legend (which is based on fact) of the Fuentesanta, a spring which was buried by two volcanoes and which has been the object of unstinting searches (because its medicinal waters are much sought-after) since the eighteenth century. These searches were always accompanied by failure until 2005, when the spring reappeared. The history of this search is in itself a novel on the island's desire to bury the failures of its past; when we travel across the island they have rediscovered it and are acting as though they had found the Holy Grail. 'It is the best water in Europe.'

WE HAVE COME DOWN INTO THE ARIDANE VALLEY; WE HAVE BEEN UNDER the shade of the Indian laurels, we have attended to a small errand to do with the wealth of the country (there are seventeen banks for two thousand inhabitants), we have looked at the Flemish art in the churches and museums, we have been to the glassblowers' works, and we have visited El Time.

El Time is wonderful, a valley out of paradise where the one unnecessary thing is the plastic which the farmers use to make bananas ripen more quickly. Before climbing up in order to see this natural monument ruined by plastic, we have paused for a moment in the hermitage of the Agony of our Lord. Canary Island pine, banana trees, cliff. Inside the hermitage an extremely sad man cries and constantly crosses himself. El Time is nearly 2,000 feet above sea level; there used to be pools here, which was why it was called the Valle de los Espejos, Mirror Valley. Now there are no longer any pools, but only this insistent plastic. Mauro says that 'the banana is the landscape'. But agricultural greed has damaged the landscape . . . As I look at this most beautiful place I can't get out of my mind the image of the man weeping in front of the picture of the Agony.

An island that looks up into the sky, but above all an agricultural island. Before taking us to La Caldera, which is like the promised land of La Palma, Maura and Malula take us along the path of the fig trees, the path of the Japanese medlars, the path of the plums . . . On some of these paths one can hear the sound of a cock crowing, and we see large numbers of drago trees; the houses crowd up to the edge of the cliff as though they were daring each other to do dangerous balancing acts. At one point I calculate how far Mauro must have walked along these paths, and I come to the conclusion, counting on my fingers, that he has walked 7,181 miles in fifty years. He laughs. 'Probably,' he says.

We have come through Santo Domingo, where next to a sixteenth-century hermitage they feed us with pork at tables covered with red, white and blue check tablecloths, and once again it is as though we are in an old Italian *trattoria* where they serve old fashioned Canary Island food, simple and well-seasoned, tasty and straightforward. Then we walk past French cliff, Galician cliff and the cliff of Mankind . . . I ask Mauro a question:

'Of all the places you have walked through, which is the one where you would most like to live?'

He replies immediately, without pausing for a moment.

'La Caldera. There are always places in La Caldera that you have never seen before. The more I walk the more there is still left for me to walk in La Caldera.'

And here we are; he has taken us very early in the morning to

La Caldera. There are athletes, who are training here for elite competitions. La Caldera is a prehistoric dip in the ground filled with majestic trees, a hole majestic in itself which makes you feel like some
wretched little shrub among all the green shades of this green place.
It is true, with every minute that passes, La Caldera de Taburiente is
a new space, a place you must discover once again. You hear the silence. Mauro is right: a journey like the one we have taken all over
the island, crossing the paths that are like the palm of someone's hand,
all this is only a moment of preparation for going down to La Caldera.
I wanted to cross it, as he did, by secret paths on which the foot of
man barely fits, and I have not dared do it. I am not ready to be like
Mauro, but I admire his light feet; he is seventy years old at least, and
he walks as though he had just come into the world. Here inland one
breathes a special air; silence is a food of the air.

THEN MAURO TAKES US TO SANTA CRUZ DE LA PALMA AND WALKS US UP
the Calle Real, which is like the hand of the eighteenth century pointing to the twenty-first century and indicating the relics that existed
back then. At one point Mauro stops and points out a plaque to me:
'Here they established the first public non-religious school of the island.
1794 to 1994. Ayntamiento de Santa Cruz de la Palmas.' In 1774,
Mauro tells me, they also brought the first democratic government to
Spain. We walked, as we had when we walked on La Caldera, in order
to find an island which connects nature with cultural and scientific
progress, a privileged site which now looks at the land and the soil
with the pride of having been a pioneer in many things. In its peace-
fulness it is as though it had always been there, waiting, but always
for a time that was yet to come, like Mauro and his paths.
    Then we went to eat fried squid facing the sea, with Pilar Rey
and Antonio Abdo, both of them poets, and Mauro and Malula. Talking about the French Revolution, which came here via the sea, and
about the relationship of the Islands with the masonic lodges in Cuba,
and about the great number of places from which the Islands' inhab-

itants came (Ireland, Andalusia, Extremadura, Galicia, Portugal), and about the tradition of the Dwarves, originally figures created to insult Napoleon, which are now brought out once every five years, when the Virgin of the Snows is brought down to the city, and about the 1885 creation of the Cosmology, one of the entities which connects La Palma to the culture of the rest of the world, and about the shipyards, and about the splendour of the nineteenth century . . .

But above all we speak about the landscape. La Palma is its landscape, here it is as though landscape were organising your life: cliffs and pine trees and green valleys, the architectural marvel that is La Caldera, which seems the mould from which Mount Teide was cast. From here, out of this silence, the sky appears to be a roof. You hear the cawing of the rooks. In the midst of the light which the pine trees allow to pass through them you see the rock, the greenery, the smooth cliff, the innumerable paths, from a hillock you see an arch, a fantastic amphitheatre filled with sunlight . . .

Mauro points out a stone monolith. He says that if the monolith falls then the island will collapse.

I believe him, because on La Palma everything is true.

And truth comes from the sky, just as the island did.

THE BEACH IN THE CITY

Gran Canaria. Like a half-closed fist, Tejeda is where it breathes, Agaete, Arucas, Teror and Firgas are where it drinks, and it bathes in Las Canteras, on the Playa del Inglés and at Maspalomas. Las Canteras is a glorious beach, a perfect band of yellow sand that lies in a semicircle in front of Las Palmas itself. The poet of the city, Manuel Padorno, who lived right here, in this corner of the sea, in a white house with blue doors just above the rocks, next to the sand where he came to bathe his feet every morning, wrote as follows: 'Beach ahead of me, the great open abyss. | I breathe the sun. I am diluted, | start to dissolve, slowly, at each step | in an endless draught, which flips me round, | which disassembles me, which fans me out | in all directions, turning round and round.'

An endless beach, an adventure. If I were asked to choose a landscape, or seven landscapes from the seven islands, then this would be one of them; I could live here forever, just looking out. The Las Canteras beach. Behind it is the city, the Port of Light, with its hubbub, with its wild and outlandish nightlife, its perpetual carnival, but here is the beach, which is the horizon for Las Palmas, the point where the city breathes, the city with sand in its lungs.

It is among the most beautiful of all the landscapes of all the islands, the most open, the exact symbol of the Islands' vocation, the search for an eternal horizon; the beach at Las Canteras is like a point of entry for the islander's gaze, onwards into the open sea and back

into the city which was made to look at the sea and to live from it . . .
Here we can spend all our time, from morning until night, and nothing will ever be the same for a moment, not the horizon or the sand
or the sky or the sea which beats with a violence that is calmed by an
artificial sandbank built in order to retain in this point the effective,
unfathomable harmony of a truly happy beach.

Manuel Padorno speaks again, the man who lived his nights of
alcohol and poetry next to this beach at dusk: 'Spreading me out with-
out mercy, leaving me | along the whole stretch of Las Canteras.' The
beach is like a totem, and emblem, like a dream where one can live.

LAS PALMAS, THE CAPITAL OF THE ISLAND, IS A COMBINATION OF ADVEN-
TURE, history and silence; Vegueta is the island's Spanish history, and
from this point it might also have gathered its history of silence; this
part of town is preserved as though a miraculous hand had stopped
all the speculators of the past and the present in their insatiable
predatory lust. Here, in Vegueta, and in the streets and houses of La
Isleta, which is on the other side of Las Palmas, the night never ends,
as though there were a ceaseless energy in the island; I believe it
comes from the contagious, eternally living landscape of the Las Canteras beach.

The island is silence in Ariñez, by San Mateo and Santa Brígida;
it is the agricultural murmur of Sur, it is Maspalomas, that still wild
beach, where the dunes carry out their ancient mission to turn all of
nature into a living painting, always the same, always changing. The
apex of the island is Roque Nublo, in Tejeda. This monolith is the geographical and sentimental symbol of Gran Canaria. It is surrounded
by other rocks, by Fraile and Bentryga; the first looks like a seated
friar, hence the name, *fraile* meaning friar, and the second was a sacred
spot for the first people of the Islands, who left their archaeological
relics here, which attain their character as that of history assimilated
by the men of today in the legendary Painted Cave at Gáldar, as
though this were the one spot where there communication could be

established between the mysterious past of the island and the people dedicated to unveiling its mystery. In Cruz de Tejeda the traveller may rest: there is the Tejeda hotel, whose surroundings were called a petrified storm by Miguel de Unamuno.

I sit down to look here, and looking at this landscape causes me nostalgia and melancholy. I am looking at the cliffs of Tejeda, and seeing memories.

MY FIRST MEMORY OF GRAN CANARIA COMES FROM MY YOUTH, AND THE island is still in my mind as an island made of air. This was because I came by boat, at night, enjoying the wind on the deck for the whole length of the journey from Tenerife, and when I arrived into the damp morning of Puerto de La Luz, which was a hodgepodge at that time, filled with dangerous people and sailors passing through, I was set down in a village which ever since then I have associated with the air. It was Tafira: I have come through it once again now on this trip.

There are lots of places in the Canary Islands where the air appears to be the essence of the space, the material out of which they are made: the air, the breeze, the wind, the distinct grades of the air; not the land, not the cliffs, not even the sea which, along with the wind, is what feeds my memory of the Islands because I have lived in the wind for more than twenty years now, in El Médano. But Tafira, on the road to Las Palmas and Santa Brígida and San Mateo, was the place where I first understood the metaphorical nature of the air, as though it were a fresh and dry gust of air that helped one sleep, helped one breathe, helped one love and also remain on the Islands. It is an air which, on the calm nights or melancholy mornings of the Islands, gives one the sense of eternity which is contained in all happy moments on similar lands.

Then I left Tafira, I returned to Tenerife; since then I have been back many times to Gran Canaria, and there has always been a hand in my memory, dragging me back to this blessed place which helped me to love the airs of the island more and to know, for the first time, what is most essential about it, the air of the island, the air of the north, the air that carries you over the peaks, from San Mateo to Tejeda. Tejeda may be the most beautiful village on this island of villages.

To get to Tafira I went through Bandama this time, by the capital, the place where I am now writing this passage; and here I am, standing in front of the beautiful beach of Las Canteras, an urban beach which is still the one that inspires poets and other artists, which is still the same as it was back when it was surrounded by huts and shacks; now Las Canteras, down there, the roar of its waves softened by a natural stone barrier, is surrounded by large buildings, all of them much taller than the beach deserves. But there is no way back from this now. When you say that you are in Las Canteras, on the beach, people usually say that it is a broken place, aesthetically wrecked by the excessive construction which has destroyed the Spanish coastline, and the coastline of the Islands above all. But here I have grown used to looking at the sea, the sand of the sea, this beach that is more than two miles long, its sand made damp by the waves but also by this climate with its low blood pressure which brings the low-hanging clouds that the locals call 'donkey belly'.

The donkey belly is, although it might not seem so, a blessing; here, under these clouds that from Tejeda seem like a grey blanket, the climate is benign, is sweetened by the clouds, is a caress of calm air, sometimes a little unruly, but always much more habitable than the high temperatures which one can suffer in Maspalomas, where the sun is hardly ever dampened. Here the sun is made slightly wet, and we, who walk along this beach surrounded on all sides apart from the sandy one by tall buildings, enjoy the weather, as though the air of Tafira made it all the way down here.

Las Canteras is a spectacular beach; I was told that one of the psychiatrists of the island, Rafael O'Shanahan, makes his more disturbed patients come here to calm their nervous fears, and he prescribes them three hours sitting in front of the sea, or three hours per day walking on the yellow, damp and yielding sand. Other people have done the same, people who were not mad. They were poets, yes, like Manuel Padorno, who was born on Tenerife, lived in Barcelona and Madrid, and came back here at the beginning of the 1980s in order to regain the vision of the beach on which he had been happy in his childhood and his youth, and where he was once again happy as an adult, windswept and far from the capital. On this beach, on its sand, among its rocks, looking out at its sea, Padorno wrote the most beautiful lines that have been written to the Atlantic since the time of Tomás Morales, the great singer of this ocean which is made majestic in Gran Canaria, like an embrace of salt and water which never releases the island and which can be seen from all points, for the island is a round rock.

THE ISLAND IS A ROCK, A HUGE ROCK WHICH HAS, IN LAS CANTERAS AND the southern beaches, from San Agustín to Maspalomas, the sea that bathes it, the calm Atlantic. The sculptor Martín Chirino—who is now eighty-five years old but who grew up here, on Las Canteras itself, in Portugal Street, very close to the house where Padorno last lived—drew a rock made of spirals (his metaphor for the island is composed of spirals) and gave it the title 'My Fatherland is a Rock', summoning up some verses of the poet Nicolás Estébanez, a citizen of Tenerife from the middle of the nineteenth century who fought in the war of Cuban independence. The metaphor, this rock, is not a lyric accident, or a transposition of the definition which Estébanez was trying to set down; it is simply a description. If you stand at the top of Tejeda, with the two symbols of Gran Canaria, Roque Nublo and Roque Bentayga, surrounding you, themselves surrounded by intricate cliffs of immense natural power, then you will understand perfectly the fascination which Chirino finds in the word 'rock' as applied to the reality of our fatherland. As though the island were, in dreams but also in the reality as drawn by Chirino, a series of concentric circles, a spectacle which is perfectly summed up in Chirino's drawing. A rock.

Gran Canaria is a rock, there is no doubt about it. The composer

Néstor Álamo, who wrote some of the greatest folksongs of the Islands
in the twentieth century, songs which have been performed by an out-
standing folk group, Los Sabandeños, dedicated a song to Roque
Nublo, the chief point in the island's symbolism, which situates it once
and for all where it will always be. Roque Nublo, Roque Nublo, lyri-
cal lunar rock. It is a stone, a rock balanced in the air of these hastily-
sketched mountains drawn as perfect peaks which show as a series of
little points from which, here and there, larger sharp points stick up,
the prolongations of this upright peak, this rock which stands in
miraculous balance.

When we were there the last time, it was raining in Tejeda and
on Roque Nublo, and it is not very common to see the fog dissolving
and pouring down in this landscape. It is the village of the island
where it rains the least, my friend Ángel Marrero told me, who has
lived here always, because he says that one sleeps better here than in
any other place on the whole island. It rains more in Maspalomas,
which is the landscape where all the sun and the sand is concentrated,
and it rains much more in Las Palmas, the capital of the island, than
it does in Tejeda; when the island is in shade, something which happens a lot in Las Canteras, Tejeda will still be bright and illuminated,
Ángel says. It must be the truth. But up there, that day, it was raining,
and the wind was blowing, and at one point, looking out at the extraordinary landscape round Roque Nublo, towards the cliffs of
which Néstor Álamo sang, I felt the tremendous impression that this
rock, this majestic cliff, was going to fall with all its weight into this
volcanic cone, equally deep and equally majestic, from which we were
observing this damp nature.

Up there I felt a sensation, and I was looking at the landscape
through the windows of Fina's house, a young historian who has con-
verted a nineteenth-century house into the Casa de la Tea, where she
hosts foreign visitors (from Holland, from England and from Germany;
she prefers the Dutch, because the Germans complain a lot; the English,
she says, keep themselves to themselves) who are now trying in vain
to protect their pale faces from the sun which is promised, sometimes

falsely, by the tourist brochures. But they are intellectuals, or at least they look like intellectuals, and soon they hide themselves away from the wind and the rain and sit down to read large books. I was looking out through Fina's windows, as I said, to see if the Roque Nublo of the songs and of reality, the rock of the island's dreams and of the reality of the stones, this huge monolith that seems so weightless, would fall down on us, in the volcanic cone. Just as the Finger of God fell down in the middle of a storm onto Agaete: it was a rock called El Dedo de Dios, the Finger of God, and it looked very like a huge finger, warning men of the wickedness of the earth. The storm finished off the Finger of God, and now all that remains of this miraculous rock, which a divine thunderbolt split and broke, is nothing, air, the pure air of the island.

I was talking about the air, and my memory of the air as the clearest sign of the memory of rock which makes up the island of Gran Canaria. Now I want to recover my air: I have left the capital behind me, its main symbols being this fantastic beach, welcoming and fascinating, the place where the sea comes to rest, where poets and other men come as well, and the Vegueta district of the city, where the city was founded before other similar cities were founded in Columbus's New World. I would live in Vegueta, but in the street, under its old streetlamps, walking from the Columbus Museum (history states that Columbus lived here) to the CAAM, the Modern Art Museum, entering as I did so into silent taverns, visiting the noisy market where I sometimes came in the mornings to bring milk from Aríñez, a village next to San Mateo, set amidst the reedbeds and banana plantations and eucalyptus trees and pines and old houses and the smell of the morning air . . . You can see, from the roads which used to be simple earthen paths, the most exuberant gardens of the whole island, as though they were the fortifications of old secret houses, beautiful remnants which one walks through as though one were always in a garden. This garden is what the air of Tafira preserves, the air I have come looking for, and which I have found once again in Gran Canaria.

BUT I STILL HAVE NOT RETURNED TO TAFIRA, I HAVE TAKEN LOTS OF detours; Tafira is a word which defines the whole island, Gran Canaria is a rock called Tafira or Tejeda, a rock made out of the air which I remember being used to construct these places. And Bandama is made of this air as well. Bandama is a natural wonder, they have told me; sometimes, when people tell you things like this, you later fall all the way down the slide to disappointment, and it was with this feeling, of being ready to be disappointed, that I climbed up to Bandama, on the way to Tafira, the spot I was look-ing for on Gran Canaria to help recover my lost time, as though air were my madeleine.

I made it to Bandama. This rock, Gran Canaria, is in some geo-logical respects similar to La Gomera, or La Palma. Distances are short, curves are eternal; on La Gomera and La Palma they have cut out a lot of tunnels, but Gran Canaria does not have so many of them; and so, in order to get to Bandama, and to carry on to Tejeda, passing through all the villages on the mountainside, you have to follow the twisting fingers of the island, and so once you reach Ayacata, the vil-lage where the composer Juan Hidalgo—another of the artists formed by Las Canteras—put his purple house, you are already feeling a little dizzy, first of all at the naked beauty of the landscape and secondly because of all the twisting and turning you have been forced to carry out. In Bandama, there is a kind of balance which also causes vertigo from time to time. The volcanic crater is like the result of a bomb going off, opening a two-hundred-metre deep hole at the bottom of which you see a house where someone has dared to decide to set up home, far from the world, enjoying this, a paradise inside a pit, a strangely naked pit, without any trees or any other protection than that offered by the air.

I carried on from Bandama, surrounded by the air of Tafira, until I reached Tafira; I had been there several times before, years after my adolescent experience with the air of the place, to visit the poet Pedro Lezcano, who breathed in this air and put it in his poems. He travelled along this road and restored his tired eyes, and even shed a tear, because one of his daughters had died up here, and he spoke of this with a pain which is not calmed by any landscape, or any kind of air: 'I should have gone first.' Sometimes one goes out looking for landscapes or air, and finds memories; suddenly, as I reached Tafira, this memory upset my soul, the memory of seeing this man crying, in the midst of all the branches that crisscrossed the courtyard of his house, in front of some stranger who had come to listen to him. Pedro Lezcano crying . . . The Islands are not simply the journey from one emotion to another over dried-out landscapes, or wet landscapes, or sun-kissed landscapes: they are the experience which you have had faced by other people.

And so, to a certain extent, I walk with Pedro over these landscapes, although he has already taken the path into the shadows, following his daughter. In Tejeda, which was my destiny as I walked over Chirino's spiralled rock, I met Ángel, who took me to his farm from Fina's rebuilt house. There it was that I recovered my desire for landscapes, because he told me a very simple story: his farm is called Mister John. It owes its name to an old farmer who when he was sixteen decided to leave Gran Canaria and go and live in the United States; when he was fifty-two Mister John came back a multimillionaire and bought a farm among the cliffs; the people thought, most likely with some reason, that he had gone mad. But he overcame his supposed madness with inviolable decisiveness, and made this place into a little miracle of the agriculture and livestock business. He died at the age of ninety-four, rich and having made this corner of Tejeda richer.

Destiny has decreed that Ángel should now be the owner of Mister John's farm. He showed me the rooms that the old farmer had built in order to receive people: before such a thing as a fitted wardrobe had made it to the island, the farmer had one imported here, and he imported fridges, and new ways of dealing with his employees. He was a revolutionary in Tejeda; listening to its history, seeing the chopped flesh of those cows whose melancholic tiredness lights up the rocky landscape, and he entered once again into the world, and breathed the air of the rock, among these fabulous cliffs which Néstor sometimes hymned in the voice of Alfredo Kraus. Cliffs like the ones at Tejeda, as the song goes.

LET'S GO BACK TO THE BEACH AND LEAVE THE CLIFFS BEHIND US, LET'S GO back to the sea in the midst of the fog. The poet Manuel Padorno made Las Canteras into the symbol of the whole island: 'I wanted to find myself here; to find where I am; I a place without form or any figure, I no appearances, no customs: nothing at all of this. I Living here makes me doubt myself.' It was in this doubtful happiness that Padorno lived by the sea until his tired heart gave way in May 2002. He sang the island, just as Tomás Morales did, just as so many others did. And he was our contemporary. It is very often that my memories of Las Palmas de Gran Canaria are touched with my memories of him. He represented the calm days and wild nights which started at midnight, drinking in places which no longer exist: Utopia, Gas, bars which were an extension of the bars I knew in the outskirts of Ripoche and of the Parque de Santa Catalina on the first times I visited Las Palmas de Gran Canaria and the island seemed to be a place where all the lights of the night, all the forbidden lights of the night, were concentrated.

And so I took away from the city the impression that it was an endless place, open at all hours, its dives and discos and cabarets always ready for continual festivities. A city by the sea whose old town, Vegueta, was the perfect place to relax after so much excitement. And as I experienced it like this, this is how it lives in my own mythology, my dreams of the spots I have revisited on this journey.

THIS TIME, WHEN I ARRIVED I IMMEDIATELY WENT TO PUERTO DE LA LUZ in the evening; they took me over to the Russian boats that had been there ever since Russia stopped being communist; the crews did not go back to their country, the boats were not reclaimed by their owners; a friend of mine, the director Carlota Nelson, discovered them and filmed a documentary about them in which the poignancy of nightmares is balanced with the lucidity of those who do not want to take back things which they do not know are theirs. And the crew were living their lives as *clochards* in these boats which are no-man's-land and which decay hopelessly inside the huge bowl of Puerto de La Luz. Carlota told me what she had seen when she first encountered these men in their crazy boats. 'Everything moves. The constant crunching noise sounds like a dog barking to warn you of danger. After a few minutes your hands lock from the effort of holding onto rusty cables. The visitor to the boat must learn to relax. Seven metres down there is a bath of tar, seawater and gasoline if you allow yourself to let go. One more jump and you are on the aft deck. You are now on the *Geminis*. This is another world, remote but incredibly close to our own. The day was covered in dull cloud.' The story seems almost unreal, Carlota says, 'but even though it is hidden, it is an integral part of Puerto de La Luz'. This is the modern landscape, the concentration of a century's emotions which were released in this way, people on the margins after living their whole lives in the communist empire, as mysterious and authoritarian as it was transparent and disorganised.

The pier that I now saw here also seemed to me to be a symbol of Puerto de La Luz, this spot that is so cosmopolitan and so open to individual strange histories. I was in these boats, and saw their savage detritus, scrutinised the gazes of their peaceful inhabitants, as though they were the denizens of a phantasmagorical city; people who had been abandoned by the ignoble twenty-first century, which had left people homeless, like beggars, simply because of their inability to tack to the winds of their current century. What better place than Puerto de La Luz to serve as a symbol of the diaspora, not just the Soviet diaspora, caused when the Russian Revolution finally burnt itself out?

And now, Ignacio Aldecoa comes back into the equation. This was another time, the Puerta is now like some kind of futurist composition, a mishmash, which contains the noise of the past within it as well, these 'dogs barking to warn you of danger'. The Basque sailor

Aldecoa saw something else: 'Puerto de La Luz is like a breast, Usebio has written. The large ships come in here and are suckled from the petrol line. Boats from all over the world. Petrol tankers and cargo ships and transatlantic liners. One boat is painted a delicate violet all the way down to the Plimsoll line, the same violet that nineteenth-century women would use for the ribbons round their necks. A blue-grey petrol tanker bids farewell with a long blast on its siren. In Puerto de La Luz the colours of the boats have a special kind of force and power. The large orange letters on a Dutch boat gladden the eye of anyone who sees them. An English boat, under the Plimsoll line, shows four foot of emerald green paint. But the most common dress code is for the boats to be black down to the Plimsoll line, and then red down to the keel. The boats are always dressed in sports clothes.'

This is how Aldecoa saw it, like a painting, but reality imposed itself on the scene and now this diverse and enormous port, filled with Koreans and Senegalese and Russians and Japanese and Islanders, is another matter entirely; it looks much more like what Carlota Nelson described than what the Basque writer saw, back when the pier was a place to go for a stroll and look for points to note down just as I am searching for them now.

THIS TIME, AS ALMOST ALWAYS HAPPENS, I STAY CLOSE TO THIS SPOT, CLOSE to the landscape which is so deeply tied up with the island, the landscape of El Puerto. I stay in a hotel from which one can see the whole of the Las Canteras beach, from the house where the tenor Suso Mariátegui used to live, to the restaurant where we would eat parrotfish and drink white Lanzarote wine, to the house of the poet Padorno, close to the Alfredo Kraus Auditorium, named after the finest interpreter of the Tejida cliffs, the subject of Néstor Álamo's song 'Roque Nublo'.

In the morning my friend Diego Talavera comes to find me. He is a journalist. He wants to take me to see something he has always recommended to me: an area of his home town, Telde, which he wants to use to connect this place with the diverse history of the Islands that stand like statues in the ocean and which nonetheless have been penetrated by so many influences and affected by so many emigrations.

He takes me to San Juan y San Francisco de Telde. He tells me that Telde is the first of the districts of El Sur, and forms a part of the quartet of the great cities of the Islands, along with La Laguna, Las Palmas de Gran Canaria and Santa Cruz de Tenerife. One has to be very careful about these questions on the Islands, because ever since the days of antiquity the larger islands, Tenerife and Gran Canaria, have fought among themselves to establish primacy, and so it is better to use alphabetical order when talking about such things. Let us say then that Telde is the third city . . . even in alphabetical order, with the first two by that criterion being Las Palmas and Santa Cruz.

The conversion of Telde, Diego says, started a century before the conquest. It was on the coast near here that a group of Mallorcan friars landed with the aim of creating a bishopric on the Fortunate Isles, the first city and the first bishopric on the Islands. After the Conquest of Gran Canaria, Juan Rejón sent a troop of soldiers out to build a fortress in Telde, one of the towers of which was used as the belltower for the basilica of San Juan Bautista, which was built at the end of the fifteenth century. It was the initial foundation of what is the current church, where the Christ of Telde stands, made by the Tarasco Indians of Michoacán in Mexico, using millet paste as their building material, so that the statue is very light despite its size: it weighs fifteen pounds and is about six feet tall. The figure has been in Telde since before 1550. The populace believe that the colour of the image changes, as indeed it does, but there is no miracle involved in this: it is because there are variations in the material used to make the statue.

Next to the San Juan district, Diego shows me San Francisco, another part of the town which one reaches by following the course of a rudimentary aqueduct. This whole part of town is filled with little earthen houses, whitewashed, like the houses in Lanzarote; the little streets are paved with cobblestones; all you ever hear here are footsteps; the whole district is silent, like a church or like eternity. The streets are pedestrianised. This district came into being because the Mallorcan friars discovered a spring of water here and set up a convent, which they called the convent of Santa María de la Cabeza. What is left of this is the church of San Francisco. They taught philosophy and logic classes in the convent, and there was also a class on offer on the restoration of bibles and other holy books. So this was the first place in the whole of the Islands where they taught classes in higher education.

In 1836, when the so-called Confiscations of Mendizábal took place in Spain, as a result of which the church lost a good deal of its property and privileges, the Franciscans were expelled, although the area was kept almost exactly as they had left it. The name of the district is a reminder of their presence.

Before leaving this place, which seems like a brief history lesson on the influences that have gone into making the Islands, Diego points into the distance, to the Telde districts of Cendro, Tara and Caserones. He says that in the pre-Hispanic period about ten thousand people lived there.

And from here we went to Bandama. Is it good to start a journey through the Islands with this area of pure air and cosmopolitan history, the journey to the centre of the island, to Tejeda, the kingdom of fog, and we passed through a village called Las Brumas, or Fog, a fact which I have noted down here. At the end of the nineteenth century the Englishmen who had come to the island set up the first golf club in the whole of Spain here; back then, when trade with Africa was just beginning, the citizens of Gran Canaria became so anglophile that they even instituted the custom of afternoon tea, just like the subjects of Her Majesty. The Englishmen had, just as in Puerto de la Cruz on Tenerife, an Anglican church, and here, like a relic of that anglophile period in the life of Gran Canaria, one can still see the elegant golf club which we looked down on from the Pico de Bandama, 1,900 feet above sea level, next to the Bandama Caldera, thirty-three hundred feet across and six hundred and fifty feet deep. We saw more from this vantage point: across a landscape which contained plains and valleys and cultivated land we saw the Isleta, Puerto de La Luz, as well as the inclement donkey belly of cloud softening the climate with its foggy weight, making the island liveable. We were turning up the road to Bandama and along with us, taking photos and turning as we turned, came many Russians, much more domesticated than the ones whom Carlota recorded in their messy floating refuges.

We have passed through Jinámar, where in the Spanish Civil War the people who were disaffected with the Franco regime were discharged; I saw a building designed by the regionalist architect Miguel Martían Fernández de la Torre, an old abandoned house that still had his style and his imprint on it, and a few of the English chalets which fill the landscape with the frank innocence which these lands had until the hyperconstruction that now threatens to fill all the Islands with cement got under way.

The road we were following combines palm trees with land sown with prickly pear; sometimes there are eucalyptus trees, as there are on the Vega de San Mateo, and sometimes there are curves, and nothing else, which surround a field whose mingled scent reaches all the way to us. At the peak, which is where we are now standing, the trees are hit by the musical wind; and further up, standing up straight, showing its beauty in all its aspects, is the object of our voyage, the handsome Roque Nublo, standing next to the rock which they call El Fraile; the Dedo de Dios is no longer there, it was struck down in a storm. They are figures in brown stone, tall and final, which are the greatest symbol of the mountainous landscape of Gran Canaria, always the same and yet always changing, protected by their cloudy or clear fogs; a symphony of mountains round a village, Ayacata, where Juan Hidalgo composes his avant-garde music in his violet house. When we walked past, the house was covered in a huge black cloth; it is a sign that it is not there, that here is not a trace of the unusual colour of the house filled with nooks and crannies. They say: 'It is not violet; it is lilac. The house is painted lilac.' It must be, I suppose. Memory always changes the colours of things.

Down below us is Artenara, the stone fortress which so enthused Unamuno, after seeing the rock of Bentayga; we are, as the Basque philosopher who discovered Fuerteventura both for its pleasures and for his poems, facing a petrified storm; it is not strange to be here and think that the ancients adored stone. The stone that you find in Gran Canaria is solemn, and definitive; there is no sense of weight about it, it is simply there; there is no sense of lightness either, so firmly is it planted on the ground. Like the island, perhaps: Gran Canaria is heavy and stands in the very middle of the sea, defying the sea. Jules Verne, who mentioned the island in one of his books, said that 'Gran Canaria is a summary of other islands. If it does not possess a peak as imposing as that of Tenerife, it does at least hold a good position relative to all the rest. It is the island with the most inaccessible coasts, the best protected valleys, the deepest ravines and the most curious natural peculiarities.'

A summary of other islands, perhaps, but Tejeda is without a doubt the stone capital of the archipelago, the place where this febrile manufacturing island can pause for breath, always occupied in look-ing for its own stones. Tejeda is in front of us, under the Roque Nublo. Fina, the woman who rules over this restored nineteenth-century house where Ángel and Diego are taking us now, says that Oliver Stone has just come through, passing through the Roque in order to look for rest. Fina says that we are in a privileged spot, 'because no one has ever wanted to buy this landscape', and so it has always re-mained how it was, 'ever since the island had a history'. You can breathe here and feel yourself the owner of the air, she says, and she recommends that I come back, 'because it is a good place for asth-matics like you to visit, for anyone who suffers from lung problems. What the hell, it's good for everyone,' she concludes.

It's raining, I say, pointing out the obvious. 'And a good thing too, or else we wouldn't have such good *papas* as the ones they grow in Tejeda.' Later, Ángel takes us to see the *papas* he has harvested in the middle of Mister John's farm; he shows us the animals he raises, he shows us the cheeses he makes, and he makes us stroke the potatoes. Here, every year, he organises World Potato Day. As it is raining, we get the impression that Tejeda is a land of water; however it is rather a land of sun and *papas*, in the shadow of Roque Nublo. Ángel says: 'The more years that go by, the more I fit in with this landscape.'

He says this as we sit in front of two dishes which we have been served in the restaurant where he has taken us, a humble little place where everyone knows him by name. On the table, *ropa vieja*, which is a stew made from the meat left after stewing pulses, served with chickpeas and strips of steak. The wine is called Peña Rajada. As it is raining, the meal seems to be giving us a refuge; if the sun were shining then the meal would interrupt our day. Food that you eat where it is wet has a certain air of welcome, of comfort, of a meeting with friends where everyone in the area participates in a ceremony which the rain makes even more solemn.

I HEAD BACK TO LAS CANTERAS, THROUGH THE REEDBEDS AND THE bougainvillea; unlike up in Tejeda, the sun is shining here, the donkey's belly has gone. The sun is a spectacle when the sands begin on this wonderful beach. 'In just one part of the beach | the sun is special: not a lot of people know that. | It is a very precise spot. Bear it in mind,' the poet Padorno says. 'Look for it with care. Your body will turn golden, | shining and of a very high quality; your skin will turn very soft, | the colour of sunflowers, | giving an immense seductive capacity | to even the bluer parts of your body.' 'This is the part that will bewitch you,' is how the poet finishes his poem 'On the Secret Part of the Beach'. And that is where I am headed. To the landscape which he nourished by day to dream of at night.

It was milky in the morning, but the landscape which the poet described is now, this afternoon, startled. A man has drowned, they have surrounded the place of the accident with a coloured rope, and policemen are moving around the area, chattering, along with by-standers and medics. The curiosity we feel in the face of death. The next morning, when I have woken up in front of this piece of land, there is no rope anymore and no bystanders; there is nothing; death has left a dull noise in the sea, a piece of forgetfulness; now the sea is white and majestic, its noise is the only thing that sounds anything like itself; the sand is browner because of the water thrown onto it during the night. Sunday laziness fills the beach's loneliness and at that instant, for a second, it has become the memory of the deaf tor-ment of that death.

At this precise moment, when day is breaking, the seagulls are screaming like madmen, they are like 'the constant crunching noise [. . .] like a dog barking to warn you of danger' in the Russian boats that Carlota Nelson visited. In front of this landscape large boats are passing, and little boats, and pleasure boats; Las Palmas is a city made out of the sea; the sea defines it and holds it tight, it spends its life looking at the sea. This morning they took us back to Telde, but today we are going in search of a sandwich, one that sounds good, a ham sandwich in a place called Jasmina, but Jasmina is closed today; we will never experience the legend ourselves; they say that everyone eats here, from truck drivers to the President. We did not get to eat it, but as we were travelling with Elsa Guerra and Joaquín Casariego, both architects, we went to another centre of the island's energy, Vecindario, where the best wind on the island blows, or at least where you can best appreciate it; here the city blends in with the wind farms. We go to Agüimes, travelling through the village of Los Corchillos (palm trees, white houses) and we see above us, majestic, presiding over the island like another totem, the fortress of Ansdite, from which the first settlers were hurled after being taken captive by the conquistadors.

There is a party in Agüimes today, and people are out in the streets. The seventeenth-century houses are all spruced up and they are serving a good local wine in the bars, with very dry, very cured cheese. It is dry, and hard, and sharp, and yesterday this cheese won one of the island's regional prizes. There is sacking hanging from the balconies, and onions and garlic and pineapples . . . This is the way in which the land makes itself appear present on the occasions when these villages, these introspective island villages, want to show off their beauty, to show that they live off the land. I ask the locals what the best thing about Agüimes is, and they reply in the same way as any Canary Islander or Cuban replies to such vague questions: 'A little bit of everything.' They have oil, but not olives, 'well, some years yes and some years no'. An old man comes in, like in the Wild West; he says nothing, but the barman pours him a rum. He drinks it in silence, then he touches the empty glass with a finger and gets served another shot. He says nothing. I look at the houses: they have lizards drawn on them, like some kind of decoration. It is a fetish. And then the people go to Mass: it is Sunday, the village is *en fête*. The architects tell me that their church is one that dates back to the eighteenth century, the church of San Sebastián, an example of Canary Islands neoclassicism; there is a square filled with tall trees, like the square in San Sebastián de La Gomera, and from the direction opposite to the one in which we are travelling there approaches a white cow, enormous; it weighs a ton, the driver says.

We have gone through Arinaga and we are going to the deep south of Gran Canaria: this is San Bartolomé de Tirajana, which is the village that comes after Arguineguín. The landscape is brown and dry. Tourists have softened it somehow, finding their solitude and sun and apartments here ever since the 1960s. The construction started in San Agustín, which is where we now are, drinking coffee in a place called Bahía Feliz; you can smell the building developments all around you; the beaches are all happy places, just like the bar where we are sitting; the road carries on as though we were in a never-ending development, until Maspalomas leaps out at us round a curve. Maspalomas is a stretch of sand which is still fairly overwhelming, in spite of the hotels that have been built here, in spite of the roads and freeways. There was nothing here in the 1970s, it was a seascape of interminable dunes, from San Agustín all the way to the lighthouse of Maspalomas. But now cement has become an important part of the landscape, although I think of it as an inviolable landscape, the landscape of Maspalomas. It has to cohabit, of course, with the blight that is shopping centres, with the establishments that drag tourists to wherever they think they should go, but the landscape is wise, and the beach has known how to hold its ground, it knows how to be open and secret at the same time, an interminable dune which is the aim of this journey. Elsa and Joaquín show me the building which was the start of the touristic development of Maspalomas, discovered as an essential part of the island in 1959 as the expansion to the south began, when the International Maspalomas Canary Islands Coast Competition was announced. The competition was won by some French architects; the first building they built was called La Rotonda, right next to the sea; the next building was Oasis, a hotel built by the Spanish architects Vázquez and Molezún. Now the Oasis honours its name; here it is, noble and all the more noble if one looks around it, with its palm trees and its gardens, decorated with a mural painted by Maolo Millares, the painter from Las Palmas who was, in the second half of the twentieth century, an emblem of Spanish avant-garde art.

I ask Elsa, when we are parked and looking at Maspalomas, what is the best thing about the landscape of Gran Canaria which we have seen, from the mountains down to the sea. 'The sea,' she says, 'the sea in Gran Canaria is astounding. In Tenerife the things that are astounding are Anaga, Almáciga, Antequera, all that mountain range. But here it is the sea.'

When faced with Maspalomas, I surrender.

Faced by this luminous sea, with the night falling, in Gran Canaria, the island of Agfaete and Arucas, the island of unsociable or astonishing shadows of history; faced by the mysterious sonority of Roque Nublo, I surrender, this is my landscape, the sea, this insatiable and continually transforming landscape which combines and separates the Islands. I surrender to Maspalomas, to the sea at Lanzarote, to the mountain range of Anaga, to the organs of La Gomera, to Famara on the way into the port of La Estaca, to El Hierro, to the seas at Gran Tarajal, to Puerto de la Cruz, to all these seas; I have come in search of the centre of the earth, to recover the smells, the tastes, the landscapes of my childhood, of my infancy, the areas of the world where I lived and dreamed, and I find myself in front of the sea, and I know, as any islander truly knows, that this is the one landscape which summarises all the rest.

Igancio Aldecoa has the right words with which to finish a journey: 'An island may perhaps be a parenthesis in the monotony of the sea, like a lake is a parenthesis in the monotony of the land.'

THE LONELINESS OF AN ISLAND, THE POWER OF THE SEA AS IT TRIES TO beat it down, the air, the wind, the land which is either fertile or sterile, the men and women who are both humble and proud. A sentimental journey surrounded by the sea, by the sun, by rain, by leaves which in the summer rot down into an ochre and sleeping land. The Canary Islands. A fragmented history in the Atlantic, which the doves that come and go from its ruined or pure shores see growing, all the way from the top of Mount Teide down to the shore where children learn to say 'sea' or 'beach' or 'mother'.

At the end of a journey I feel as though I had disembarked from a ship, at dawn on some island.

An island is a parenthesis. But it is also a rock, and I cling to it like a child.

WHEN I STARTED WRITING THIS BOOK I REMEMBERED A PHRASE THAT THE Catalan writer Josep Pla put at the beginning of his beautiful book about Cadaqués, his beloved homeland. The old master said that there would certainly be a more beautiful book out there, 'a more eminent one', than one he was about to start, but that this was his book. This is what I wanted to do with this complicated journey around and to the depths of my own land. When I was finishing it I came across a couple of lines from a poem by the German poet and editor Michael Krüger, a friend of Peter Mayer, the editor who commissioned this book on the Islands from me. The lines run as follows, and I have put them as the epigraph to this volume: 'Sometimes my childhood sends me | a postcard: Do you remember?' Well, this is what the book is about, this book which I now bring to a close: the postcards sent to me by my childhood, and by life itself.

El Médano, Tenerife, 11 November 2011